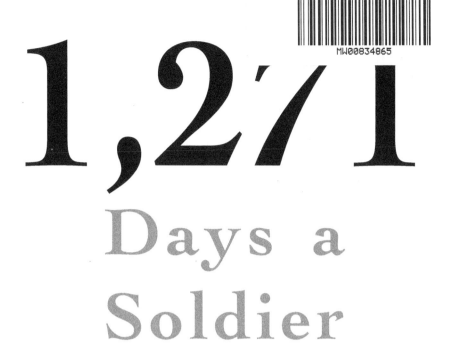

# 1,271

## Days a
## Soldier

The Diaries and Letters of
**Colonel H.E. Gardiner**
as an Armor Officer in
World War II

Edited by Dominic J. Caraccilo

UNG
UNIVERSITY *of*
NORTH GEORGIA™
UNIVERSITY PRESS

Blue Ridge | Cumming | Dahlonega | Gainesville | Oconee

Published by:
University of North Georgia Press
Dahlonega, Georgia

Printing Support by:
Lightning Source Inc.
La Vergne, Tennessee

Cover and book design by Corey Parson.

ISBN: 978-1-940771-82-3

Printed in the United States of America

For more information, please visit: http://ung.edu/university-press
Or e-mail: ungpress@ung.edu

Publisher's Note: UNG Press respects the editor's transparency in publishing Gardiner's letters as he wrote them, noting but not correcting spelling and word choice errors and not identifying but correcting only punctuation errors. That transparency extends to cultural, social, racial, and gender attitudes current in this era, attitudes that to our current era may seem erroneous but from which we may still learn.

UNG
UNIVERSITY of
NORTH GEORGIA™
UNIVERSITY PRESS

Blue Ridge | Cumming | Dahlonega | Gainesville | Oconee

For Karen: My Wife, My Life

and

to the soldiers of the 1st Armored Division

# Acknowledgements

Especially helpful in this endeavor were the Special Collections Section of the U.S. Military Academy Cadet Library, which initially located the manuscript for me. *1,271 Days a Soldier* has been a quarter century-long endeavor, and many have touched, encountered, and inspired its completion along the way.

A special thanks goes to the late Dr. Martin Blumenson, American military scholar and historian who authored, among several other classics, *Anzio: The Gamble that Failed* (1978), *Kasserine Pass* (2000), *The Patton Papers* (2009), and *Salerno to Cassino* (2015). Dr. Blumenson served as a historical officer with the Third and Seventh Armies in World War II and inspired me to study World War II history and sent me a letter on May 19, 2002, urging me finish and offering his pen as a lead. It is my great misfortune that he passed before this work could come to fruition.

Finally, a thank you to Colonel Gardiner's niece, Mrs. Patricia Issel from Lexington, Kentucky. Pat's assistance has been invaluable as she provided insight, original documents such as photographs and articles from Gardiner's collection, and the excitement and friendship any author would cherish taking on such an insurmountable endeavor.

# Table of Contents

## 1. Prelude to Conflict: United States and Ireland

## 2. North Africa

## 3. Italy

# List of Figures

# Foreword

In his seminal work, *The Face of Battle*, John Keegan studied three battles that occurred in the same geographic area but were separated in time across five centuries. Although Keegan identified changes in technology and tactics that occurred over time, his study revealed one striking continuity:

> What battles have in common is human: the behavior of men struggling to reconcile their instinct for self-preservation, their sense of honor and the achievement of some aim over which other men are ready to kill them. The study of battle is therefore always a study of fear and usually of courage, always of leadership, usually of obedience; always of compulsion, sometimes of insubordination; always of anxiety, sometimes of elation or catharsis; always of uncertainty and doubt, misinformation and misapprehension, usually also of faith and sometimes of vision; always of violence, sometimes also of cruelty, self-sacrifice, compassion; above all, it is always a study of solidarity and usually also of disintegration for it is toward the disintegration of human groups that battle is directed.[1]

In *1,271 Days a Soldier*, Colonel H. E. Gardiner's experience reveals a human and personal perspective on the most destructive war in history. The editor, Dominic J. Caraccilo, has transformed Colonel Gardiner's

---

1    John Keegan, The Face of Battle, (London: Viking Press, 1977), 83.

journal articles and personal letters into an invaluable resource for researchers and a compelling story for those who want to understand better the trials, tribulations, emotions, sacrifices, and rewards associated with service across four years of war from the United States to Ireland to Africa to Continental Europe.

After the Japanese attack on Pearl Harbor on December 7, 1941, America mobilized. The U.S. Army grew 44-fold, from 190,000 soldiers to almost 8.5 million. Virtually every American had a family member in harm's way and made a deep emotional investment in the Army. During World War II, the U.S. military sustained almost 300,000 battle deaths and about 100,000 deaths from other causes. Those who returned from the war after experiencing tough, harrowing fighting rarely spoke of their experiences. That is why Colonel Gardiner's personal account has proven invaluable in understanding at least one officer's odyssey. Now this edited collection makes his story accessible to general readers as well as researchers and historians. As the World War II generation fades into the twilight, Caraccilo has given Americans an opportunity to understand better how brave soldiers and officers like Colonel Gardiner helped save the free world from Nazi Fascism.

Gardiner's account remains relevant beyond its contribution to historical understanding. His story helps us understand the Army as a living historical community. 1,271 Days a Soldier sheds light and understanding on the character, commitment, and ethos of American soldiers today. At a time when few Americans are directly connected to our professional military, Colonel Gardiner's story may help American citizens understand better the warriors who fight in their name.

H. R. McMaster
Lieutenant General, U.S. Army (Retired)
26th National Security Advisor to the President of the United States

# Preface

In the mid-to-late 1990s, I served as an Assistant Professor for Systems Engineering at the U.S. Military Academy at West Point. During my tenure on a campus rife with history, I came across the boxed diaries, letters, and papers belonging to Colonel Henry Edward (H. E.) Gardiner in the Cadet Library Archives. What led me to peruse the top floor archives, tucked away in the centuries-old historical repository, was a parallel effort to edit and publish *Surviving Bataan and Beyond: Colonel Irvin Alexander's Odyssey as a Japanese Prisoner of War* (Stackpole, 1999). Much like the effort I put into editing Alexander's story, capturing Colonel Gardiner's notes, diaries, letters, and manuscripts was, while daunting, an intriguing prospect for a book. In fact, *1,271 Days* was slowly coming to realization in draft form when, in 2001, the War on Terrorism shifted my attention to fighting a war and subsequently penning works associated with strategy and combat. As a result, this work was put into abeyance until now.

My original interest in transforming a historical set of disparate notes and diaries came from a colleague in the late 1990s: then-Major Thomas T. Smith, who edited *A Dose of Frontier Soldiering: The Memoirs of Corporal E.A. Bode, Frontier Regular Infantry 1877—1882* (University of Nebraska Press, 1994). Smith told me that if I wanted to succeed in providing a quality edited version of these types of volumes, I would have to become an expert on the topic. This proved true with the Bataan book and, in similar fashion, with the Gardiner story. Whether I have become an expert or not, I will leave to the reader.

I learned from my work on *Surviving Bataan and Beyond* that—despite having written my own combat memoir and infusing my own experiences in other works during my three decades of writing about strategy, operational art, and my own military service—editing someone else's experiences is far more difficult than my own. After spending nearly two decades on this manuscript, I can affirm that compiling a text to make up *1,271 Days* was no small task.

While it is important that the reader understands the daily entries coupled with a paralleling operational and strategic history of World War II, this book is more than just a historical chronology of a U.S. Army colonel's war tenure. It is about the perseverance of an army officer determined to capture his experiences every day for nearly four years. While other WWII accounts exist, few cover a mid-level officer's daily experiences in multiple theaters.

In the late 1990s, I was given the opportunity to provide "50 years ago this month" World War II additions to the *VFW Magazine*. Readers' interest in those accounts eventually led to a two-set volume titled *The Faces of Victory* (Addax Pub Group Inc., 1995) which recounted the salient battles in the Pacific region and on the African and European continents. While there was great interest in the war's Golden Anniversary, one can expect that interest in the Diamond Anniversary will be just as great, if not more.

The ranks of veterans who served in World War II are quickly diminishing, a loss which draws an added interest to their historical legacy. According to U.S. Department of Veterans Affairs statistics, 496,777 of the 16 million Americans who served in World War II were alive in 2018 and their number was decreasing by almost 400 a day.[2] One can expect a similar peak of interest in stories that involve this vanishing population.

2    Hollis, John D. "Honor our WWII veterans while they are still among us," retrieved on October 17, 2019, from https://www.washingtonpost.com/opinions/2019/05/26/honor-our-wwii-veterans-while-they-are-still-among-us/

The diaries kept by World War II soldiers are very rare, given that keeping a chronological journal was generally forbidden due to the danger of its falling into enemy hands. Gardiner's work is one of the few that made it through the war intact.

Dominic J. Caraccilo
Editor

# Introduction

This work is the definitive account of Colonel H. E. Gardiner's World War II service. Coupling the chronology provided with daily entries, it offers a paralleling perspective of Gardiner's combat and personal experiences in line with the events of the Second World War. This edited version, complete with the editor's extensive footnotes, places Gardiner in step with the famous, and sometime infamous, personalities and events of the war.

*1,271 Days a Soldier: The Diaries and Letters of Colonel H .E. Gardiner as an Armor Officer in World War II* is a selection of journal entries and personal letters neatly summing up Colonel H. E. Gardiner's experiences during the Second World War. His recollection of his duty in the United States, Ireland, Africa, and on the European continent is unique in many respects, not the least being the intriguing first-hand experiences of an operational level ranking officer in multiple theaters over the span of three and a half years during the Second World War.

In its rawest form, the Gardiner odyssey is a commonly used reference and resource for scholars, historians, and laymen. References accredited to the Gardiner diaries and letters frequently find their way into military history manuscripts and as supporting evidence for larger volumes of work. Indeed, one can find Gardiner's experiences cited in countless volumes, most notably about the notorious actions at the Kasserine Pass.

From the shock of the initial volley of violence registered by Gardiner during the Day of Infamy radio broadcast to the final days of the war while operating on the "soft underbelly" of Hitler's Europe, these diaries and letters cover the prelude to and the fighting in the African and European theaters. The historical perspective makes this work interesting, but the human perspective of a midlevel officer makes *1,271 Days* a rare find. The diary entries and letters are written with all the emotion of someone who endured nearly four years of high-intensity conflict, coupled with long periods of boredom and interjected with periods of frivolity.

Much research and cross-referencing were needed to fully identify who the various individuals in the diaries and letters are; to explain what the strategic, operational, and tactical strategy of the war or battle was at any given time; and to clarify any other ideas that left the reader begging for more information. Detailed footnotes, photographs and captions, and maps put each journal entry in context so the reader may gain a better appreciation of the full spectrum of war that was unfolding at any given time in the work. The footnotes provide encouragement for the reader to study the readily-accessible referenced citations while reading the book to attain a better understanding of what took place, when, and by whom.

As per the original manuscript, entries with a date to the left indicate a dairy entry, while letters are indicated by a date Gardiner justified right. Unless there was a salutation, the letter was written to Gardiner's mother.

## Henry Edward (H. E.) Gardiner

Henry Edward (H. E.) Gardiner was born in Montana on June 30, 1905. He was raised on a ranch near Anaconda, attending a country grade school and the Anaconda High School. In 1928, he graduated from Montana State College where he took the required two years in infantry ROTC. That same year, he entered Cornell University, from which he received a law degree in 1931, and became a member of the Chicago Bar Association. Prior to moving Chicago in 1934 to serve as council for the Anaconda Wire and Cable Co., Gardiner had been employed in the legal department of the Anaconda Copper Mining Company in Butte, Montana.

Figure 1: Lieutenant Colonel Henry E. Gardiner bivouacking during pre-deployment training during the Louisiana Maneuvers (Photograph from the Patricia Issel Collection)

Gardiner enlisted in Troop C (popularly known as The Chicago Black Horse Troop) on November 25, 1935, and was serving his second enlistment as a sergeant when he was commissioned as a second lieutenant on June 11, 1940.[3] He was promoted to a First Lieutenant on August 23, 1940.

3    Elting, John R. (1988). *Military Uniforms in America: The Modern Era from 1868*. Presidio Press. p. 92.

At the time of Pearl Harbor, Gardiner was a First Lieutenant commanding a troop in the horse squadron of the 106th Cavalry (Horse-Mechanized) stationed at Camp Livingston, Louisiana.[4] He was called to active duty on November 25, 1940, when Troop "C" of the 106th Cavalry, an Illinois National Guard unit from Chicago, was inducted into Federal Service.[5]

In January 1941, the 106th Cavalry, which comprised a horse squadron from Chicago and a mechanized squadron from downstate Illinois, moved to Louisiana to train. During the summer of that year, Gardiner attended the Cavalry School at Fort Riley, Kansas, as a student taking the basic course. Upon graduation, he was promoted to captain on December 13, 1941.

At the outbreak of the war, he was assigned to the Fifth Corps Headquarters, and, in May 1942, he was deployed overseas with the 13th Armored Division. Gardiner was promoted to major on October 21, 1942, and then lieutenant colonel on January 27, 1943. He served as a battalion commander and regimental executive officer until his discharge at the rank of colonel in October 1945.[6]

In February 1943, then-Lieutenant Colonel Gardiner was awarded the nation's second highest combat award, the Distinguished Service Cross (DSC), for actions as a Lieutenant Colonel in command of a squadron in North Africa (see Figure 2 below).[7]

---

4    Camp Livingston, Louisiana, located about twelve miles north of Alexandria, Louisiana, was created in 1940. First known as Camp Tioga, it was renamed Camp Livingston in honor of Chancellor Robert R. Livingston, negotiator of the Louisiana Purchase. The camp formed part of a larger complex of military bases in Central Louisiana that included Camps Claiborne, Polk, and Beauregard, as well as Esler Field, retrieved on October 30, 2019, from http://encyclopedia.densho.org/Camp_Livingston_(detention_facility)/

5    Before World War II, the 106th Cavalry was a National Guard unit based in Chicago, Illinois. Prior to World War I and the Spanish American War, it had been known as the 1st Illinois Volunteer Cavalry. The 106th underwent several different reorganizations until September 1, 1940, when it was re-designated the 1st Squadron, 106th Cavalry (Horse-Mechanized). The 106th was inducted into federal service on November 25, 1940 in Chicago. The Regiment moved to Camp Livingston, Louisiana, on January 3, 1941, under command of V Corps. *Armor: The Cavalry Journal* 48: 93 (1939), retrieved on October 30, 2019.

6    Favager, D. J. *The History of the Gardiners of Whitchurch, Liverpool and Wallasey: Volume 2: Liverpool.* (Kindle Direct Publishing, 2019), location 3756 of the Kindle Edition.

7    For more on the actions taken to earn such a distinguished award, refer to Gardiner's diary input dated February 4, 1943, retrieved on October 31, 2019, from http://valor.militarytimes.com/recipient.php?recipientid=31043'

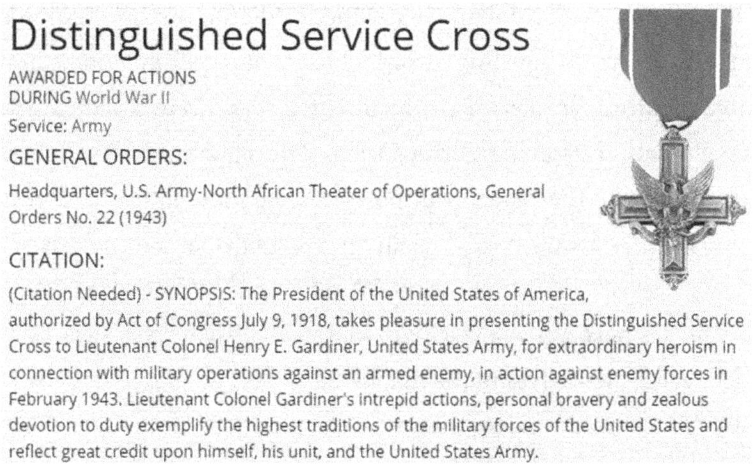

# Distinguished Service Cross

AWARDED FOR ACTIONS
DURING World War II

Service: Army

### GENERAL ORDERS:

Headquarters, U.S. Army-North African Theater of Operations, General
Orders No. 22 (1943)

### CITATION:

(Citation Needed) - SYNOPSIS: The President of the United States of America,
authorized by Act of Congress July 9, 1918, takes pleasure in presenting the Distinguished Service
Cross to Lieutenant Colonel Henry E. Gardiner, United States Army, for extraordinary heroism in
connection with military operations against an armed enemy, in action against enemy forces in
February 1943. Lieutenant Colonel Gardiner's intrepid actions, personal bravery and zealous
devotion to duty exemplify the highest traditions of the military forces of the United States and
reflect great credit upon himself, his unit, and the United States Army.

Figure 2: Distinguished Service Cross citation for then-LTC Henry E. Gardiner

Starting with his college days, Henry kept a diary. During the war, this practice was followed where permitted and when conditions would allow. Infrequently, there were breaks in the continuity of this diary-keeping due to the conditions of combat, a need to move hastily, and his convalescing after being wounded. At times where an entry was attempted, by his own admission, the contents were "very sketchy" and Gardiner filled any noticeable gap in entries with extracts from letters he received and wrote to family and friends throughout the war. Perhaps Gardiner got his passion (or least a keen interest) in journal keeping from his paternal grandmother who did the same during her trip "up the Missouri" with Gardiner's paternal grandfather in 1879, when the family migrated from Fort Benton, Montana, some 200 miles north into Bozeman, Montana.[8]

The following are extracts from the countless letters and diary inserts transposed from by Colonel Gardiner's office secretary upon his return from the European Continent in 1945. In discussions with various acquaintances, the name of the secretary remains unknown. I can only assume that her work in transcribing the letters and diaries resulted in

---

8    Gardiner, Henry E. "Interview with the Montana Historical Society with Michael Malone," Montana State University and Bill Lang, Montana Historical Society. (Bozeman, MT: November 10, 1987), 1.

a transposition of the documents without edit. As in any manuscript, there are errors in spelling, word choice, and punctuation. In this edition, I address word errors with corrected versions in square brackets. For punctuation errors, I correct them throughout without the need to identify each. The reader will note that, in some letters and entries, Gardiner writes about "peeps" when referencing what we know as ¼-ton trucks or "jeeps." This is not a typo. World War II soldiers did in fact call their vehicles peeps.[9] I will clarify in more detail such references as these as they reveal themselves in the manuscript.

By his own admission, Gardiner decided not to include portions of his documents that were intimate, personal, or (what he claims) inappropriate as part of the original transcribed manuscript. One can surmise what was not included, and I would venture to say that, after reading the entire manuscript, the reader would agree that it was minimal or, in any case, insignificant.

I intend not to publish here every letter and written entry into a body of work but to provide a manuscript rife with history identifying Gardiner's odyssey. What follows are salient entries of Gardiner's diaries and letters that I chose to tether together chronologically, providing the reader a sense of what it was like for Gardiner during his 1,271 days as a soldier.

---

9    Many soldiers referred to what is commonly known today as a Jeep (¼-ton truck or M151) as a "peep" since the vehicle was considered to be a reconnaissance car, as in "peeping" on the enemy. Larger ½-ton or ¾-ton Command Reconnaissance cars were often called "beeps" for "big Jeeps." A May 2, 1942, *Colliers* magazine features an article called "Our Fighting Men" and is about vehicle names and a need to standardize such. This article claims that a survey was done asking soldiers to write in and vote for names for vehicles, and the results were reportedly as such:

      Peep, name for the ¼-ton Bantam, GP (General Purpose)
      Jeep, name for the ½-ton reconnaissance command car
      Weapons Carrier, name for the ½-ton open cab Dodge
      Pickup, name for the ½-ton closed cab Dodge
      Carryall, name for the ¾-ton Dodge ambulance

# 1

## Prelude to Conflict: United States and Ireland

December 7, 1941–November 7, 1942

*{The attack on Pearl Harbor on December 7, 1941, quickly ended two years of neutrality and the U.S. entered the war. Most Americans are surprised to discover that the first U.S. soldiers to enter the Second World War were forward stationed in Northern Ireland. By September 1942, the role of the U.S. troops in Europe had intensified. Much of (U.S.) V Corps who made up the first wave of troops into Ireland were bound for Operation Torch, the name of the operation to liberate North Africa. Gardiner deployed in the first movement of soldiers to Ireland from the U.S.. He was the aide-de-camp to the Commanding General and then found duty with the 13th Armor Cavalry Regiment. Gardiner's eventual battalion command time was with the 2nd Battalion of the 13th Armored which deployed from Ireland to Northern Africa in 1942. The following entries describe his experiences from the beginning of the war in December 1941 to the beginning of his combat experience in Northern Africa.}*

## War Breaks Out, Immediate After Effects

**December 7, 1941**

A friend came to my tent to listen to the New York Philharmonic program. When he switched the radio on there was a news broadcast in progress which seemed to be discussing the Far Eastern situation in much the same vein as has been typical the past few days, until we were shocked out of our somewhat indifferent attitude to hear the almost unbelievable news that the Japs [sic] had attacked Honolulu this morning and that a bombing raid was still in progress.

The accounts would indicate that our forces were caught completely unaware and that the casualties among the military forces and civilian population would run into the thousands. Two troops of the mechanized squadron were on their way to New Orleans shortly after midnight for reported duty around the dock area.[1]

## December 8, 1941

There was a different attitude of the men when they fell in for reveille this morning, it being one of seriousness and earnestness. At noon, today a group of us gathered in one of the officer's tents to listen to the President ask Congress for a declaration of war against Japan which was almost immediately forthcoming. This evening there was a regimental retreat at which time we were addressed by the Colonel who gave us something of a fight talk regarding the war. The band played and everyone was very grim.

## December 9, 1941

The camp is bubbling over with rumors and we undoubtedly contributed to them today for I took the troop out on an all-day trailer march and we went thru [sic] the main camp with the kitchen truck and the combat truck in addition to the horse trailer with the men sitting with their heads over the top wearing steel helmets. The various units of the 32nd Division have been scattered up and down the Mississippi to guard bridge power plants, etc. and one infantry regiment went out of here by rail.[2] Their destination being, we understand, California. Civilian clothes

1    Gardiner was stationed with the 106th Cavalry conducting training at Camp Livingston at the time of the attack on Pearl Harbor. During the war, New Orleans was a major port of embarkation for troops and equipment destined for overseas deployment. For more on troops and cargo transported during World War II, see http://www.usmm.org/armycargo.html

2    The 32nd Infantry Division had seen intensive combat in France during World War I and inactivated in April 1919. During the years prior to World War, II it was much a paper tiger and then on October 15, 1940, as part

are out now and as I packed mine up the evening preparatory to sending them to Chicago, I felt I was making a definite break with the past. Heard the President address the nation tonight saying what is an obvious fact that we are now fighting Germany and Italy just as much as Japan.

### December 10, 1941

The Colonel had proclaimed today a holiday which started off with what might be considered a regimental review. The first item on the program was a baseball game between the officers and the non-coms. All officers played and I was in center field for two innings. Got to bat once, secured a hit and scored. During the course of the day several drinking parties got well underway in the officer's tents which I think is bad because it was apparent to any enlisted men who were about, but they can't do such things without getting in trouble.

### December 11, 1941

In preparation for a Special Court Martial that is coming up I made a trip to Camp Claiborne this morning to interview some MP witnesses.[3] One regiment of the 34th Division moved out yesterday for the west

---

of the eighteen National Guard units being brought onto active duty, it was federalized and found its headquarters in Lansing, Michigan. At the time, it comprised National Guard units from Michigan and Wisconsin. While it was authorized to have a peace-time strength of about 11,600 soldiers, like almost all units in the National Guard and the Regular Army prior to World War II, it was not at full strength nor was it assigned all the equipment it was authorized. To ensure its level of training, the division was scheduled to receive a year of training in Louisiana. In October 1940, the division began a six-day motor march to Camp Beauregard, Louisiana. On January 26, 1941, the 32nd Division relocated to the recently completed Camp Livingston, about 15 miles (24 km) northeast of Alexandria, Louisiana, where it spent the next sixteen months training. During the summer of 1941, the division moved to Camp Beauregard, Louisiana, as part in the Third and Fourth Army maneuvers—nicknamed the Louisiana Maneuvers—which provided the army high command a good look at the preparedness of the regiment. The first test, which was held near Camp Beauregard, was conducted June 16–27 and included the 32nd Division as well as the 37th Division from Ohio. From August 16–30, the maneuvers expanded to include the 34th and 38th Divisions. During September, the largest maneuvers were held with the Seventh Corps of the Second Army, opposing the Fourth, Fifth, and Eighth Corps of the Third Army. The Grand Rapids Guard was part of the Fifth Corps. It was the largest maneuver of its kind in the history of the Army and included some 100,000 men. What Gardiner is referencing here was the effort to protect internal U.S. infrastructure from potential enemy harassment/attacks. After the Attack on Pearl Harbor, the division was one of the first activated for federal duty. "Division History: 32nd Infantry Division," retrieved on February 15, 2018, from http://www.lonesentry.com/usdivisions/history/infantry/division/pacific/32nd_infantry_division.html

3     Camp Claiborne was a U.S. Army military camp during World War II located in Rapides Parish in central Louisiana. *The Camp Claiborne News, 6 July 1944*, retrieved November 7, 2019, from http://www.campclaiborne.com/

coast.[4] Germany and Italy declared war on the US today and just to make sure that there was no slip up, US declared war on them.

## December 13, 1941

This noon the Colonel was holding a conference with the unit commanders in his quarters when the phone rang and the party on the other end of the line told him to keep everyone in camp and to report to Corps Headquarters. A quick check showed me that I had ninety-two men in camp ready for duty, so I put them to work packing up. They didn't get very far along however before word came to alert the first squadron. The second squadron however continued to pack up and are standing by ready to roll. My orders came thru [sic] promoting me to the rank of captain of Cavalry and I was duly sworn in my commission to date as of yesterday.

## December 14, 1941

The second squadron continues to make preparations to leave and they were busy this morning loading ammunition. In view of the clothing that is being issued to them it would look as though they were headed for service in the tropics.[5] All of the men from the second squadron who are on leave have been called back.

## December 16, 1941

Ran a few hours behind in sleep last night for I had taken over yesterday afternoon as O.D.[6] and made a couple of rounds during the night. They have jumped the number of posts up to fifteen since the

4    The 34th Division was subsequently activated on February 10, 1941, with troops from North Dakota, South Dakota, Minnesota, and Iowa. The division was transported by rail and truck convoys to the newly constructed Camp Claiborne in Rapides Parish, Louisiana near Alexandria. Henry Blaine Davis, Jr. *Generals in Khaki.* (Raleigh, NC: Pentland Press, Inc., 1998), p. 43.

5    The initial plan was for his unit to invade North Africa directly from the U.S., therefore the initial issuance of "tropic" or warm weather uniforms.

6    Office of the Day (O.D.) is a managed duty that puts an officer available to manage any issues that may come up in the period of his watch.

declaration of war and all men are now supplied with live ammunition. Found on visiting the posts after dark that the boys were on their toes and challenges were prompt and business like. Speculation continues to run high as to the destination of the second squadron. At first with the issue of cottons and their getting ready for yellow fever shots it looked like the tropics. Now they have been ordered to draw three blankets and a comforter per man and Sibley stoves, so that looks like some northern spot.[7]

## December 28, 1941

A convoy left late tonight for New Orleans with the luggage of those men who are sailing and all of the vehicles that they are taking with them, the principal item being fifty scout cars. A group of us stay-behinds were designated to go along as observers, and I was assigned to ride in scout car.

## December 29, 1941

The ride through the night was cold but uneventful. All serials closed up about twenty miles out of New Orleans for breakfast. After some hot coffee and scrambled eggs, we felt much better. Pulled into our parking area near the Army Wharfs on the Mississippi at eight. All of the rolling stock that is to be shipped was left sitting to be loaded by a labor battalion when the oars arrive to move it. There was no restriction placed in our moving about and we inspected the variety of equipment that was going aboard the steamer at the wharf which will carry out units, so far as the personnel and luggage is concerned, when they move. We saw men engaged in the process of mounting two 37 mms. on [bow] and a 75 mm. on the stern.

---

7    Henry Hopkins Sibley (1816–1886) graduated from West Point in 1838 and served in the 2nd U.S. Dragoons and served in the Seminole War. In 1856, he patented the "Sibley Tent", which could accommodate 20 soldiers and their gear and was widely used in the frontier afterwards. Sibley also invented the "Sibley Stove" to heat the tent. These sheet iron stoves were being used until the advent of World War II. "Sibley Tent Stover," retrieved June 17, 2018, from http://www.afn.org/~micanopy/html/sibley_tent_stove.html

*{On the first day of 1942, the Declaration by United Nations was agreed upon during the Arcadia Conference in Washington, D.C. Representatives of twenty-six Allied nations pledged to employ their "full resources" until victory was won and not to make any separate peace agreements with Axis powers. Forty-seven nations would eventually sign the agreement by the end of the war.[8] On the very next day, Japanese forces occupied Manilla.}[9]*

**January 1, 1942**

A radiogram came in late yesterday afternoon that today would be a "Day of Duty." It was after four when I got to bed so it took considerable effort to crawl out of my nice warm bed on to a cold floor at six-thirty. While at the stables I received a call that there would be an officers' meeting at eight o'clock and it being just about then that I commandeered the manure truck for a quick ride up to regimental headquarters. It was a rather bleary-eyed bunch of officers that faced the Colonel. He said he wanted by noon a list of the number of men that would be required to bring the troops up to full strength and the items of clothing and equipment that would be needed to fully supply our present number where they were short plus that required for the new men. There seems to be some thought that the V Corps was getting ready for a major move of some sort.

**January 3, 1942**

Went on as officer of the day yesterday and was fortunate in that the Friday-Saturday trick is the light one of the week, for you are relieved at noon. It was a rather interesting tour for the troops that are bound overseas left last night and there was a lot of celebrating prior to their departure. The men were hauled in trailers and would have a cold ride down. There was a ceremony yesterday in honor of the departing squadron and the finish of it was to have the unit which was leaving and those who were

8    "1942: Declaration of the United Nations," retrieved on November 7, 2019, from https://www.un.org/en/sections/history-united-nations-charter/1942-declaration-united-nations/index.html

9    Stanley Sandler. *World War II in the Pacific: An Encyclopedia*. (New York: Garland Publishing, 2001), p. 830.

staying pass by each other in a single file and all shake hands. I was busy taking movies, so I didn't get a lame hand as some of the boys did.

**January 6, 1942**

Was awakened at two o'clock this morning by the orderly who stands by in the regimental headquarters during the night with the news that the M.P.'s had a "B" trooper in the brig and wanted us to come get him. I sent the first sergeant and one of the officers in after him. His offense seems to have been merely loitering after the curfew. At seven o'clock this morning I tried a boy as summary court officer, for having been loitering on his post while on guard. He pleaded guilty, his story being that he had gone into a furnace room to get warm. I sentenced him to 15 days of hard labor and a forfeiture of $15.00 of his pay. Rode with the troop this a.m. The horses were more than frisky for it was good and cold.

## Aide to the Corps Commander

**January 9, 1942**

Found a note that the Colonel wished to see me. He said that General Daley who commands the V Corps was looking for a captain as an aide and if I were interested, he would recommend me.[10] He said it should mean an almost immediate move abroad, so I said I'd like it. Was told to report down to Beauregard for an interview with Capt. Peca, the General's present aide.[11] Did so and he called me back later in the afternoon to say the job was mine.

---

10    Major General Edmund L. Daley commanded V Corps from March 17, 1941, to May 6, 1942 as the Detachment Commander who remained at Camp Beauregard, Louisiana. After hearing numerous rumors of morale problems within the command, Chief of Staff of the Army George C. Marshall suggested that Daley "analyze" his command techniques to see if they might be a cause. The chief of staff relieved him in March 1941. In lieu of Daley, Major General William S. Key deployed a detachment of the V Corps to Ireland and commanded until Major General Russell P. Hartle assumed command of the operational corps. "United States Forces in Northern Ireland," retrieved on November 8, 2019, from https://history.army.mil/reference/ireland/IRECHR.htm; "Letter from General George C. Marshall 3-198 To Major General Edmund L. Daley, May 18, 1942," The George C. Marshall Foundation, retrieved on November 8, 2019, from https://www.marshallfoundation.org/library/digital-archive/to-major-general-edmund-l-daley-3/

11    Captain Peter S. Peca became a notable Air Defense officer retiring as a Colonel in 1962. United States Military Academy Association of Graduates memorial, retrieved on November 9, 2019, from https://www.westpointaog.org

## January 12, 1942

Checked in as per instructions and was assigned a desk opposite Capt. Peca's in an office which connects with the Chief of Staff's office and Gen. Daley's office. Am being quartered in the General's cottage and have the luxury of a tub bath. Meals are at the camp officers club. I didn't do much today but sit and listen to the hum that was going on around me. The aide's office sort of acts as a clearing station for visitors to the Gen. and the Chief of staff and there was a stream of them today. Saturday night there was a riot in the colored section of Alexandria and some twenty odd Negro soldiers suffered gunshot wounds, most of which being minor in nature. The reports of the affair were however grossly exaggerated, and Gen. Krueger was here all day getting an investigation of it underway. He is the Commanding General of the Third Army so there was much bustling about it.[12]

Figure 3: Lieutenant General Walter Krueger (left) with General Douglas MacArthur (center) and General George
C. Marshall (right), U.S. Army
(Photograph from the Army Signal Corps Collection in the U.S. National Archives. Photo #: SC 183951)

12    General Walter Krueger (January 26, 1881–August 20, 1967) is best known for his command of the Sixth United States Army in the South West Pacific Area during World War II. In 1941, he assumed command of the Third Army, which he led in the Louisiana Maneuvers. In 1943, he was sent to General Douglas MacArthur's Southwest Pacific Area as commander of the Sixth Army and Alamo Force, which he led in a series of victorious campaigns against the Japanese. Kevin C. Holzimmer. *General Walter Krueger: Unsung Hero of the Pacific War.* (Lawrence, Kansas: University Press of Kansas, 2007), pp. 66, 69–70, 73–76.

## January 13, 1942

I'm afraid I will soon get back into some bad habits of sleeping late for the office force or rather the staff doesn't put in an appearance before eight o'clock. Capt. Peca and I had lunch today with the General and the Chief of Staff, a Col. Kneubel who is a very aggressive hardworking officer.[13] One of our callers was a Brig. Gen. Davis who is the only colored general in the Army.[14] He was down here in connection with the investigation of this riot.

## January 14, 1942

Lunched again with Capt. Peca, the Chief of Staff and General Daley. Made myself somewhat more useful today now that I'm catching on to the routine and getting to know some of the staff. The movement and it is a case of maintaining the status quo. I did that one better by getting my bedroll rolled and stenciled and my foot lockers packed for shipment. I'd hate to have to carry all I am required to take not to mention that which I am authorized.

## January 15, 1942

Capt. Peca was out of the office a good share of the day and I found myself talking to generals on the phone and answering calls of the Major General and the Chief of Staff. After all they aren't any more than the equivalent of executives of various capacities in civil life and in some individuals, I've bumped into since landing in this office the capacity has been marked limited. Letter orders came through from the Adjutant General's office in Washington for me which read in part "Proceed to Ft. Dix, New Jersey, for transportation to station outside continental limits of the United States."

---

13    Colonel John H. Knuebel was the V Corps Chief of Staff, retrieved from https://www.unithistories.com/officers/US_Army_officers_K01.html#Knuebel_JH

14    General Benjamin O. Davis was the first African American general officer in the United States military.

## January 18, 1942

Was invited to join the General, Mrs. Peca and the Captain at the General's cottage (my quarters) and then we went over to the officer's club for Sunday dinner. The General enjoys a drink and is quite a kidder. Mrs. Peca is an army girl, attractive and pleasant. In my contact with radio people and the few actors I've known I've been impressed with the narrowness of their conversation. That is, it is always about themselves, their work, or others in the same business. That is to a less degree true of the medical profession and in all three the wives chime in along the same lines. I find that the regular army is given to even a closer circle in that respect I think the legal profession is much more cosmopolitan. Lawyers do not as a rule discuss their work at home and the families have no particular bond with other lawyer families.

## January 19, 1942

We are getting all cluttered up again with generals. The 28th Division which is the national guard of Pennsylvania is moving into Livingston and Beauregard and the Major General and a Brigadier with that outfit called on General Daley this morning.[15] The move of the V Corps out of here according to some guessers has been delayed because of the lack of bottoms to transfer it to its overseas destination.[16]

## January 21, 1942

I certainly wish we could get rolling. There isn't much activity around the general's office right now and we don't seem to be doing anything towards knocking out the Axis.

---

15    The 28th Infantry Division is oldest division-sized unit in the armed forces of the United States. Prior to deployment, it trained under the command of then-Major General Omar Bradley. It landed in Normandy some six weeks after D-Day. "Pennsylvania Army National Guard," retrieved on November 13, 2019, from https://web. archive.org/web/20131022103608/http://pa.ng.mil/ARNG/28ID/Pages/default.aspx

16    The term "bottom" most likely refers to the flat-bottomed landing craft, vehicle, personnel (LCVP), or Higgins boat. It was a landing craft used extensively in amphibious landings in World War II.

### January 22, 1942

Was sent up to the airport to pick up Brig. Gen. Jones and his party, arranged lunch for them with the C/S and after they completed their conference with Gen. Daley, I took them back to the airport. Our Corps is "reinforced", [one] of the attachments being a sizable Air Force and Gen. Jones commands the same which is now in the process assembled around here.

### January 23, 1942

A new program has been adapted in connection with the Headquarters Company since I came over here and they are now drilling all of the office help, cooks, chauffeurs, etc., an hour each afternoon. This morning I was over watching them on the parade ground when Capt. Peca asked me if I would like to drill a platoon for a while. Don't know how much knowledge I conveyed as to the intricacies of the Calvary's version of infantry drill, but I was good and hoarse when I finished. The 106th group which left here are now writing back and they seem to be comfortably stationed on the Pacific side of the Panama Canal Zone where they are doing patrols duty from their vehicles.

### January 25, 1942

Mrs. Peca called this a.m. to invite me to have dinner with the General and my other boss. She also said she was inviting Patricia who came out and returned under her own power. It was a gorgeous warm day and we had some drinks out on the porch of the cottage. Learned that the General likes scotch so broke out a bottle that I had packed away in some woolen goods that I had stored in my footlocker as a sort of hedge against the time when we might be where liquor is scarce. There is a stable maintained here on the post where eight saddle horses are boarded. Two of them are the generals but he never rides, and I've been told that I may use them if I so desired. Took my saddle over to the tack room and unpacked my boots and a pair of breeches that I had in one of my footlockers. Getting readjusted in that respect will probably precipitate an order to move out.

## January 26, 1942

Got up at five-thirty and was saddled and riding by six. It was a foggy morning, so I moved in darkness until about the time I returned to the stable which was at seven. Rode a mare of the General's. She has a good mouth and is well mannered but is too fat and not so sure of her footing on rough going. This noon there was a luncheon at Camp Livingston which was in the nature of a get-acquainted meeting between the 32nd division and the newly arrived 28th. General Daley was the guest of honor and Capt. Peca and I attended. There were a number of short speeches. This afternoon there was a review of the 28th Division in honor of the Division's retiring commander. His successor, Gen. Ord was also on the platform as was Gen. Daley. The aides were in the rear ranks.[17] It was entirely a movement of foot troops and I thought they appeared very ragged particularly when one takes into consideration that they have been in service for almost a year.

## January 27, 1942

Rode again this a.m. and with a cloudless sky the visibility was better, so I covered more ground. The War Dept. announced that American troops had arrived in Northern Ireland under the command of Gen. Hartle.[18] The number of men was not given nor the outfits that they represent. While every effort has been made to keep the plans of the V Army Corps secret, I have known since the day that Col. Johnson asked me if I were interested in becoming Gen. Daley's aide that the V Corps was bound for Ireland. Gen. Hartle commands the 34th Division, which

17    Major General James G. Ord (USMA 1909) commanded the 28th Infantry Division and was Chairman of the Joint Brazil–U.S. Defense Commission during World War II. Stetson Conn and Byron Fairchild, Office of the Chief of Military History, Department of the Army, *The Framework of Hemisphere Defense* (1960), page 319.

18    General Russell Hartle was in command of the 34th Infantry Division while the 34th was on maneuvers in Louisiana. Following the Japanese attack on Pearl Harbor, war plan MAGNET Force (the Allied program to start the build-up of U.S. ground forces in Northern Ireland) was activated. Pursuant to that war plan, in January 1942,

was formerly at Camp Claiborne, of his force some four thousand are now in Ireland and the balance are still located at Ft. Dix, N.J. Gen. Daley will still command the V Corps when it gets across.

## January 28, 1942

Quite a substantial flow of the Generals in to see the General. There have been two head loppings since I've been in the office. The major one was when the Commanding General of the 32nd Division was relieved of his command and todays victim a mere colonel.[19]

## January 29, 1942

The papers and radio continue to feature the arrival of troops belonging to the American forces in Ireland. Apparently, the intention is to capitalize on the propaganda values of this move and try to get across to the German people that another A.E.F. is on the way and that an allied victory is now a certainty. One amusing feature of the whole thing has been the howl that has been put up by the Irish Free States so called statement at not being consulted. The 32nd is undergoing another change of hands and the division passed in review before the retiring commander this afternoon. They made an excellent appearance [as] far [as] marching, uniform and equipment was concerned.

## January 31, 1942

Rode a different horse this a.m., and my arms got something of a workout for he had considerably more get up and go than the mare I've been riding. There was a long-distance call this a.m. for the general from

the 34th Division under Hartle's command was the first U.S. division shipped overseas to Northern Ireland as part of that plan to begin the European Theater of Operations (ETO). Hartle would proceed Daley as the Commander of CV Corps. *Codenames Operation of World War II*, retrieved November 13, 2019, from https://codenames.info/operation/magnet/

19    Major General Irving A. Fish commanded the 32nd Infantry Division until March 1942 when Major General Edwin F. Harding assumed command. Harding deployed the Division to the Pacific Theater, most notably to New Guinea where he led Americans in the first battle against the enemy in World War II at the Battle of Buna. In December 1942, Harding was relieved of command by General Douglas MacArthur for a lack of progress and ineffective leadership. Dominic J. Caraccilo, "The Battle of Buna," *Infantry Magazine* 83, no 3 (May–June 1993), p.21.

Washington which started things buzzing in certain directions and from what drifted my way it would appear that our move was on the front of the agenda again. I understand that tea is a rather scarce article in the direction we are going so I purchased two tins to keep the whiskey company that I already have in my footlocker to be used for barter purposes with the natives.

### February 2, 1942

There is nothing like the Army when it comes to everyone putting on a little more steam when their boss puts in an appearance. Gen. Krueger flew in from his headquarters this a.m., and it was Gen. Daley who met him and was going the "Yes Siring." I don't doubt [that] when Gen. Krueger is equally on his toes when Gen. Marshall gives them a visit. This evening Gen. Daley gave a dinner at the Bentley for Gen. Krueger and the other Generals in this area and the Chiefs of Staff. He footed the bill although we ate and drank in separate rooms for a party for the aides.[20] In sizing them up I would say they would sort of match their respective bosses as to apparent capabilities.

### February 3, 1942

The Federal Govt. has just completed a housing project between here and Alexandria which is to provide homes for the families of non-commissioned officers stationed in this area. Gov. Jones of Louisiana had invited Gen. Daley and the other military big wigs to attend the dedication ceremonies and we went down and helped provide a backdrop for the governor's speech. The La. Adjutant General then entertained at cocktails following which there was a luncheon.[21] Seems like losing a lot of defense

20    The Bentley Hotel is a classic Renaissance-style hotel located near City Hall in downtown Alexandria in central Louisiana. National Park Services NPGallery Digital Asset Management System, retrieved on November 15, 2019, from https://npgallery.nps.gov/AssetDetail/NRIS/79001084

21    Samuel Houston Jones was the 46th Governor of Louisiana for the term from 1940 to 1944. The Adjutant General was Brigadier General Raymond Fleming, Barry M Stentiford, "Forgotten Militia: The Louisiana State Guard of World War II," *Louisiana History: The Journal of the Louisiana Historical Association* 45, no. 3 (2004): 323–339, retrieved November 17, 2019, from www.jstor.org/stable/4234033

hours of busy men but politics still seems to be an important consideration ever since the shooting started. The 28th division entertained Gen. Krueger at their mess tonight and Gen. Daley attended. The only speech that was given was by Gen. Krueger and it was an excellent one. He has the reputation of being a tough soldier and I have yet to see him smile. While a couple of years older he appears younger than Gen. Daley and is more vigorous.

**February 5, 1942**

Gen. Krueger left by plane this afternoon for his home base. We didn't see him at the office. Gen. Daley's chauffeur has been taking him around and I asked him about the Third Army's Head Man's activities. He was constantly on the go while here and when he saw some instruction which he didn't like, he stepped in and demonstrated how it should be done. At one place he took a rifle away from a man and ran thru the bayonet course himself.

**February 6, 1942**

There is a copy of the plan covering the mission of the Corps making the rounds of certain individuals on the staff and I examined it. When not in the hands of specific individuals it is kept in the safe. It goes into the most minute drill of the whole thing. The force involved is about 25 percent larger than I had imagined. Am now seeing the G-2 releases which come in daily from Washington and contain intelligence information regarding the enemy gathered from operatives on the spot. It is secret information and has to be passed from hand to hand by designated officers. Much of it reflected in the general news stories that appear in the press but there are some fascinating items of news that won't be for public consumption until after the war.

## February 9, 1942

Certainly not much electricity if any being saved by the "wartime" that went into effect during the night since the army has already gotten up in the dark and now that is just prolonged for another hour. A flash came in that this Headquarters was to be out of here by the 16th but I received no word as to how that was to affect my program. This country still doesn't realize that it is at war at least other than there is some fighting on the other side of the world, a few subs being sunk in our front yard and tires and automobiles are not on the market. For the most part people continue to go about their business or pleasure as formerly and talk about the war but think of it as a sort of a spectacle that they are watching like a football game, with maybe a relative here and there on the team but that's about it.

## February 10, 1942

It is now set that the V Corps headquarters is being moved from here to Camp Dix the first of the week, but I'm no longer scheduled to go with the General's car since a convoy is being made up.[22]

## February 11, 1942

This "wartime" has knocked out my riding in the mornings and I've packed that equipment away. Am back in a rut of getting no exercise and I'll soon be as soft as a civilian. Much activity about the Headquarters with files being packed boxes being numbered and cubic contents determined. In my own personal baggage allowance as things stand now, I still have considerable space left. Before clearing the Port of Embarkation, I hope to have every [niche] filled with some article of contraband that will help

---

22    Camp Dix became Fort Dix on March 8, 1939, and the installation became a permanent Army post. During and after World War II, the fort served as a training and staging ground during the war and a demobilization center after the war. The first troops from Fort Dix arrived in Northern Ireland in February 1942 and finished the staging in Northern Ireland by the end of May 1942, eventually entering combat in north Africa late in 1942. *History of Fort Dix New Jersey—50 Years of Service to the Nation 1917–1967.* Prepared by the Information Office, United States Army Training Center, Fort Dix, New Jersey 08640, retrieved November 26, 2019, from http://whitedeercafe.blogspot.com/2017/05/history-of-fort-dix-part-i-1917-1967.html

overcome the handicap I may have with the ladies because of not speaking their native tongue or dialect.

## February 12, 1942

Went with the General when he inspected the local induction center which is now processing two hundred men a day. It is a highly systemized [smooth] operating set-up and should give the men a very favorable impression of their first few days in the Army, particularly as to cleanliness and the quality and quantity of the food. Criticism of the U.S. war effort is becoming more vocal and will increase as news of reverses continues and there is nothing to chalk up in the way of any offensive action of importance.[23] We are handicapped by having an administration which is trying to carry on an all-out war program and still adhere to the eight hour day, forty hour week, or time and a half overtime where that is exceeded with the important of political stooges and bureaucrats still running the important government agencies.

## February 14, 1942

Since I have been pretty much well alerted to move for some weeks, it didn't require much effort to break camp this afternoon and load on to the northbound afternoon train. This marks a very definite milestone in my career. It isn't so important if I visit Alexandria again or when what happens from now on in my career as a soldier. To this point it has been a pleasant case of mock war, but I will soon be in the theatre of operations and probably in the combat zone before many months. I will look back upon my stay in Louisiana with a great deal of pleasure.

---

23    For more on the popular opinion on the war effort in 1942, see "American Popular Opinion and the War Against Germany: The Issue of Negotiated Peace, 1942" by Richard W. Steele, *Journal of American History*, Volume 65, Issue 3, December 1978, pages 704–723, retrieved November 26, 2019, from https://doi.org/10.2307/1901419

# Fort Dix, New Jersey, and Inspection Trips to V Corps Units

Figure 4: V Corps Patch

**February 17, 1942**

Took a Pennsy train to Trenton and a bus from there to Ft. Dix. Got off at the Post Headquarters and found I was a long way from my home base but was fortunate in securing transportation and taken up to the new V [Corps] headquarters. Our offices are to be in four converted barracks buildings, and I gave the men who are fixing things up some ideas as to how we would like the General's set up and the aide's. I have a room in a two-story barracks building close to the office which is filled up with officers from the staff. The camp area as a whole has a rather rundown looking appearance and is bleak, windy and cold.

**February 18, 1942**

Received a very complete assortment of knitted gloves, scarfs, socks and sweaters from Aunt Annie which should take me *unfrostbitten* thru a winter in Iceland.[24] Took the General's car and two chauffeurs into N.Y. this afternoon.

**February 19, 1942**

Met the General on his arrival in New York from Detroit where he has been spending a day with his younger son. He had suggested quarters

---

24    Aunt Annie, the only sister of Gardiner's father. According to Patricia Issel, Gardiner's niece, she was "a spinster and artist, who lived with her parents in St. Catherine's, Ontario. She was rather stern, but much loved by her nephew and nieces." Interview with Patricia Issel on February 24, 2020.

at the Commodore, so we had rooms there with a connecting bath.[25] We drove over to Brooklyn to the Port of Embarkation from which many of the task forces which are being sent out are dispatched. A large contingent of ours had cleared out during the night. The question of how fast the other elements will move is entirely one of securing the necessary bottoms. Over to Governor's Island where the General paid his respects to Gen. Drum.[26]

### February 20, 1942

We are rolling at eight this morning and went straight up to West Point. The General has a son who is a captain and is an instructor there and he caught him in between classes and had a short visit with him and spent a little more time with his family, i.e., wife and two children. He then called on the superintendent of the Academy and we headed down stream again.[27] Quite a thrill to visit the Academy in uniform and to go into buildings and rooms that you would normally never enter as a civilian visitor. The General talks a lot about the days when he was a student at the military academy and I never tire of listening to his stories. We reached Dix late in the afternoon. Among the staff who were lined up to meet the General was a Capt. Dreyer who is carried in the staff roster as an aide who has been in Washington working in the construction quartermaster's office up until a month ago.[28]

---

25    The historic Commodore Hotel, opened in 1919, became the Grand Hyatt in 1980 when Donald Trump converted it as such. It is scheduled to be demolished in July 2022 as a key element in an overall development project. "Grand Hyatt New York Shares Update on Timing Around Proposed Redevelopment Project," retrieved July 30, 2020, from https://www.hyatt.com/en-US/hotel/new-york/grand-hyatt-new-york/nycgh/news-events

26    Lieutenant General Hugh A. Drum was the Commanding General of First Army and II Corps Area (Governors Island, NY). He later commanded the New York National Guard and became President of the Empire State Building. Fort Drum is named after the General.

27    The Superintendent of the U.S. Military Academy at that time was Lieutenant General Robert L. Eichelberger who went on to command the 8th U.S. Army in the Pacific Theatre.

28    Brigadier General Christian F. Dryer later served as an Air Force Officer in Great Britain and later in North Africa, retrieved on November 26, 2019, from https://www.af.mil/About-Us/Biographies/Display/Article/107211/brigadier-general-christian-f-dreyer/

## February 21, 1942

The Carpenters were more than busy during the time I was in New York and the General's office had been completely worked over and his present set up in some respects is better than it was at Beauregard, It is now Major Peca and a number of other officers have been promoted a grade. The General and I left right after lunch for Washington with two drivers. We put up at the Army-Navy club and I had an excellent dinner there with the General following which he went out to call on the family of his son who is stationed here.

## February 22, 1942

The Chief of Staff arrived in time to join us for breakfast and we went out to the War College and spent until mid-afternoon closeted with different members of G.H.Q. particularly those who are tied in with our plan. It appears that our task force is one of two that have been set up and the other group has not sent any troops overseas while of course we already have some on the spot.[29] The big problem is shipping, and it is becoming more critical for the public is not being advised as to the seriousness of the present submarine campaign.[30]

## February 23, 1942

While Washington is swamped with employees and hangers-on brought in by the war activities every indication points to an aggravation of that condition rather than any remedial steps. Lumber and materials are being assembled in the parked area around Washington's monument, on either side of the reflection basin in front of the Lincoln Memorial and

29    Since January 27, 1942, Major General Russell P. Hartle (Commanding General, 34th Division) had been in temporary command of U.S. Army Northern Ireland Force as an additional duty because the V Corps Commander (Major General Edmund L. Daley) never deployed. Headquarters, U.S Army Northern Ireland Force (USANFI), *United States Forces in Northern Ireland,* retrieved on November 26, 2019, from https://history.army.mil/reference/ireland/IRECHR.htm

30    The German U-boat, or submarine, threat in the spring of 1942 was at its height because of a large gap in mid-Atlantic air cover putting shipping vessels at risk. Once the United States entered the war, U-boats ranged from the Atlantic coast of the U.S. and Canada to the Gulf of Mexico. John P. Vanzo, "U-boat Attacks during World War II," *New Georgia Encyclopedia,* January 31, 2011, retrieved on November 26, 2019, from https://www.georgiaencyclopedia.org/articles/history-archaeology/u-boat-attacks-during-world-war-ii

in all other open areas with the view of erecting temporary structures to house the additional workers that are swarming into the city. Have been impressed by the number of young majors and lieutenant colonels I have seen in the street. Apparently knowing the right people and being close to the throne brings rapid promotion for certain individuals. Undoubtedly many are capable, but it is rather unfair to those who will be and are ducking the bullets. A very pleasant but uneventful drive back to Ft. Dix.

### February 24, 1942

I had been told in Louisiana that Capt. Dreyer while being carried as an aide would not function in that capacity since he had been brought into the staff to do engineering work and had been listed as an aide to fit him in since there was no vacancy as of the time in the engineering section. It was also stated that he would probably have gone overseas by the time we reached here. He is, however very much on the job and all primed to be of whatever service he can. I told Major Peca that I would like to have an understanding as to how things stood, for I was afraid that Capt. Dreyer and I might get stuck in the door while both trying to beat the other into the General's office when he rang. The Major said he would be the head man handling certain personal affairs for the general and that Capt. Dreyer would be next in line and from now on we should alternate on the outside trips.

### February 25, 1942

One thing that stood out in the conversations in Washington Sunday was the salesmanship that the American Force Commander in Ireland expected to perform in persuading De Valera to open up the ports of Eire to Allied shipping.[31] Drove into New York this afternoon and we put up at the Commodore again.

31    After the establishment of the Irish Free State, a set of deep-water Treaty Ports (ports of "Eire" or, in English "Ireland") were retained in accordance with the Anglo-Irish Treaty of December 6, 1921, by the United Kingdom. These ports were initially used to support the World War I conflict with German U-boat incursions. Their control went back under the newly formed Ireland in 1937 and Éamon de Valera, the leader of the newly formed Fianna

**February 26, 1942**

Made a trip over to the Port of Embarkation with the General this a.m. It is a very busy place and heavily guarded although I think an enemy agent could get a pretty picture of what was going on from the windows of any one of the many apartments that front on that area. Out unit maintains a staff there for liaison purposes and to be of assistance when part of our force clears thru there.

**February 27, 1942**

We made a leisurely trip back to Ft. Dix arriving shortly after noon.

**March 3, 1942**

Accompanied the General and the chief of Staff on an inspection of the FA [Field Artillery] units belonging to the 34th division which are still here.[32] It was more of an area inspection and a check-up on housekeeping. The General checks the fingernails of the cooks, looks in all the iceboxes, criticizes the presence of newspapers in offices, takes exception to old material on bulletin boards and gives the impression of a tough thorough inspector.

**March 4, 1942**

I went along as a door opener and sort of a direction finder on another inspection this morning which was made of the units of the infantry regiments of the 34th which haven't moved overseas yet. They had not only been forewarned of the General's visit but had been tipped off as a result of yesterday's visit as to what was expected, and things were

Fáil party at the time and essentially the Prime Minister of Ireland, continued to maintain Irish neutrality during the war but turned an eye toward the Allied use of the ports. David Freeman. "Winston Churchill & Eamon De Valera: A Thirty Year Relationship," The Winston Churchill International Society, (2008), retrieved on November 27, 2019, from https://winstonchurchill.org/publications/finest-hour-extras/churchill-and-eamon-de-valera-thirty-year-relationship/2008

32    The 34th Infantry Division Artillery consists of Headquarters and Headquarters Battery, 34th Infantry Division Artillery, 125th Field Artillery Battalion (125th FAB) (105 mm), 151st Field Artillery Battalion (151st FAB) (105 mm), 175th Field Artillery Battalion (175th FAB) (105 mm), and 185th Field Artillery Battalion (185th FAB) (155 mm). Minnesota National Guard 34th Infantry Division Artillery, retrieved on November 26, 2019, from https://minnesotanationalguard.ng.mil/documents/2018/10/34th-infantry-division-artillery-history.pdf/

more than shined up. This morning, prior to the reporting for work, the staff was formed and marched at attention about the area for twenty minutes to sort of limber us up. The General and I left right after lunch for Indiantown Gap, Penn., where the 37th division is now stationed.[33] Had dinner with the staff of the 37th and then the General visited several of the Divisional schools that were in action. This is a most attractive camp, and everyone is comfortably fixed.

## March 5, 1942

The morning was given over to inspecting mess halls, regimental headquarters, barracks buildings, etc., and then a drive through some of the training area. We left right after lunch for N.Y.C.

## March 8, 1942

There is a new War Department order out on saluting to the effect that enlisted men and officers will exchange salutes wherever they meet which abrogates the old rule that you were not required to salute in public places. There has been pretty good distribution on that order for in walking about the city today I was saluted by soldiers at every turn. The General picked me up at the hotel early in the evening and we proceeded to Dix stopping for supper enroute.

## March 9, 1942

The corps staff is playing host to a group of visiting officers from the other divisions and there were over two hundred and fifty officers fell in this morning for the usual staff morning hike or march about the area. There is a program of instructions and orientation and I attended this morning's sessions. This afternoon the commanding generals of the 32nd

---

33    The 37th Infantry Division was a National Guard division from Ohio, nicknamed the "Buckeye Division". The Division served in the Pacific Theater during the war. Major General Robert S. Beightler commanded the Division during its entire period of Federal service in World War II; one of only eleven Generals to command their divisions for the entire period of the war. History of the 37th Infantry Division, retrieved on November 27, 2019, from https://history.army.mil/html/forcestruc/cbtchron/cc/037id.htm

and 37th divisions reported in, so the aide's office was pretty well filled up with aides. I sort of functioned as chief bartender at the General's cottage when he entertained the visiting generals and the aides before dinner.

**March 10, 1942**

All of the visiting officers and the staff of officers were given an examination in map reading this a.m. When I completed the course at Riley and wrote in the final exam last summer without mistake, I thought I was fairly proficient, so it came as something of a shock to learn how much I had forgotten about the subject because I far from distinguished myself. Saw two very interesting training films and got a little more than the usual exercise. All of the officers attending these conferences were given a brisk half-hour march this a.m., and I played in the touch football game this afternoon.

**March 16, 1942**

For selfish reasons I have been letting no opportunity go by the boards to be just a little more useful to the General than anyone else when it comes to "aiding" him without adopting the "yes man" or valet approach of some of his staff which does not however describe the approach of the other two aides. I came into the picture with the understanding that I was to sort of take over from Major Peca and I'm not going to be relegated to third place just because I was told that is where I am to fit in.

**March 18, 1942**

The purpose of our trip up here was to visit the 32nd Division which has recently moved to Camp [Devens] from Camp Livingston.[34] [Devens] is some thirty-five miles NW of Boston. Major General Harding picked

34    There were three divisions that were sent to Fort Devens, Massachusetts, for training for the war: the 1st, 32nd, and the 45th. The Fourth Women's Army Auxiliary Corps (WAAC) Training Center was also built on the installation, and it officially opened on April 1943 (WAAC would later become known as the Women's Army Corps just three months later). Fort Devens was also used to hold prisoners of war, with over 5,000 German and Italian soldiers held in a temporary camp in the installation. The POW camp remained in operation until May 1946. Retrieved on December 2, 2019, from http://armybases.org/fort-devens-ma-massachusetts/

us up at the hotel this a.m. From the way things were turned out at Camp I don't think there is much question but when the Commanding General of the 37th Division passed on what the General liked and didn't like. There was a lot of snap and polish and there were bands playing all over the place and the General was highly pleased with the appearance of the organization.

**March 20, 1942**

The war seemed a little closer last night with the camp in total darkness and the sirens howling. Wonder how long before we will be experiencing the real thing. The whole Atlantic seaboard is having practice blackouts. The G-3 section put the staff members through an examination this afternoon designed to determine how observing you were and how well you could follow rather involved instructions. I made it around the prescribed course all right but where we were required to estimate ranges, found myself missing badly as to the mid-distances although I judged those up to six hundred yards reasonably accurately as I did those over three miles.

**March 22, 1942**

The General spent the morning at the office reading the Sunday papers which sort of immobilized me in that I was there when he came in, so I stayed until he left. His principal diversions are working crossword puzzles. He is able to delegate most everything and claims that he doesn't devote five minutes time to administrative matters each day. There is no time lost in making decisions and the C/S gets an almost immediate yes or no on the things that he takes into him. The General's system is fine so long as he has a capable C/S. As to that, there are times when I have my doubts.

**March 23, 1942**

The General over the weekend decided to pay a visit to Fort Knox and see something of the 1st Armored Division which is stationed there and which according to the plan is to make up a part of our force. It is due to start moving toward Dix shortly. The C/S and our G-4 were included in the expedition and we caught a mid-afternoon train out of North Philadelphia.

**March 24, 1942**

The General was met on our arrival in Louisville this a.m. by the Commanding General of the 1st Armored Division.[35] Just as we entered the Ft. Knox Military Reservation, we were greeted by a guard of honor in halftracks which after being inspected roared into the Post ahead of us. After a short visit at the Divisions H.Q.'s we went on an inspection trip of Division and Post. An Armored division is a tremendous outfit and the equipment that they have represents a staggering tonnage. Saw some of the newest tanks which are being turned out, but which are short of ordnance. There was a noticeable high degree of esprit throughout the Post. A luncheon with all of the generals on the Post in attendance, a few brief calls and we were on our way to Cincinnati via motor.

**March 27, 1942**

The morning walk and drill was augmented for the first time with some calisthenics. I wish they would put some of that in the schedule every day.

**March 28, 1942**

If it weren't for the trips, I make with the General this job would be a deadly one for there is less going on in this office than there was at Beauregard. The General is a great believer in delegating authority and is able to operate the show without much effort on his part. He doesn't or hasn't passed any of the military end on to me. There is a lot of

35    The 1st Armored Division, nicknamed "Old Ironsides," was first commanded by Major General Bruce R. Magruder. Retrieved on December 2, 2019, from https://army.togetherweserved.com/army/servlet/tws.webapp. WebApp?cmd=PublicUnitProfile&type=Unit&ID=252

incompetence in high places in this organization and it makes me pretty unhappy at times to see the way things are handled.

## April 1, 1942

Was given the job of guide for our platoon at drill this morning. That was my assignment back when I took drill at Montana State College, in 1923 and 24. Am wondering how I look now in comparison.

## April 2, 1942

The members of the staff are being given a practical examination on map reading and I was scheduled to take it this morning. Will have to do so however when they have a make-up for the absentees, since I was detailed by the general to entertain his active twelve-year-old grandson during the morning. We walked and drove about the reservation and took a swing out by the airport and artillery range. This camp is mushrooming all over the place and I was very much impressed by the extent of the work that was being performed at the airfield.[36] Joined in the touch-football this afternoon and loosened up some of the muscles that I toughened up or rather laid up when I played last Tuesday. Took the grandson to a Post movie.

## April 3, 1942

An argument which started between a colored soldier and a white soldier as to priority in a line at a telephone booth in a pool hall just off the reservation started a riot last night. When it was over there were two dead colored soldiers and one white MP had been killed. None of the men involved belonged to our unit.

---

36      Fort Dix was expanding so rapidly during the early years of World War II that surrounding towns, such as Pointville and New Hanover, passed out of existence by the end of 1942. "History of Fort Dix New Jersey—50 Years of Service to the Nation 1917–1967." Prepared by the Information Office, United States Army Training Center, Fort Dix, New Jersey 08640, retrieved on December 6, 2019, from http://whitedeercafe.blogspot.com/2017/05/history-of-fort-dix-part-i-1917-1967.html

## April 6, 1942

The reason for this trip was to visit a detachment of about a thousand engineers of ours and a group of doctors and nurses who are at Ft. Edwards [NY]. They were with the last convoy that started out but the ship they were on developed trouble a couple of days out and they had to turn back. The colonel had reported that their morale was pretty low, and they thought that they were sort of being forgotten and asked the General if he wouldn't come up and inspect them. We drove from there into Boston stopping off to take a look at the Plymouth Rock.

## April 8, 1942

The 1st Armored Division which we inspected while out at Knox is a part of our task force and is now in the process of moving into Ft. Dix, for transshipment. Several convoys have arrived. They are a cocky outfit and are sort of the opinion that the Corps will revolve around them and the general has been fully aware of that attitude.

## April 10, 1942

I was given the third platoon to drill this morning for our usual half hour tour of the campus. It had been raining hard all night and the ground was muddy and it was cold. Though a little double timing would start the blood pounding so warmed them up that way and then marched them across a sodden parade ground to see those elements of the 1st Armored that have arrived. The other two platoons stayed on the hard-surfaced roads and I got a lot of dirty looks from my command.

## April 11, 1942

There has never been any doubt in my own mind how much happier I am in the Army today than I would be in civil life. The men who it is really hard on are those who want to get into uniform but can't, particularly the younger fellows.

## April 14, 1942

Now that the nice weather is at hand, I'm getting pretty sick of this sitting in the office all day. When the time is opportune, I'm going to ask for a transfer back to troops. The General and I caught an evening southbound train out of Trenton.

## April 15, 1942

We unloaded at Charlotte, North Carolina, this a.m., where we were greeted by the Commanding General of the 73rd FA Brigade which is one of our outfits which has just come north from Camp Shelby.[37] They are in a tent camp. There was a particularly fine-looking guard of honor lined up at the entrance to camp and they were on their toes all the way through to give the General a favorable impression, and they succeeded in doing so. They had a special tent with his name out in front of it rigged up for him, the band played outside of the mess hall while we were at lunch, etc. Was impressed by the excellent physique of the men.

## April 16, 1942

We detrained at Trenton at 5:40 a.m. We could have caught a later train out of Charlotte with a correspondingly more seasonal arrival, but the general was anxious to be here first thing this morning so that he could make his usual pre breakfast inspection of the early morning drill. He wanders all over the area jumping on those commanders who he feels do not put enough drive into their drill of instruction. One thing which irritates him very much is to see soldiers with their hands in their pockets. He sent me out twice to correct men that he spotted from his window and he summoned one battery commander whose men he thought were particularly bad in that respect and gave him a very rough going over.

---

37    The commanding general was Brigadier General William A. March.

## April 17, 1942

The staff was invited to send ten officers over to the artillery range by the Armored Division to go through a school that they were giving their men. I wasn't included in the ten designated but secured permission to go along so borrowed a pair of coveralls and spent the morning learning something about the operation of the M-3 tank which is listed as a medium tank and with crew of seven and ammunition on board weighs forty-two tons.[38] On one trip I fired the 75mm three times, once while the tank was moving and the 37mm twice, once while in motion. I also acted as assistant gunner while another officer fired the same course. They have an autogyro stabilizer on each gun which of course simplifies immeasurably training it while in motion. The noise wasn't near as bad as I had expected it to be, but I did get my head cracked pretty hard several times since I didn't have a crash helmet.

Figure 5: M3 Lee Tank and Crew in Souk-el-Arba, Tunisia, November 26, 1942
(Photograph from the Patricia Issel Collection)

38    The M3 Lee Tank, officially Medium Tank, M3, was an American medium tank used during World War II. In Britain, the tank was called by two names based on the turret configuration and crew size. Tanks employing U.S. pattern turrets were called the "Lee," named after Confederate general Robert E. Lee. Variants using British pattern turrets were known as "Grant," named after Union general Ulysses S. Grant. Steven J. Zaloga. *M3 Lee/Grant Medium Tank 1941–45*. (Oxford, United Kingdom: Osprey Publishing, August 10, 2005), p. 4.

## April 20, 1942

As the result of an unsatisfactory officers' barracks which the General visited yesterday, the Colonel of that regiment was relieved of his command. The General is all over the area in the morning and sails into any one where he feels that they are not conducting themselves or their drill properly. Whenever a soldier is found with his hands in his pockets, coat unbuttoned, or similarly out of step, or doesn't salute promptly and properly, he is ordered to the Corps Headquarters and his commanding officer sent for to get him and receive a dressing down from the C/S.

## April 21, 1942

Major Dreyer and I asked if we might have permission to go out and watch one of our artillery units which is now firing, in action and the General readily approved. Was very much surprised to see the extent of the range facilities here.[39] We spent most of our time at the observation point from which the fire was being directed and I learned a lot about how fire was brought down on a point particularly when viewed from an angle as this was. I must say though that I was not favorably impressed by the apparent ability of the junior officers who were working on these problems. The Armored Division was also firing and have trouble with starting fires since the countryside is very dry. When they do start a fire break and scattering dirt on the flames.

## April 22, 1942

The General has shown an increasing tendency toward "toughness" and this morning had all the staff routed out for a 7:00am formation and sent them on their way to inspect the units in the area. Since the

---

39    During World War II, Fort Dix trained and processed personnel, including ten full divisions, for operations in every theater throughout the world. Peak loads in all respects exceeded those of World War I. Several encyclopedias and military reference volumes credit Fort Dix as "the largest army training center in the country" during the Second World War. *History of Fort Dix New Jersey—50 Years of Service to the Nation 1917-1967.* Prepared by the Information Office, United States Army Training Center, Fort Dix, New Jersey 08640, retrieved on December 14, 2019, from http://whitedeercafe.blogspot.com/2017/05/history-of-fort-dix-part-i-1917-1967.html

normal formation time has been over it was announced that from now on reveille would be observed by all the staff which means up and in motion by 6am. That won't be any hardship on me for I've been getting up at 6:15 regularly now.

**April 23, 1942**

Was told by our Adjutant General that they obstacle that my promotion had run into was the fact that I had not served for six months in grade which is the prerequisite apparently for a move from one bracket to the next. That means if that is the only thing in my way that I will qualify on the 13th of June. If things run true to form, however there will be something else popup about that time. Went out this a.m. and watched a battalion of 105mm's belonging to the Armored Force fire. They are on self-propelled mounts being halftracks and they gave the impression of a great flexibility and fire power against moving targets. I don't know whether my trigonometry could be brushed off sufficiently to make me an artillery officer, but I certainly liked the looks of that outfit. I'd much rather be firing at a tank from one of those than to be in a tank trying to get hit by some anti-tank weapon.

**April 25, 1942**

When I headed down towards the General's cottage at ten to seven as has now become my morning routine, I passed the same sentry who had challenged me when I came in at 4. He recognized me and said, "You look just as fresh as if you had ten hours of sleep, sir." I may have looked that way in a poor light, but I certainly didn't feel that way. My tour of inspection with the General lasts for about an hour and forty-five minutes and a lot of it is at the trot for he continually sends me off to round up some outfit or round up some officer so that I get a very fair work out.

## April 26, 1942

I was waiting for the General when he came out from mass at 7:45 a.m., and we had breakfast together. The plan had been to be heading for Washington before nine, but all units were drilling this a.m. and the General couldn't resist the temptation to go watch them for a while, so we were somewhat delayed in getting underway. We did a quick job of freshening up on arrival at the Army Navy Club in Washington and then went out to the Army Navy Country Club to a dinner party at which there were three other Major Generals and I was the only thing as low as captain.[40]

## April 28, 1942

We sent the car on ahead to Philadelphia last night and caught the train up there which gave us a longer stay in the City. On the way over to Camp which we reached at one a.m., the General told the Chief of Staff that he thought there should be a practice alert, so we were all called out at five a.m. and ordered to report immediately in full packs to the main headquarters.

## April 29, 1942

There was a large-scale moving day here most of the daylight hours with the result that many barracks which have been well lighted up for some time now are dark. Don't know just how many were getting away but they cleaned out all of the balance of the Division which had gone across and started in on the Armored Force and took a fair chunk out of our staff. There were convoys rolling by here all afternoon taking the men down to the railroad from whence they were being shuttled to the P.E.[41] There was no cheering or band music. Such movements are very commonplace here and besides they do not wish to attract attention to them by any sort of a display.

40    The Army Navy Country Club has offered active military, former military, and military-minded customers a place to enjoy the elegant facilities, fine dining, golf course, bar and lounge, hotel rooms, and a vast array of social and networking events. Located in Arlington, Virginia, it was founded in 1924.

41    The New York Port of Embarkation (NYPOE) was a United States Army command responsible for the movement of troops and supplies from the United States to overseas commands during World War II. In June 1942, many troops started departing through the newly activated Camp Kilmer, New Jersey.

## April 30, 1942

Took my usual cross-country run as the General made his inspection this a.m. The General became particularly provoked when he discovered five unshaven men in one platoon this morning so ordered that unit and its officer to camp for a period of one week. Over to Philly this evening with the General where we boarded a Boston sleeper.

## May 1, 1942

We were met at the station in Boston that a.m. by Maj. Gen. Key who commands the 45th Division, a National Guard outfit which we have secured in place of the 32nd.[42] This division just completed its movement into Ft. Devon yesterday and the General wanted to have a look at them before he got away. Gen. Key had been well advised as to when the General wanted, and he found few things much pleased with what he saw. This Division draws a large number of troops from Oklahoma and some units have as high as seventy percent Indians on their roster. The troops were a good-looking bunch of well hardened men and they were putting lots of drive and feeling into their bayonet drill. We drive down to Springfield where we caught a train back into NYC.

## May 2, 1942

We went over to the Port where we learned that our number was about up on the takeoff time.

## May 4, 1942

I'll not only be completely satisfied that the General is going to make this trip until the boat is out of sight of land. Word came from Washington that a further reduction was to be made in the age of field officers and all

42    General William S. Key commanded the 45th until October 1945. See footnote #28 for more on the 32nd command relief. The 32nd was reassigned to the Pacific Theater and the 45th replaced the 32nd for the African/European fight. Flint Whitlock, Flint, *The Rock of Anzio: From Sicily To Dachau, A History of the U.S. 45th Infantry Division* (New York City, New York: Basic Books, 2005), p. 7.

those above that would have to be put on less active duty.[43] If strictly applied, that would mean the loss to the armored division of practically all of their regimental commanders since the top age for colonels would be forty-five. It would be pretty ruthless to arbitrarily enforce that, would badly disrupt things for the time being and would certainly cause a lot of heartbreaks.

## Relieved as Aide and Assigned to G-1 Section

**May 7, 1942**

Well the roof certainly came crashing in this morning. When I stopped in at the Generals as is my normal routine, he informed me that he had received a radiogram last night relieving him of command of the V Corps. It was a well held secret during the day and I don't believe anyone on the staff besides the General, the C/S, the Deputy C/S, and myself knew of it. The General was pretty much broken up and didn't come near the office. He assumed that I would go with him wherever he was reassigned, but I told the C/S that it might be constructed as not being loyal but since I had taken this job primarily because I had been informed that it meant a move abroad, I didn't want to get left behind now. The C/S told the General that I wanted to go, and he said fine he wouldn't stand in my way if I wanted to make it. Naturally I am very much disappointed at this change of events and of course with it has gone my glimmering prospect of a promotion.

**May 8, 1942**

The C/S assembled all the officers at nine this a.m. and informed them that General Daley had been sent on a "secret mission" and was no longer

---

43    There may have been some confusion as to how The Selective Training and Service Act of 1940, known as the Burke–Wadsworth Act, was interpreted when the U.S. entered World War II when it stated that all men from their eighteenth birthday until the day before their forty-fifth birthday were made subject to military service. After the U.S. entered World War II, amendments to the Selective Training and Service Act on December 20, 1941, made all men between the ages of 20 and 44 liable for military service. It appears that the interpretation was that you could not serve if you were older than 45 years of age, which was not the case. Selective Service System, "Selective Service in Peacetime First Report of the Director of Selective Service, 1940-1941," (Washington: Government Printing Offices, 1942).

with the Corps. The staff has been picked by the General and most of the staff has gone up one grade since they have been with him. He has been highly regarded by all of them and there are many heavy hearts among his officers today. I made numerous trips to the General's cottage escorting visiting General officers who wished to pay their respects, running errands for him, and taking down the mail. Orders came through relieving me as aide and assigning me to the G-1 section. I certainly have no desire or intention of remaining there and Gen. Daley said that both would "get me across." Much speculation as to the reasons for the General being relieved. Age, of course is one of the foremost, walking on the armored forces toes is another, and a third is that it will prevent complicating a situation where he would be in Ireland as a junior commander to Gen. [Chaney] in London, who while his junior, would actually command the General.[44]

## May 9, 1942

Made a number of trips down to the General's cottage. He has had no further word as to his status. We were restricted to camp tonight, and all outgoing messages, mail, telegrams, etc., are now taboo.

## Overseas via the "Queen Mary"

## May 10, 1942

This could be the last day for me to have trod on American soil and in any event, it will probably be a long time before I walk on the home turf for tonight, we are sleeping on board the Queen Mary.[45] At four-thirty this afternoon we lined up out front of the barracks at Dix and loaded down

44    General Daley was 59 years old in May 1942. "U.S. Army Officers 1939-1945," retrieved on January 19, 2020, from https://www.unithistories.com/officers/US_Army_officers_K01.html#Knuebel_JH. Headquarters, United States Army Forces in the British Isles (USAFBI) established under MG James E. Chaney by reorganization and expansion of the Special Observer Group. United States Forces in Northern Ireland, retrieved on January 19, 2020, from https://history.army.mil/reference/ireland/IRECHR.htm

45    Gardiner is referring to the first voyage of the two former British passenger liners (*Queen Mary* and *Queen Elizabeth*) on their high-speed unescorted shuttle runs to move American forces to the British Isles. The first cruise for the *Queen Mary* arrived in Firth of Clyde as it sailed from New York on May 10, the fourth increment (10,000 men) of the MAGNET Force. United States Forces in Northern Ireland, retrieved on January 19, 2020 from https://history.army.mil/reference/ireland/IRECHR.htm

with our full field equipment, piled aboard trucks which took us down to a railroad siding where we boarded a train which ran us into a ferry-siding Hoboken. There we boarded a ferry and sat watching the New York skyline fade away as darkness set in before proceeding up the river and past where the Normandie [sic] lay on her side to the pier where the Queen Mary was berthed. We went aboard immediately and proceeded directly to our staterooms. I am in a stateroom on the Main Deck which in peace time carried two but has been triple decked to carry eight. Surprised to find we had mattresses, sheets, pillows and pillowcases, towels, etc. We eight captains turned in since the orders were to stay in our staterooms. Spent an hour with the General just before we left. He is quite reconciled to being left behind now but is hoping that he will get some command that will keep him in the field and not pigeon-holed in an office.

**May 11, 1942**

Was surprised on awakening to find that we were still at the dock although it wasn't for long since we pulled into the river exactly at 8 o'clock and headed downstream. I was down in the dining room having breakfast when we cleared Manhattan and through a porthole had a good look at the Statue of Liberty who seemed to be cheering us on our way. We weren't allowed on deck until we were out of sight of land. Found on my first trip out on deck that there were three destroyers tagging along with us, a Navy blimp overhead and two planes which kept swinging around and around us. The ship's staff captain addressed a meeting of all the officers on board and discussed the precautions we must take to minimize the loss of life in the event of an attack.[46] He had an attentive audience for he spoke with authority having come through two torpedoing's in this war already, one in which some three thousand were lost when the Lancastria went down

---

46   The ship Captain was Sir James Gordon Partridge Bisset who would captain both *Queen Mary* and *Queen Elizabeth* on a total of sixty-six wartime voyages during World War II. John Edwards, "Commodore James Bisset," *Ocean Liners Magazine*, retrieved on January 19, 2020, from http://oceanlinersmagazine.com/2015/07/15/commodore-james-bisset/

during the evacuation of France.[47] Drew the midnight to three a.m. blackout patrol watch on the sun deck. It was a clear but cold night and I made good use of all of the warm clothes I had along with me. My duties consisted of a continuous patrol to observe for violations of the blackout of which I observed none. About all you could see on deck were the dim white blurs which marked the life preservers of the men on guard.

Figure 6: *RMS Queen Mary* was converted to an American Troop Carrier during World War II (Jason Ponic, "Whatever Happened to the RMS Queen Elizabeth, RMS Queen Mary's Sister Ship?" OwlVacation, retrieved December 29, 2019, from https://owlcation.com/humanities/RMSQueenElizabeth)

## May 12, 1942

Meals are served at two sittings and all of us in our cabin are in the second which means breakfast at eight-thirty, so we sleep fairly late. I set my alarm clock however so as to be the first one in the bathroom. We had no aerial escort this morning and our three destroyers after a salute of a blast from their whistles wheeled about at noon and started back home leaving us completely on our own. I spent most of the day on deck. There was a practice boat drill and it was pretty ragged although somewhat better than the one held yesterday. We have 9,660 officers and men on

47    The *Lancastria* was sunk on June 17, 1940, off the French port of St. Nazaire while taking part in Operation Ariel, the evacuation of British nationals and troops from France, two weeks after the Dunkirk evacuation. For more on this tragedy see Brian James Crabb, *The Forgotten Tragedy: The Story of the Sinking of HMT Lancastria*, (Lincolnshire, UK: Paul Watkins Publishing, 2002).

board, which is a record load for the old girl. Quite a valuable cargo to be entrusting to her sole care but I guess those who have charge of such matters know what they are doing. The lifeboats if everyone was launched and all were filled to capacity, could not handle a third of the men on board. There is considerable armament, every gun with the exception of a six-inch naval piece on the stern being primarily used for use against aircraft. The principal defense against submarines and hostile war craft is speed. There are frequent changes of course although none of them sudden. Our principal direction of travel has been northerly, and it has been getting colder all of the time. Most everyone turns out for four o'clock tea.

**May 13, 1942**

The amazing thing about this trip continues to be the meals. It would appear that there has been practically no change if any in the quality, variety or quantity of the food. There is a new printed menu for each meal with several choices of entrée. The linen is fresh and plentiful and the waiter service of the best English steward standard. The weather continued to freshen throughout the day so that we were getting something of a roll by afternoon and a few of the boys elected to go without dinner and some of them lost their lunches. I had no difficulty but continued to spend a lot of time on deck. It was almost a gale where one rounded the sundeck just under the bridge. We had both a boat drill and an air-raid drill. The latter consisted of running everyone below decks. Would be quite a mess if someone slipped a torpedo into us just after we had all responded to an air-raid warning. Aside from the air-raid and boat drills there hasn't been anything in the way of training. The officers have been playing cards and sleeping. At teatime today an enlisted men's orchestra provided music and this evening the band played. The main lounge hasn't been touched all of the nice overstuffed furniture still being in place. We sighted a lone freighter bravely plowing along on its own.

*{Much of the content from May 14–17, 1942, was on Gardiner's experience aboard the Queen Mary.}*

## V Corps Headquarters to Ireland

**May 18, 1942**

A cabin boy came around with hot tea as we were getting dressed and that constituted our breakfast supplemented by the biscuits which we took from the can of our "C" ration. The first glimpse of Belfast was a gloomy and rain-drenched slip into which our boat moved. Just on the next dock they were completing the unloading the last of the tanks which had come over on a "sea-train" for the Armored Division. There were a group of officers down at the wharf to greet us as we came off the gangplank. We were put in buses, the side curtains of which were drawn, and after a short run were unloaded on the grounds of the estate or an estate of Sir Thomas Dixon.[48] It didn't take much time to set up camp for our bedrolls and foot lockers have yet to arrive, so we were issued blankets until our rolls put in an appearance. The officer who has been holding down the G-1 office in addition to many other duties since the first units came over and took Col. Holmes and another officer and myself for a sort of orientation swing around the countryside. Called on Gen. Hartle. He has been in command of the American Forces over here and has now been designated as the Commanding General of the V Army Corps. I told him what I knew of Gen. Daley's being relieved.

**May 19, 1942**

The four blankets that I had last night were none to many and I was very happy to see my bedroll and "A" footlocker came rolling in today. The four bottles of liquor that I had packed in my bedroll for the General came through still a one hundred percent proof. The Corps

---

48    Thomas Dixon was a Northern Ireland politician who made his grounds and home available to U.S. forces and its leadership.

Staff is scattered pretty well over the countryside with the C.G. and Administrative units here. The junior officers are quartered in Nissen huts which are quite satisfactory.[49] The principal shortcoming in that setup is the distance one must go to the latrine. The main house which is a fine big structure serves as the offices for the staff here and the residence of the C.G. and the colonels and lieutenant colonels. We all mess in the same dining room and the food has been very good the only deficiency of any consequence that I have noted to date being the fact that there is no butter on the table. The huts are scattered about the main house so as to take advantage of the cover offered by the trees and the shrubbery.

## May 20, 1942

There is a very large volume of work going through this office each day and I can see where I can be more than busy in short order. Am certainly going to try to avoid getting to be one of the regulars in the department and there was one item that went through today that was a tantalizing prospect for a diversion into the kind of work that I would like. An American Commando unit is to be made up from men in this force and the first group will train with the British to be attached to them for a period after their training is completed.[50] I was given the file on the matter to write a letter to the Commanding General of the 34th Division and the 1st Armored asking them to submit the names of a lieutenant colonel and a captain to study the British system with the view of being in position to line up a group to serve as the cadre for our own force. The directive said that the average age of the British commandos was twenty-five. I'd probably be too old for the captain and of course I'm a long way from a lieutenant colonel.[51] I realize of course that at thirty six I'm not as

49    The Nissen huts were one of the very first metal Arch-Style Quonset huts.

50    Gardiner is referencing the U.S. Army Rangers who trained in Northern Ireland before the European Invasion. For more on this see, Dominic J. Caraccilo, *Forging a Special Operations Force: The US Army Rangers* (Warwick, UK: Helion & Company, 2015).

51    This included the selection of Lieutenant Colonel William O. Darby, a plank holder in the formation of the

capable of rough going as I was ten years ago although I think I am, and it might be that the physical output required is more than I could produce. Took a two hour brisk walk this evening.

## May 21, 1942

Yesterday morning for a half hour everyone wore their gas masks at work that being standard operating procedure for that day. You were required to keep them on while using the telephone and they were surprisingly of little trouble so far as making yourself heard was concerned. When I last said goodbye to the General, he said that General Hartle would now be authorized three aides and he might take me on. My visit with him was of the briefest and carried no indication on his part of any such prospect. He now has one aide who is a regular army captain being a West Point graduate. They are pretty much behind on some regulations over here and he learned yesterday for the first time that he would not be able to function in that capacity after June 30, there being an AR out ruling our regular army officers as aides after that date.

*{Entries from May 23–29, 1942, are omitted as they were mostly associated with administrative Army topics}*

## May 30, 1942

By next Memorial Day the United States will have many more war dead to honor than it has today. There was no official notice of the day taken in this command it definitely being a day of duty. I miss the troop activity that we had around Dix. There I got considerable exercise just from saluting but here it is seldom I have occasion to do so. The shift which will move the "Force" Command to Lurgan and place the "Base" Command here started to get underway today.[52] Have had my eye on a modern-day Rangers.

52     In January, the Headquarters for United States Army Northern Ireland Force (USANFI) was officially established at Wilmont House (seven miles southwest of Belfast); Headquarters of Northern Ireland Base Command (Provisional) was activated at Wilmont House under the command of Brigade General Leroy P. Collins (former

more desirable hut and in all the moving in and out that was going on today I arranged to be shifted into it.

Figure 7: Wilmont House where the United States Army Northern Ireland Force was headquartered (Public Domain)

## May 31, 1942

There wasn't much work accomplished in the office this morning for that group which constitutes the major portion of our force was moving out. Colonel Holmes who is the section chief and who has been a most pleasant person to work for headed the departing G-2 section with three assistants. That leaves me behind with a Lt. Colonel Lamb who has been running the G-2 and the Adjutant General Offices since the first units of our outfit came over here in January of this year. Don't know how long I'll be here for I received a note back this afternoon from my friends with the Armored Division saying that he had fixed a place up for me in the 13th Armored Regiment and if I would initiate transfer proceedings they would be approved from that end. Colonel Holmes has indicated that he would approve a request for a transfer but there will be one obstacle to clear and that is Colonel Kneubel. I am rather afraid he may be inclined to spike it for I think he feels that I ran out on the General when I didn't stay behind with him. Two officers and I started out hiking after lunch and three and a half hours later were on top of the highest place of ground in this area being a Mt. [Divis] which is back of Belfast. Had a wonderful view of the country and could see Scotland. Walked down into Belfast where we had dinner.[53]

## June 1, 1942

Initiated a request for transfer to Armored Division. Colonel Holmes, who was here this afternoon, said to clear it through Col. Lamb and he pigeon-holed it. I don't think he is anxious to have any change until someone of the over aged grade officers is brought in here to help. Dropped a note to the C.O. of the 13th Armored Regiment advising him that I had started a request through for a transfer.[54]

## June 4, 1942

This morning before I got out of bed, I looked out the window to the north and could see as I have been able to the past several mornings a whole flock barrage balloons floating over Belfast. On clear nights they seem to run them up regularly after dark. Some of the old age officers that have been relieved are showing up at this headquarters for reassignment. It is a tough break after bringing and organization to this point to have it taken away from you just because of an arbitrary limitation that says you are too old for the job.

53    Divis and Black Mountain are the highest points boasting views across the north. Divis, or Dubhais, means 'black ridge', referring to the dark basalt bedrock found in the area. Divis and Black Mountain rest in the heart of the Belfast Hills providing lookouts over the Belfast cityscape. Divis stands at 478 meters (1,562 feet) and Black Mountain at 390 meters (1,275 feet). Belfast Hills Partnership, retrieved on January 20, 2020, from http://belfasthills.org/visiting/divis/

54    The Commander of the 13th Armored Regiment at the time was then-Colonel Paul Robinett. He authored a well-known book titled *Armor Command* that chronicled the war from the U.S. to North Africa and on. Brigadier General Paul McDonald Robinett, Armor Command, (Washington, D.C.: McGregor & Wheeler, 1958).

## June 5, 1942

There was much chasing about by certain of our staff today for we were entertaining a Lt. General, a visiting Major General and about a half dozen Brigadier Generals. They were of the party which had recently come over to London, the head man in this group being the Chief of the new Service and Supply setup.[55] It is rather interesting to sit back as a spectator and see the aides and colonels scurrying about and wonder how you looked when you were functioning in a somewhat similar capacity. Things are all too peaceful and pleasant and I have a feeling that the honeymoon is about over so far as I am concerned. I left the office at five this afternoon, went over to my hut, stripped and stretched out in a blanket in our backyard and spent an hour reading Kipling's "Departmental Ditties and Barrack-Room Ballads". With all that I have to learn about an armored regiment, let alone the regular routine of work that one runs into, I don't expect to have any spare time when I get over there.

## June 6, 1942

The shriek of air raid sirens had us throwing up the window blinds and rushing for our steel helmets and gas masks. We were looking pretty grim until one of the older settlers announced the usual first Saturday of the month practice alert. There are six war correspondents and photographers who are quartered in mess with us. Our Corps Commander seems to be very willing to be photographed and quoted. I think one of General Daley's first acts would have been to order this group to find some place to bivouac completely independent of our headquarters.

55    The Commanding General of the Army Services of Supply, redesignated in 1943 as Army Service Forces, was Lieutenant General Brehon B. Somervell. "US Army Officers 1939–1945," retrieved on January 20, 2020, from https://www.unithistories.com/officers/US_Army_officers_S01.html; and John D. Millett, *United States Army in World War II: The Army Service Forces*, (Washington, D.C.: Center of Military History, 1987), p. vii, retrieved on January 20, 2020, from https://history.army.mil/html/books/003/3-1/CMH_Pub_3-1.pdf

## Assignment to the 13th Armored Regiment

**June 7, 1942**

In the official mail this a.m., I received copies of the following extract from a special order dated June 5th; "Capt. Henry E. Gardiner, 03937013, Cav., HQ. USANIF and V Army Corps (Reinf), is Reld for Asgmt and duty with this HQ. is Assgd to the 1st Armored Div. and will report without delay to the CG thereof for duty." When I showed it to Col. Lamb, he said I couldn't leave until my relief showed up and was broken in. The breaking in won't consist of any more than showing him where to sit, pointing out the telephone and the "In" and "Out" baskets. Have stood by the past two nights for Col. Lamb while he was off the post, so he suggested that I use an excuse the fact that I had to pay the Armored Division a visit and take the day off. I secured a car and drove down to the 13th Armored H.Qs. and advised the adjutant that I expected to be in tomorrow or Tuesday. Had one of my fellow hikers from last Sunday along and we drove into New Castle, parked the car and proceeded to hoof it to the top of St. Donard.[56] Elevation 2,796. It rises abruptly from the sea and was quite a stiff climb taking us two hours and forty-five minutes. We had lunch on top of our PX supplies that we had drawn the last time. A marvelous view but interrupted by rain showers. Amazed by the stone wall that the City of Belfast had built along the skyline of the Mourne Mountains to protect its watershed. Must have been an early day example of a WPA [Works Projects Administration] project.

56    Slieve Donard is the highest mountain in Northern Ireland and the wider province of Ulster. *High Point Ireland*, retrieved on January 23, 2020, from at https://www.highpointireland.com/province-high-points.html

Figure 8: The red dot shows the location of Slieve Donard (Public Domain)

## June 8, 1942

Quite a volume of work cleared through our office today and I was of some assistance moving it along. Found time to make two calls to the organization of the man that is coming in to take my place, who is an over age major, to inquire when he was going to report in. That put enough heat on him so he showed up this evening and I advised the Armored Division that I would be putting in an appearance on Wednesday morning which in principle was agreeable with Col. Lamb, so everyone is happy at the moment. Learned that the General's present aide who is now a major but who was a captain when I arrived is going to command a "Ranger" or "Commando" unit of some four hundred and fifty men which is being assembled this week from volunteers out of our present force on this side. This war is catching me like many others just a little too late on the age side since you are supposed to be twenty-five or to have the blood pressure of one that age to qualify. There is nothing like patting yourself on the back but that is just the sort of a job I was made for and I know I could do a better job than the man who is starting out to run it. However, the fighting that they will do, while spectacular and the basis for many post war stories, will only be on the fringes.[57] We in the outfits like the first 1st Armored will really make the holes and roll up the flanks and cause whole armies to collapse while they will principally give officers of the day sleepless nights.

## June 9, 1942

While this elimination of over aged officers is costing the army a lot of experienced officers, it, of course, is weeding out some that should be on the shelf and should have been there long ago. The trouble is now that they are going into responsible positions but not where they will have to exert themselves physically. The major who is taking over in my place is a case in point. He was battalion executive in a field artillery outfit, and he would appear to have had but an eighth-grade education and is not to have learned since he completed that. It is certainly a reflection on the National Guard and the regular army for the past two years that they have permitted a man to get into and retain a position of responsibility who is so lacking in ability native or instilled. Paid my mess bill, straightened up

---

57    This is an interesting observation as the unit Gardiner is referring to eventually became the famous "Darby's Rangers." Captain William Orlando Darby was chosen to command the newly formed Ranger unit. On June 19, 1942, the 1st Ranger Battalion was sanctioned, recruited, and began training in Carrickfergus, Northern Ireland. When the U.S. Army decided to establish its Ranger units, Darby gained a desired assignment to direct their organization and training. Many of the original Rangers were volunteers from the Red Bull, the 34th Infantry Division, a National Guard division, and the first ground combat troops to arrive in Europe. Deploying his Rangers across Europe at salient points in the fight, Darby ultimately succumbed to wounds received by indirect fire during an attack on Trento, Italy, on April 30, 1942. Dominic J. Caraccilo, *Forging a Special Operations Force: The US Army Rangers*, (Warwick, UK: Helion & Company, 2015), pp. 26–27.

with the PX office and packed up to the point that about all I have to do is roll my bedroll, spit on the fire and call the dog and I'll be on the way.

### June 10, 1942

Said a few goodbyes after mess and loaded my effects into a pickup truck and in company with another officer who had some business to transact at my destination, started out for the Armored Division head-quarters. Found them just getting established in Castlewellan, which is a lovely place with extensive grounds all about the estate and a magnificent view of the Mourne Mountains from the main front rooms. The boys are living in a regular Hollywood set. They didn't know much about the fact that I was due in so told me to go down on the 13th Armored Regiment where I reported to the C.O. He said he was undecided where to place me yet but for the time period I could work with the Headquarters Company. For the most part the Armored Force didn't like General Daley so it re-mains to be seen how warmly his former aide will be received. In addition, a new officer in a regiment, particularly when he happens to rank some-one else, is not exactly the most welcomed person in the world. Spent the afternoon getting acquainted with the routine of the H.Q. Company and this evening I attended an hour's tank drill which consisted climbing in and out of a tank simulating going in and out of action.

### June 11, 1942

Stood reveille with Headquarters Company and went through some rather mild calisthenics which were given by one of the officers. This place is known as Camp Ballykinler and was one of the British modern peace-time garrisons.[58] There are many two-story and some three-story large brick buildings which would prove an excellent target for any enemy bombers that might come over. All of the building that has been done here recently is of the same sheet iron and corrugated iron construction

---

58   Also referred to as Abercorn Barracks, Ballykinler Barracks installation in Ballykinler in County Down, Northern Ireland. It was used as a brutal internment camp during the Irish War of Independence in 1919. In

so much of which is seen about the war-time camps on the island. These buildings are quite well scattered and shouldn't prove a very remunerative target. I made another fruitless trip over to Castlewellan to try and check in this morning, but everyone was out again. This afternoon I clambered about one of the light tanks with which H.Q. Co. is equipped and got a few pointers from one of the mechanics as to what makes the wheels go around. The adjutant told me after dinner this evening that I had been given temporary command of Service Company until the return of the present C.O. who had just gone to the hospital with the yellow jaundice.

## Service Company, 13th Armored Regiment

**June 12, 1942**

Service Company wasn't standing reveille this morning or really doing much of anything besides maintaining the outpost line since the Company went on that tour of guard duty yesterday afternoon. If this officer is in the hospital any length of time, I should get in pretty good hiking condition for the Company area is on the extreme end of the regimental area from the officers' quarters and close to fifteen minutes' walk away. There are three officers on duty in the company now and while pretty green from the standpoint of service, would seem to be above the average of the regiment on capabilities. They are in one of the sort of housekeeping officers' quarters and I moved in with them. In an armored regiment it is quite apparent that the part of Service Company is an important one in view of the fuel and ammunition that must be hauled. The Company has a compliment of sixty-eight trucks but about a half of them have not been received

World War I, the 36th Ulster Division did much of its training there. In World War II, the camp continued to be a military training establishment and the North Irish Horse record moving there to take over Valentine Tanks and convert to an armored regiment. Troops from the United States, including those from the 1st Armored Division that Gardiner is referencing, also trained at Ballykinler. *Ballykinler Camp: The First Seven Decades, 1900–1969*, retrieved on January 23, 2020, from http://www.downcountymuseum.com/getattachment/Collections/Down_Survey/Ballykinler_Camp_compressed.pdf.aspx from shipment as yet nor has a lot of other equipment. The men are in barracks that are reasonably satisfactory, but the latrine facilities are pretty rugged. They consist of buckets under wooden holes which are picked up daily by a civilian which eliminates an unpleasant detail for someone. The first sergeant, mess sergeant and truck master are all old regular army sergeants with many years of service in the horse cavalry so we should get along.

**June 13, 1942**

It is really a great pleasure to be back again where there is a band playing in the morning, drilling going on all over the place and you find plenty of saluting to do again. There is an American anti-aircraft regiment stationed here for training under the British. Around noon each day planes come diving in over the camp to give the gunner some live targets to train on. The regiment's tanks are dispersed about the camp in a very business-like way. We are right on the seacoast and there is barb wire all over the place. Over to Castlewellan again for a perfunctory call on the Commanding General and the Chief of Staff. It isn't so long ago when I looked through the glass partition in General Daley's door and saw him give them both a very chilly reception designed to sort of let them know that they were just like any other division commanders. Gen. Ward was very cordial and said that he was glad that I wanted to join the Division.[59]

*{The letters, diary entries, and discussion from June 14 to July 28, 1942, focused on the daily training in Northern Ireland as well as mundane past time events and actions in preparation for the unknown.}*

---

59    Major General Orlando Ward was the second officer to the 1st Armored Division. He supervised the deployment of his division across the Atlantic to North Africa, which was brought piecemeal (with a layover in Northern Ireland) as part of Operation Torch and subsequent operations. The failure of 1st Armored to arrive intact and deploy as a single entity would have important consequences as Gardiner explains later in this work. 1st Armored Division History, retrieved on January 23, 2020, from https://army.togetherweserved.com/army/servlet/tws.webapp.WebApp?cmd=PublicUnitProfile&type=Unit&ID=252

**July 28, 1942**

My boss in many respects is really Major Bruss who is the regimental S-4 and an individual who isn't the easiest to get along with.[60] He took me over to Castlewellan this afternoon for a conference on supply dealing largely with our next maneuver. They lay a lot of beautiful plans and outline a nice standard operating procedure but in the field, there is just a lot of it that will break down. The recreation officer arranged a dance tonite which was participated in jointly by Service and H.Q. Co. We pooled the men's beer allowance for this past week and made it a treat on the Company fund. The girls were local A.T.S.'s. and there were not near enough to go around.

**July 29, 1942**

I stayed with last night's party until almost the close when I pulled out because I preferred to have some of the junior officers help shoo the boys home so I could be the upper court if there was any difficulty and the cases had to be heard before me. My acting first sergeant was not in line this morning and I found him in bed very sick as a result of mixing his drinks last nite. Informed him that his one chance had gone and if he slopped over again, I would replace him. What really burned me up however was to find that six of the boys who were on pass had not returned and haven't to the present writing. Am certainly going to try to make them feel that their extra holiday wasn't worth it. On the basis of company punishment, it is pretty difficult to take away privileges since there are so few that the boys have. We have an allotment of a thousand rounds of .45 ammunition for training purposes and I had the boys on the range firing that today with the pistol and the Tommy Gun. This evening's school proved to be

---

60    Hyman Bruss would eventually command the 2nd Battalion, 13th Armor and be relieved in command in Tunisia because of poor performance that led to a defeat at Djebel bou Aoukaz on December 6, 1942. Later in this work, Gardiner offers a detailed depiction of his interaction with Bruss and Bruss's action in battle. Gardiner would replace Bruss in command of the 2nd Battalion. *13th Armored Regiment in Tunisia Part II*, retrieved on January 25, 2020, from https://www.flamesofwar.com/Default.aspx?tabid=112&art_id=581; and Rick Atkinson, *The Army at Dawn: The War in North Africa, 1942–1943, Volume One of the Liberation Trilogy*, (New York, New York: Henry Holt and Co., 2002), p. 228.

of more interest than usual, it is dealing with the sighting of the 37 mm and the 75 mm in the tanks. We did quite a bit of dry-running on the anti-tank range at targets moving at different speeds in various directions.

**July 30, 1942**

My six wandering boys were on the line this morning. Two of them have ratings which I intend to revoke but I didn't pass judgement on the group because I wanted to find out the mechanics of busting them.

**July 31, 1942**

Find that the six boys who were A.W.O.L. will be red lined on this month's payroll which means missing pay day and is considerable punishment in itself. I started them in this evening signing in every hour from six thru ten with the charge of quarters. At ten o'clock they stood a full field inspection outside of their shelter halves in which they will be required to sleep. Then they are to report to me at 5:45 a.m. in the morning. Have made a deal with the utility officer to put them on a coal hauling detail during the daytime. That is the program for a week with certain additional labor details thrown in. The first sergeant who has been in the hospital came back today to say good-bye and check in his equipment for he is being sent back to the United States since the doctors say he is no longer fit for field duty. Took him up to see the Colonel since he has been in the service longer than any other man in the regiment having served twenty-eight and a half years. The Colonel called me back afterwards, said he [thought] it would be appropriate to arrange some sort of a little farewell ceremony and wound up by ordered a regimental review on Sunday in his honor. This evening's officers' school so far as the section I was in was concerned ran for three hours. It was a course of instruction in the light machine gun in which we fired at different types of targets on four different ranges. Some of our officers are surprisingly ignorant on the subject of machine gun fire.

*{From August 1–9, 1943, Gardiner continued to prepare himself and his unit; most of the letters and diary inserts during this time frame discuss the daily activities.}*

**August 9, 1942**

This has been a day of noteworthy events. To start with, I had eight hours sleep last night for the first time since joining the 13th. That came about by virtue of our going back to daylight savings from "double" daylight savings which we have been operating under since our arrival. The development of the twenty-four hours, however, was my hearing via dinner table conversation that I had a new job which was confirmed shortly thereafter by my receiving a copy of Special Order No. 175 which among other things stated "R.3. Capt. Henry Gardiner, 0-397013, 13th Armored Regiment, is relieved from assigned to Service Company and is assigned to Headquarters, 2nd Battalion." That is definitely out of a clear sky of a shift for the better or not. The captain who is following me into Service Company is an officer I haven't liked, and, in my estimation, which of course may be slightly prejudiced, I think Service Company is considerably the loser in the swap. As to whether the 2nd Battalion has gained anything by this shift is probably likewise very doubtful when viewed from the standpoint of the boys who are already over there.

## Second Battalion, 13th Armored Regiment

**August 10, 1942**

I went down to Service Company as per usual and while we were going though calisthenics spotted the Colonel approaching and went over and reported him. He said that I had been transferred to the 2nd Battalion because they were short one on their staff and that it would represent an advance forward for me. He said that he had been very much pleased with the work I had done with the Company and that the S-4 had reported that my work in the field had been entirely satisfactory. I must say that the last boost came from a quarter where I didn't expect to receive one. The 2nd Battalion which is a medium tank battalion is commanded by Lt. Col. Wells, a regular Army officer, whom I have found very pleasant in the limited contacts that I have had with him to date. I reported into him this morning and he said to go ahead and complete my checking out down at the Company and to get busy and learn to run a medium take before I became bogged down in the routine of the office. I spent a little time this morning wandering around the 2nd Batt. Motor Park. We have been very fortunate in Service Company in having tank battalions have no such facilities and everything is exposed to the elements which means that a daily routine of cleaning all weapons has to be followed. One basic shortage is O.D. paint which makes it difficult to combat rust where the paint has been scraped off.

**August 11, 1942**

This was pay day for the regiment and since I had been named the Agent Finance Officer for the company before my order of reassignment came out, I went ahead and paid Service Company, whose payroll ran a little over $12,000.00 which represented quite a work-out with the English monetary system. My successor is giving every indication of stalling off coming over to his new job as long as possible and I spent most of the day at the Company but told the boys that now that the payroll is out of the way they could count me out. There was a regimental retreat parade this evening and Service Company was designated as Color Company. When we formed the sun was shining brightly although there were rain clouds on the horizon moving our way. Just when we came up on line it started into rain and poured throughout the ceremony so that everyone got soaked. I of course lost the press in a pair of trousers that I had been carefully nursing along until I could get another pair back from the cleaners.

## August 12, 1942

Took my maiden trip at the controls of a medium tank this morning. I ran it for a little over an hour in some fairly hilly country where they train here, and I knew that I had been some place when I finished. The mechanics of being a driver isn't difficult, but it is a tiresome job. Hope that I will be able to put in a couple of more days on one so that I can acquire some confidence in manipulating it. Colonel Wells said he wanted me to move up to where the 2nd Battalion officers are staying so I made a deal to move in with another officer. Had a visit with the Colonel and he said he wanted me to work in as S-3 and act as executive which amounts to being second in command. That calls for a Major in the T/O but that may not be forthcoming for some time. I suppose if I get that then I'll be thinking in terms of a lieutenant colonelcy but I do hope I can be a major before too long largely because I want my friends at home, particularly those that I've known more on the business side, to know that I'm getting ahead. I am going to have a great deal of work to do before I can feel that I am qualified to handle the job I'm in now.

## August 13, 1942

Poked around the Maintenance Company shops for a while this a.m. I'm not of a mechanical turn of mind although I think I can grasp the general way things mesh together in reasonably short order. The whole production program has been one keyed to the manufacture of complete units with the result that there are not sufficient spare parts on hand to service the breakdowns that are now beginning to show up. As a result, there are quite a few inoperative tanks many of which lack only a fairly minor part to put them back on the line. There just doesn't seem to be any end to the work that one has to do, and it keeps piling up. When I was a Troop and company commander, I was of the opinion that all extra details should be handled by the staff. Now I can understand why the staff feels that it should be the other way around. The afternoon was devoted to getting set to go out on a Division CPX which so far as the Battalion is concerned will just involve the command post group. Slept on the floor in the orderly room so as to be ready to move in the event the time of departure was accelerated.

*{Entries August 12–15, 1942, discuss Gardiner's various troop visits and are omitted.}*

## August 16, 1942

We didn't have long to wonder about who our new C.O was going to be for he took over that a.m. It is no other than the former S-4 under whom I chaffed while I was in Service Co. His name is Major Bruss and he was a captain when I joined the regiment and probably will soon be a lieutenant-colonel. He spent twelve years as an enlisted man in the cavalry, securing his commission thru and officers' training school about two years ago. Our Colonel knew him as a sergeant and had a high regard for his ability and has been responsible in a large measure for his rapid advance. I think we will get along all right, but it won't be as pleasant a relationship as it would have been under his immediate predecessor. The Colonel is away now in England attending a school of some sort which only runs for about a week. He took over the regiment just a short time before it left Ft. Knox. The boys all have been expecting for some time to see him made a brigadier-general, but nothing seems to come of it. I understand he is forty-seven or eight and the last word we had on the other side was that they weren't going to make any more generals above forty-five. All of this emphasis on age has made me much more conscious of my thirty-seven years. Have concluded I am just as well off by not being in the commandos for my legs aren't as good as they used to be.

## August 17, 1942

There was a meeting of the S-3's of the regiment at Mourne Park this morning to watch a demonstration put on by the Engineers and the Ordnance people of flame throwers, smoke generators, and the so-called [Molotov] cocktails. While I wouldn't want anyone using a flame thrower on me, I wasn't impressed with them as a weapon. They are too short in range and inoperative time. Saw some interesting smoke devices to shield a vehicle that was making a get-away. Went to this show with our Regimental S-3 who is a young lieutenant-colonel by virtue of four years at West Point not so very long ago.[61] The Division C.G. was there and made a few remarks. One point that touched upon was the amount of drinking and drunkenness among the men and asked for cooperation in trying to cut it down. One trouble is that it is treated too lightly by all of the officers when they have occasion to punish those who get out of line.

## August 18, 1942

The line of duty board which I was on the other nite met again this evening. Three boys had testified that the deceased was drunk, and we all agreed that his death did not occur in line of duty. An autopsy now fails to disclose any alcohol in the urine or blood, so the other two members of the board now say he wasn't drunk, and it was in the line of duty. It is just a case of their having decided that they ought to help out his family, but I am not going to allow my opinion to be changed by such considerations so will continue to hold out.

## August 19, 1942

Devoted most of the morning to working up a directive for the battalion training schedule for next week. It is quite a headache since there are so many different things going on and interruptions in the regular training program. I don't believe we are giving our intelligence service

61    The S3 was Lieutenant Colonel Edwin A. Russel. *Armor Command*, p. 26.

much credit when we are set up as though an invasion might develop on a few minutes' notice. The necessity for keeping so many units in a constant state of alertness seriously interferes with the training that you are able to give them. Heard second-hand radio reports this evening that a large scale commando raid was in progress on the French coast.[62] Perhaps my contention of last spring that an allied thrust on the continent in August of this year was to be made will not be so far off at that. Also heard that there had been a considerable force of additional troops landed in Ireland. One interesting angle was that there was included a battalion of engineers who specialize in landing operations.

**August 20, 1942**

Well the attack on the French coastline was nothing more than a raid at least that is the Allied story for the forces which were landed were withdrawn. The Germans state that they were driven back into the sea and claim 1,500 prisoners. Since some tank units were landed, I wonder whether they were trying to stay if they could but decided that the going was just too tough. The British acknowledge that loss of close to a hundred planes so it must have been quite a show while it lasted. I would imagine that a bona fide invasion would be combined with an attempt to establish beach heads at various points. They can't expect to try to put us down over there until they have a well-established port for our equipment is just too heavy for any barge landing operations.[63] Our line of duty board convened again, and the other two members became rather indignant

---

62    Operation Jubilee, more commonly referred to as the Dieppe Raid, was an Allied assault on the German-occupied port of Dieppe, France, on August 19, 1942. The main assault lasted less than six hours until strong German defenses and mounting Allied losses forced its commanders to call a retreat. Over 6,050 infantrymen, predominantly Canadian, were supported by The Calgary Regiment of the 1st Canadian Tank Brigade and a strong force of Royal Navy and smaller Royal Air Force landing contingents. It involved 5,000 Canadians, 1,000 British troops, and fifty United States Army Rangers. This was the first use of the newly formed Ranger unit in World War II. *Forging a Special Operations Force*, p. 27.

63    3,623 of the 6,086 men who made it ashore were killed, wounded, or captured during the raid. The Royal Air Force lost 106 aircraft (at least thirty-two to anti-aircraft fire or accidents), compared to forty-eight lost by the Luftwaffe. The Royal Navy lost thirty-three landing craft and one destroyer. The events at Dieppe influenced the strategic decision to invade North Africa (Operation Torch) and the eventual Normandy landings (Operation Overlord). Norman L. R. Franks, *Royal Air Force Fighter Command Losses of the Second World War, Volume 2: Operational Losses: Aircraft and crews 1942–1943*, (London: Midland Publishing Limited, 1998), pp. 56–62

when I refused to join them in their findings that the man was not under the influence of liquor and was in the line of duty. Their decision was the one of the Board's, of course, but I filed a dissent.

*{From August 21 to September 11, 1942, the diary entries focused on preparing for deployment and the administrative actions and requirements in command of a battalion on foreign soil preparing to go to war.}*

### September 12, 1942

The Major and I were out dark and early again this morning and took a different tack this time being one which brought us back through the sand dunes. He is carrying a little weight and I don't have any difficulty in outdistancing him. We picked up some replacements today in the nature of men who had transferred over from the Canadian Army. Before they send this outfit into battle, we are going to require a large number of replacements for the regiment was badly hit by men who went to the hospital with yellow jaundice and who haven't been returned to duty. Drove a light tank again this afternoon.[64] They are fun to handle because they are so speedy and responsive but if the choice is mine between them and the mediums when the bullets begin to fly, I want to be in the latter.

### September 13, 1942

This morning we shoved the battalion schedule ahead one hour so had a third of the regiment groping around in the dark at reveille. Revised the schedule so as to give the men a half hour of road work before breakfast which was set at six and drill call was at seven. While that is the schedule that the 106th used to follow, there is one feature which slows things up that they didn't have there, which is the necessity of the men washing their mess kits. It wouldn't have taken a very astute enemy agent even if

---

64    Gardiner is most likely referring to the M2 light tank which was an American pre–World War II light tank that saw limited use during World War II. The most common model, the M2A4, was equipped with one 37 mm (1.5 in) M5 gun and five .30 caliber M1919 Browning machine guns.

he were blind if he has been in the vicinity today to sense that there was something unusual in the wind. Every range was busy from early morning until dusk. We fired more ammunition from tanks that the regiment has since it came here. Had a course going during which we fired the 37 mm from the tanks and self-propelled mounts, the pistol at the .30 machinegun that is mounted with the 37 in the tank. At one point we were firing sixty rounds of 37 mm every half minute on the moving target range. Finished up the school that I have been attending by making what is known as a twenty-five-hour check of a medium tank and then spent some time in practicing the evacuation of wounded from a tank. It is going to be quite a big job to get a large man out particularly through the turret. Some of this practice and training may be obsolete soon for we are supposed to be due to receive a shipment of the new medium tanks.

Figure 9: M2A2 Light Tank. Note the 1st Armor Division patch on the turret. (Retrieved on January 27, 2020, from https://tanks-encyclopedia.com/ww2/US/M2_Light_Tank.php)

## September 14, 1942

We continued on with the same range program today adding in, however, the Thompson sub-machine gun so we were burning up the ammunition even more rapidly than yesterday. I fired a couple of clips with my new .45 pistol and didn't do so well. We are the shortest on that type of ammunition and also are receiving very little .50 caliber. How much better it would have been to have delayed our departure on the other side a short time and fired on the excellent ranges that were available at Dix and not have had to use up that tonnage in ammunition to be shipped over here for practice purposes. We should practice all we can here, of course, but only for the finishing touches and not be learning how as so many are. In accordance with the Colonel's directive all firing is being made as realistic as possible so the men wear that which they would normally have on when they go onto combat. We now have the new type of steel helmet which is referred to as the coal scuttle type, and I've been wearing it the past two days and I find that it gives me a headache which is a discomfort that I rarely suffer from.[65] It doesn't weigh but a little more than the old variety but has a different suspension system. Our tank firing went slower this afternoon and we didn't finish until seven-thirty, so we are becoming quite unpopular with the kitchen crew.

**September 15, 1942**

This morning we fired a company on the rifle range in addition to our tank firing and they did very well. The 37 mm firing has been quite satisfactory, and I think the boys could make it warmer for an opponent with that weapon. As a sort of demonstration, they ran one of the tanks along the firing line as a sort of a grand finale and plastered it with .30 caliber machine gun fire. The Colonel was a passenger in it at the time. As was expected the shots didn't much more than chip the paint on the main armament. We were disturbed, however, to find that the 75 mm gunner's sight had been knocked out which in action would have meant that the gun would have been valueless until a new sight could have been

65    When the Second World War broke out in Europe, American soldiers were still equipped with the 1917 flat helmet, the M-1917 A1. In 1941, the U.S. Army changed the helmets to the metal M1 helmet. World War II American M1 Steel Helmet, retrieved on January 27, 2020, from https://www.dday-overlord.com/en/material/uniforms/m1-steel-helmet

substituted. Furthermore, one of the observation ports on the side was knocked out. They are all periscope sights so the crew couldn't have been injured by a bullet, but it certainly shows that rifle and machine gun fire against a tank is most worthwhile if directed at the sights and ports. Spent most of the afternoon laying out a compass course which we intend to run the officers and non-coms through. If it is a normal dark night, it will take some good navigating to get around it.

**September 16, 1942**

Completed our firing for the next little while with a morning session on the rifle range. I borrowed a rifle and fired five shots from the 300 yd. range getting the bulls and two just outside. The Canadian's now announce that their casualty list the Dieppe Raid was 3,500. From all the stories we receive the Germans met them head on and they took a licking. I hope wherever they plan to send us that the scheme will be well thought out and that we can at least get our vehicles ashore and into action before they are put out of commission.

*{During September 17–23, 1942, Gardiner continued to posture his unit for an eventual deployment; much speculation as to where they would be going.}*

**September 24, 1942**

Moved the clock up an hour this a.m. so as to get our range firing details underway in good season. I went out with the tank company that started firing the 75 mm guns on a nearby range. The moving target set up isn't too substantial and we kept knocking it out. The boys shot well but not as accurately as they did with the 37 mm. Even in the limited zone that we are firing in today we found ourselves handicapped by the 28 degrees traverse of the 75 mm gun. The new M-4 tanks have a 75 mm in the turret with a 360 degrees traverse which is what we should have.

Things seems to be approaching a boiling point more all the time since we are warned that footlockers must all be packed by the 27th, etc. One of the Bn. Staff was ordered on short notice to London today. This afternoon I helped out on a firing combat course that we were firing and worked until I was dead tired running thru the sand following thru the various units that were firing. There was a Bn. party tonite which consisted principally of a good meal. The talent in the way of entertainment was supplied by the enlisted men and it was surprisingly good.

Figure 10: 13th Tank Battalion M4 tanks in Italy (Photograph from the Patricia Issel Collection)

### September 25, 1942

At officers' call this noon it was announced that all diaries (a list had been made some time ago of enlisted men who kept diaries) were to be picked up and turned over to S-1 for safekeeping. If as it appears, I'm due to go over to England, I'm going to take this with me and then turn it over to one of my friends for safekeeping. Could have been at the Home ranch from the way the Mourne Mountains looked this a.m. for they were well powdered with snow on the upper third and some of it stayed all day.[66] I

66    Gardiner is referring to the family ranch known as Mule Ranch. His father, Henry Cook Gardiner, leased the ranch from the Anaconda Mining Company sometime in the 1920s. David Favager, *War Heroes: Gardiners at War:*

spent my time on the combat range today. Things went off in good shape this morning but the Company that was performing this afternoon stuck two tanks in the first phase and it was after seven o'clock before we finally got them out. It took the assistance of two ten ton wreckers from the Maintenance Co. and I was interested to see how they worked. Both tanks were stopped by soft sand having tipped over so that all of the weight was on one track. The wreckers merely tied on to their turrets and pulled them over so that the weight was about evenly distributed between the tracks and then they walked right out.

**September 26, 1942**

No firing today but there was more than enough going on to keep everyone humping. If I survive this war and have the money someday, I'm going to have a little research into why the Army can never seem to give an order when some move is in prospect without having to change it a half a dozen times before it finally goes into effect. In connection with the impending move, there was a series of starts and stops, changes in numbers of personnel, changes in number and type of vehicles, etc. If we have any mental cases in the outfit, they will certainly show up now. I know that a lot of this is just due to incompetence and inexperience of which there is altogether too much in the outfit. However, during all of my short period of service it has been a case of "dig a hole and then fill it up". We received some replacements today and some of the men hadn't been in the service for a period of three weeks and they looked to me like they represented the bottom of the barrel. That, of course, is just criminal to send men over who may soon be in battle and who have had no more training than these fellows have.

*Extracted from The Illustrated History of the Gardiners of Whitchurch: Volume 2 Liverpool, Canada, Wallsey, and Montana.* ISSUU Publishing, retrieved on January 29, 2020, from https://issuu.com/davidgalina/docs/gardiners_ at_war_

## September 27, 1942 to November 8, 1942

During this period no Diary was kept and, but a few letters were written. This was because of the security restrictions and the lack of time due to preparations for the African invasion.

Figure 11: Marbury Hall just east of Liverpool, United Kingdom (Google Maps)

On September 28 [I] left Camp Ballykinler with an advance detail of the regiment for Marbury Hall, a large estate just outside of Chester, England.[67] The move was made by rail to the port of Larne. From there a night trip was taken by boat across the North Channel of the Irish Sea to the port of Stranraer, following which an all-day train journey was made to Chester. This trip was taken with full personal combat equipment, including emergency rations. Strict orders were given that these were not to be eaten and meals were served en route. However, these orders were not observed by all the men, giving rise to the "chocolate soldier" incident recounted in a subsequent letter.

The stay at Marbury Hall was one of around-the-clock activity. Civilian workers were brought in to assist in welding "stacks" on to

---

67    Marbury Hall was used as a military camp and later as a prisoner of war camp during the Second World War. As part of the large deception plan for D-Day (called Operation Fortitude) a phantom U.S. Army Corps, the XXXIII was created which had its HQ 'based' at Marbury Hall. This corps had the 11th and 48th Infantry Divisions, plus 25th Armored Division under its command. Thaddeus Holt, *The Deceivers: Allied Military Deception in the Second World War*, (London: Phoenix, 2005), pp.174–177.

the back decks of all tanks. These served to carry the exhaust gases up to a level above the deck of the tank so that the motor would not be affected by submerging to a depth of eight feet. The ports, hatches and gun embrasures were all sealed up to make the tanks waterproof to the point that they could be landed in the water and driven ashore under their own power. All of the wheeled and half-track combat vehicles were similarly waterproofed and dispatched to Liverpool and surrounding ports for loading.

On October 19, [I], along with the personnel of Headquarters and "D" Companies of the 13th, loaded onboard the "Durban Castle", a passenger liner, in the port of Liverpool.[68] The following day the ship sailed to Clyde where Brigadier General Oliver, the Force Commander, boarded her with his staff.[69] The "Durban Castle" remained in the Clyde for a week while the other ships of the convoy were assembling. During this period a program of training was followed which included climbing up and down scrambling nets slung over the side of the ship.

The convoy sailed on October 26, and the "Durban Castle" took up a position just astern of the flagship which was maintained throughout the voyage. The officers on this trip enjoyed meals, service and accommodations, equal to a peace-time pleasure trip. A small aircraft-carrier accompanied the convoy, a number of destroyers patrolled the perimeter of the convoy, and a heavy cruiser kept it company.

On November 1st the news was broken to us that our force was charged with capturing the port of Oran on the Algerian coast, and that simultaneous attacks would be made on Casablanca and Algiers on the same day, namely, November 8. From then on until we went ashore, our time not devoted to drill of one kind and another, lectures, inspections, etc., was taken up with familiarizing ourselves, from maps, photographs,

---

68    For more on the Durban Castle, see http://www.bandcstaffregister.com/page186.html

69    Major General Lunsford Errett Oliver was the commander of Combat Command B and took command of the larger Task Force Green during the attack in Northern Africa. He went on to command the 5th Armored Division and then the 4th Armored Division by the end of the war. *Armor Command*, pp. 9, 26, and 128 and https://www.unithistories.com/officers/US_Army_officers_O01.html

and models, with the coastline that we were to invade, the road net and terrain to the immediate interior, and our mission.

The day before we were due to enter the Mediterranean, the half of the convoy which was to proceed to Algiers split off and left us, while we cruised around for one day to give them the necessary additional time to advance towards their objective.

We passed through the Strait of Gibraltar the night of November 6. Dawn found us in sight of the coast of Spain and passing convoy after convoy of deep laden freighters which were carrying vehicles and supplies. Being slower they had sailed from the British Isles before we did. The course that we held to during the daylight hours was one which led the enemy to believe we were bound for Malta.

### October 6, 1942

*{Note: Gardiner makes an insert here stating that; except where the name of the person is given, all letters were directed to his mother}*

By the way, I've discovered that malted milk powder is a dangerous commodity when stowed in a barracks bag. I had put mine there and must have had it in a warm place because when I unpacked it, I found the cover on one can had come off and a sort of fudge had formed and run over everything.

### October 12, 1942

Spent one nite in the field this past week. A short time ago all of our men were issued two "D" rations, being six bars of a sort of chocolate bar. They were given explicit instructions not to eat them, but a check showed them that many of them had done so. At five o'clock the other afternoon, two other officers and I lined up the hundred and thirty-five out of the battalion who had disobeyed orders and marched them off. They have been told to have their shelter halves and one blanket. We marched them until eight o'clock when we halted for two hours and then moved on again until midnight when we pulled into a field and stayed until daylight. It was a miserable nite for it rained hard. Timed our march so as to get back into camp the next morning at eight-thirty. The men then put to work so they the missed two meals and walked about twenty-five miles. Believe they will think twice before they dig into their emergency rations again. These boys have been dubbed the rest as the "Chocolate Soldiers". I didn't get any more to eat than these men but didn't mind it and was able to tell how hungry they were.

### October 24, 1942

Am learning a new card game, the tuition costing me up to two pounds a nite. There are five of us who play "Hearts" after dinner every evening until ten o'clock. We play for ten shillings a game. Last evening, I broke even and the nite before I won but over the period that we have been playing I am still the loser.

### November 7, 1942

Am afraid there will have been a long break between this and my previous letter. As things look, it will be in all probability a matter of weeks or even months before any more letters will follow this. We haven't had any mail since I wrote you last, and I hate to think how long it will be before any of it catches up to us. The way things are moving much of it, particularly packages and magazines, may never catch up.

However, starting tomorrow, you should be able to keep pretty much in touch with our activities through the radio and the newspapers. In fact, you will probably be better posted as to what is going on than we are.

We are, of course, not permitted to write anything which would be of value if it reached the enemy and I hope that the censor will agree with me in that what follows is perfectly harmless.

Our trip has been for the most part a very comfortable one, and I haven't been at all seasick, although many of the men were for a couple of days. The days and part of the evenings have been well occupied in study and preparation for the events that lie ahead. The officers have been travelling first class in every sense of the word. The steward has been around to awaken us with a cup of tea in the morning and four o'clock tea in the afternoon has been one of the regular formations. Blouses were worn for dinner, there was coffee in the lounge afterwards and I have been continuing to play with my same four gambling friends each evening, with the result that I am flat broke. We weren't paid this past payday and I made the mistake of sending you a little too much money before we left. However, where we are going there should be no particular need for money. Part of our instruction has been in two different languages, one of which was entirely new to everyone.[70]

Last nite we had quite a thrill which brought everyone on deck when we saw the lights of a city. It was the first time most of us had seen any lights out in the open for over six months and it made us all a little homesick. Unfortunately, diaries are very much taboo in this stage of operations and I sent mine on to Evelyn in London to hold for me when we pulled out. Have been enjoying a hot sea water tub bath each evening and the food and service has left nothing to be desired. Please don't worry just because you don't hear from me because it will be the lack of mail facilities instead of the fact that I'm not writing. We hadn't expected to be able to leave any mail on the boat until last nite when the word came out, so everyone is busy writing now.

---

70    Although much of North Africa had not yet been occupied by German armies, it was under French control and answerable to the pro-Nazi Vichy French Government. "French Language Guide," retrieved on February 1, 2020, from https://www.eisenhowerlibrary.gov/sites/default/files/file/French_Language_Guide.pdf

# 2

# North Africa
## November 8, 1942–June 2, 1943

## The Invasion and Overland Move into Tunisia

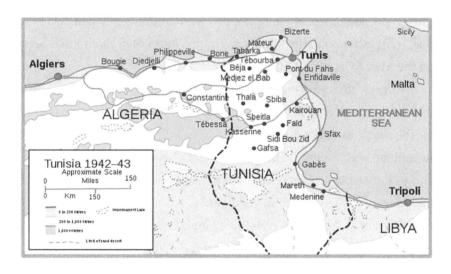

Figure 12: Map of North Africa during Operation Torch in Tunisia, 1942–1943
(Wikimedia Commons/Public Domain)

*{At this point in the chronology, Gardiner retrospectively notes that there were no diary entries kept between the period of November 8 until December 5, 1942, when he was hospitalized for wounds. During the time that he was in the hospital, while "the memory of the preceding month was still fresh," he made a record of events leading up to his hospitalization in a pocket diary. Gardiner recalled the order of events from November 8 to December 5, but he did not recall the exact dates and chose to annotate each event*

*in his pocket diary in the order of occurrence and noted each with a "?" to acknowledge the lack of exactness in the recalled date.}*

## November 8, 1942

Went on the deck to see that we were lying off a bleak rocky coastline. During the nite we had stayed up until late to listen to the President's speech announcing the invasion, but it didn't get thru. We had, also, stood on deck straining our eyes to see any signs of action as the first forces went ashore. Could see a Maracaibo just offshore with H-T's and light tanks and peeps going ashore.[1] Shells started landing about the vessels so smoke screen was laid down. Shelling stopped without doing any damage. Our boat went ashore on schedule and I jumped into water about knee-deep on the African shore at 11:00 hours.

No resistance was reported close at hand and our personnel was marched on to an assembly area just out of St. Leau.[2] I stayed with a detail on the beach to watch out for our equipment. The beach rapidly began to jamb up with supplies. The men's barracks bags began to come ashore, and we had to move them several times. A few peeps came ashore. Several outbursts of firing on planes. As darkness fell much artillery fired and flashes could be heard and seen inland and to the East. Reports came in of heavy fighting. Surf increased during the night resulting in beaching and damage of many landing craft. Difficult to round up sufficient help to unload barges. Tendency of soldiers was to shirk and let the British sailors do the work. We worked all night. Very tired after constant walking around in the soft sand.

---

1    *HMS Misoa* was a Maracaibo-class Landing Ship-Tank (LST) of the British Royal Navy during World War II. As a converted Lake Maracaibo oil tanker, she took part in the invasions of North Africa, Sicily, and Normandy hauling Heavy Tanks (H-T) and light tanks ashore. For more on LSTs see https://www.globalsecurity.org/military/systems/ship/lst.htm

2    St. Leu was where Beach Z was located and where Gardiner came ashore with the 1st Armor; see Figure 13.

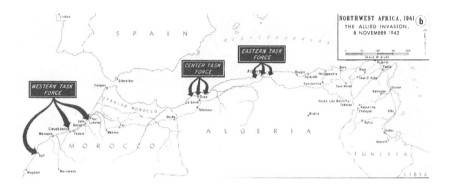

Figure 13: North African Landings: Morocco, Algeria, and Tunisia (Wikimedia Commons/Public Domain)

## November 9, 1942

Just after daybreak, two of our tanks came in on L.C.T.'s but did make it since because of the heavy surf they beached fairly well out. They would never have made it except for their waterproofing. Arzew having been captured and the beach being out of the question because of the surf, unloading operation shifted there. I went in with detail from all companies. Set up shop in railroad station. Vehicles began to come ashore in fair numbers. Drunken soldiers around docks. Outbreaks of shooting. Difficulty securing water. Large numbers of French prisoners. Natives unloading supplies. Officers' baggage comes ashore. Barracks bags everywhere. Slowness in unloading tanks. Word that French had given in.

## November ?, 1942

All tanks ashore so took peep and drove across country to Battalion bivouac site near Tafaraoui airfield. Learned we were heading eastward with a tank force and that my promotion to Major had come thru. Battalion review for General Robinett, also newly promoted. Oranges and wine. Lots of P-38's in the air. Capt. Cocke and I shared a C.P. tent with Bruss, which was blown down during a violent wind and rainstorm during the nite. Slept in bedroll first time since landing.[3]

3    Captain Philip St. George Cocke served in the British and U.S. Armies where he retired as a Colonel with the latter. *Armor Command*, pp. 80–81.

## November ?, 1942

Took off at daylight. Our route of march was preceded by a French officer advising the populace not to be alarmed. The communities turned out in mass to greet us and we were showered with fruits and flowers by cheering crowds. Saw evidence of much agricultural productivity. Lots of mosques on the hilltops. We marched with the 106th A.A. Bn. in our rear.[4] Camped just before dark.

## November ?, 1942

F Company soldiers got drunk and one shot in a brawl. Took the man who did the shooting into Algiers and turned him over to the authorities. Tanks started to load on L.S.T.'s. One E Company tank fell in water and driver drowned. Airport outside Algiers bombed at nite. Made nite trip into Algiers for instructions relative to overland move. Bruss goes by boat. I am to have charge of overland movement.

## November 17, 1942

Even if you ever gave any consideration of "raising your son to be a soldier", you probably didn't think of him as doing any campaigning in Northern Africa. Well, we're very much in the active theatre now and the papers are probably referring to the action of American tank units in Algeria and points east. When they do, that's us.

Spent the nite on the beach the day we landed; the next four on the floor of the Arzew railroad station and since then we've been traveling east and are jumping off in a few hours for another trek east.

Every meal that I've eaten since we landed, I've prepared, which has in practically every case been just a question of heating up contents of a tin can. Have been able to secure plenty of oranges, however, some tomatoes and today I bought a bunch of onions in an Arab market. We have been thru a lot of mountainous country, which is much like Arizona

4    The 106th Anti-Aircraft Artillery Battalion was a Kentucky-based unit that was eventually attached to the 45th Infantry Division during the landings at Salerno, Italy, in 1944.

or parts of California. The natives, however, come in different colors and live considerably differently.

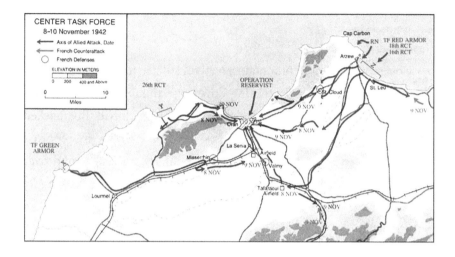

Figure 14: 1st Armor Beach Landings in North Africa (Center of Military History/Public Domain)

### November ?, 1942

Made a daylight start. We have all the wheeled vehicles and the H.T.'s. Our route took us over a high mountain range a short time after we left. Much excitement over spotting our first camels. We encountered a British tank column moving our transporters. Everyone buying eggs along the roads from Arabs and purchasing oranges and tangerines. Made camp well after dark several miles beyond Setif in a wet snow. Had to return to Setif to call Algiers and report our progress. Did so from the barracks of the local gendarme. A colorful sight. Cocke acted as interpreter. Warmed of somewhat by hospitality of the C.O. and a bottle of wine. Scrambled eggs in camp for supper. Tent up but ground soaking.

### November ?, 1942

Pulled out just before daylight stopping mid-morning for roadside breakfast. Much British traffic on the road. Checked in by phone while passing thru Constantine at hotel just requisitioned by British. Camped around cemetery about twenty miles from town, getting settled before dark. Saw some turkeys but too late to try and secure them.

### November ?, 1942

Covered many more mountains. Natives still friendly and interested. Tried out our M.G.'s while coming down one mountain. Went within sight of Bone but halted when attack on airfield developed. Bivouacked along a side road. Sent Cocke in to check on tanks. They were reported as due tomorrow. Nite air-raid on Bone. Bombers cruised around over us. Some platoons are getting so they do a real good job of cooking by pooling their compo ration and sort of work out a menu. The chocolate in the crack boxes just evaporates.

### November ?, 1942

Didn't like our bivouac so moved to a new area at daylight where there was more cover and we could disperse. The tanks joined us there right after noon. Col. Zanuck was out to see us and to check a group of photographers that were attached to us, including Director John Ford.[5] All that group were Navy personnel for the duration. Tanks had an uneventful trip along coast. Last night's bombing in Bone did no damage.

### November ?, 1942

The Bn. marched to Souk Aharas reaching a bivouac area on the local racetrack considerably after dark. It was a particularly difficult haul for the tanks being a very high mountain road with many switchbacks. The Bn. tanks are not all with us. One platoon of E Company still being behind us and F Company less a platoon. That group didn't come along with the

---

5    Lieutenant Colonel Darryl F. Zanuck was of the Signal Corps Photographic Service. (*Armor Command,* p. 78.) John Ford, an American film producer and director, was historically at odds with Zanuck over the filming of the battles in Tunisia. Zanuck is an award-winning film producer credited with the likes of *The Grapes of Wrath, How Green was My Valley, All About Eve, The King and I,* and *The Longest Day.* Ford was a film director and won awards for many of the same films Zanuck produced.

others because of a shortage of ships. Learned on reaching our stopping place for the nite that the two light Bn's had come thru here today by rail but were being tied in with a British tank group known as the Blade Force. Bruss didn't march with us having gone on ahead for orders.

### November ?, 1942

Sent Recon. Plat. on ahead of us to check on bridges that were reported not capable of handling our tanks. A terrific mountain road to Ghardimoui. I marched the column holding the speed at 10 m.p.h. Met coming downhill by British officer who said we were urgently needed at the front and to rush on. That proved to be a false alarm although we did proceed at a good rate to a bivouac site just outside of Souk-el-Arba where we pulled off the road just as the airport there was dive-bombed by Stukkas.[6] They came down thru a heavy ack-ack fire that didn't seem to faze them. H.Q. Co. set up around a cactus patch.[7] We elected, however, to go some distance from there to sleep for it seemed like such an obvious target. Two reporters called on us: [Clyde Kluckhorn] of the New York Times and Lowell Bennett of the A.P.[8] Bruss waxed strong as to how soon we would be in Tunis. Much chasing about the country for certain items, our most serious shortage being lubricating greases.

---

6    It was called the Stuka Valley (Gardiner misspells it as Stukka) for the amount of strafing done by German Ju87 Stuka dive bombers. Barbara Brooks Tomlin, *G. I. Nightingales: The Army Nurse Corps in World War II*, (Lexington, Kentucky: The University Press of Kentucky, 2001), p. 75

7    "Ack-ack fire" is anti-aircraft gunfire named after the sound it makes as it fires.

8    Bennet went on to survive eighteen months as a German POW. Ray Parker, *Down in Flames*, (Minneapolis: Mill City Press, 2009), p. 97.

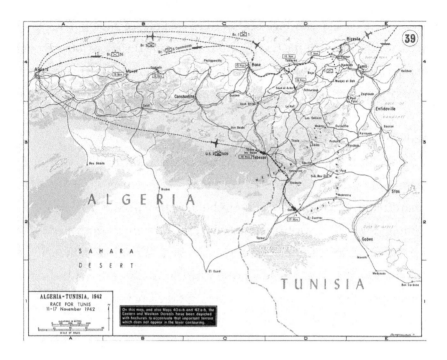

Figure 15: The Race for Tunis, November 11–17, 1942 ("Historical Resources About the Second World War," retrieved on February 8, 2020, from https://historicalresources.wordpress.com/category/ww-ii-second-world-war/ ww-ii-maps/war-maps-war-in-north-africa-and-italy/)

### November ?, 1942

The day was spent in maintenance of vehicles and trying to pick up certain supplies. The balance of E Co. closed in on us today. Maps were issued of the area in which we expect to operate. Number of camels about. Saw some suspicious lights around on the hills that we suspected of being signal lights for enemy planes which were over tonight. The gas stoves the boys picked up in Algiers do wonders towards cooking our meals.

### November ?, 1942

We moved out shortly after midnight with Bruss directing and leading the parade from the Command H/T. He halted the entire column astride a bridge when enemy planes dropped flares well in front. We pulled off the road near Souk-el-[Khemis] for breakfast and to await orders. Around mid-morning received word to proceed and Bruss went ahead. Beja proved to be as heavily damaged from bombing as any city we had seen yet. Guides met us there and headed us for Medjez-el-Bab. We began to pass a few burned out British vehicles and saw a number of large bomb craters along the road. Pulled off again to await instructions. Bruss returned late in the afternoon with orders that we were to attack a hill some eight miles down the road just as soon as we could.

Orders were sketchy and given on a 1/200,000 map. Tanks rolled forward and then column halted short of objective. Went ahead to see what the trouble was. Fortunately, the Co C.O. of the leading Co. had investigated some figures that seemed unduly conspicuous on the hill that we were about to attack and discovered that they were British troops, the hill having been taken earlier in the day.

Bruss ordered D Co. to go on by the hill despite the fact that it was almost dark. Other Co's returned to a bivouac site several miles back down the road. D Co. joined us later having been unable to see where they were going in the direction they were ordered.

Rained all night and became soaked as I had no tent. Bruss returned during the night with orders that we were to proceed at dawn. E Co. having been detached and sent on a separate mission, C Co. of 701st brought up our rear. Bruss went asleep in his tank leaving column to me.

We were ordered to take a circuitous route to get to the S.E. of Medjez where we were to join up with the British for an attack on that town. Recon fired on by French troops guarding bridge who thought we were enemy.[9] Crossed narrow bridge over the [Medjerda River] not knowing whether it would hold us or not. Recon dive-bombed but unhurt and

---

9    This was the first real battle in Operation Torch. By many accounts, the initial landings were spearheaded by the Americans as it was a political decision taken to appease the local French authorities who "could negotiate better with an American rather than a British Officer." Following the landings, the more experienced British were put in charge of the offensive with Lieutenant General Kenneth Anderson in command. Facing Anderson on the German side was General Walther Nehring, Wehrmacht General who commanded the Afrika Korps. The Allied aim was to break through to the eastern coast, where the ports of Bizerte and Tunis lay. Their approach was dictated by the landscape, which featured rugged mountains through which critical passes ran. They planned to advance on three fronts: along the road to Bizerte in the north; to Chouigui Pass in the center; and around Medjez-el-Bab in the south. Andrew Knighton, "The First Battle for Tunisia in World War Two," *War History Online*, retrieved on February 9, 2020, from https://www.warhistoryonline.com/world-war-ii/first-battle-tunisia-world-war-two.html

claimed to have knocked down an enemy plane. 701st reported they had been bombed by our planes and casualties and losses were so heavy that they were having to turn around and go back.[10]

Joined up with Br. Inf. Col. A recon made and he and Bruss evolved a plan. Br. Infantry mounted our tanks and rode to a point near Medjez where they dropped off and went into town, our tanks proceeding on out on to the flat beyond.[11] I followed the tanks in the Command H/T. The town was occupied without resistance the enemy having already retired. The Br. had been shelling it all day yesterday. Tanks pulled out to a harbor just S.E. of town. Br. Engineers went to work putting in bridge where the main one in town had been blown up. Enemy planes were over during the night and dropped bombs, some landing very close to us but no one hurt.

### November ?, 1942

Bruss away all day. We dispersed putting some tanks in position to fire if enemy counter-attacked. Bridge in and enemy bombers dived in on it several times despite strong ack-ack fire but while they came in very close failed to secure a disabling hit. All sorts of rumors about progress of other elements and discussion as to when we might be in Naples. Everyone is now digging adequate slit trenches. Some German dead reported in nearby fields.

## Fighting In and Around Tebourba

### November 29 (estimated), 1942

At daylight tanks again take up defensive positions. H.Q. Co. units dispersed in hollows. Bruss away. Stukkas again bomb bridge. Fighters dive on us and boy manning machinegun in mortar platoon killed. I stood up as plane passed over only to have to hit the dirt again as the M.G. in

10    The 701st Tank Destroyer Battalion.

11    The British Unit was the 11th Infantry Brigade Group. Charles R. Anderson, *Tunisia*, Center for Military History Publication, CMH Pub 72-12, p. 8.

tail cut loose. Bruss arrives just before dark, orders an attack out into the flat which is launched just before dark for benefit of General Oliver and staff. Danger of movement because of French outposts. Tanks all return safely after dark. We go into a new bivouac area a short distance from where we had been to avoid re-visit of enemy planes.

During the night received order to send a number of rifles, tank grenades, and an instructor to Br. H.Q.'s. Later ordered to move Bn. across river and by road to Teboura.[12] I went ahead to Br. H.Q.'s to contact Bruss and receive orders. Protested about our men having to give personal arms to Br. Reprimanded by Bruss.

Figure 16: Members of 2nd Battalion, 13th Armored Regiment in North Africa discussing operations, November 26, 1942. Standing is Sergeant N. T. Mahoney and kneeling is Lieutenant G. W. Williams. Lieutenant Colonel Gardiner is bending over on the right reviewing the map. (Photograph from the Patricia Issel Collection)

12    Teboura is twenty miles from the capital city of Tunis. This was the location of a battle between the Axis and British troops lasting from November 29 to December 4. The British Hampshire Regiment held the town for several days until it fell to the Germans on December 4. The battle is commemorated in the name of a road in Southampton, England called "Tebourba Way." Rick Atkinson, *An Army at Dawn: The War in North Africa, 1942–1943: The Liberation Trilogy*, (New York, New York: Macmillan Publishers, 2007), p. 222.

Ordered to bring Bn. forward to point south of Tebourba where Br. Liaison officer would guide us into bivouac. Realized as daylight broke that we had missed him and gone on by the point and were in wide-open country. Deployed Bn. off road and went ahead to contact Bruss. Ordered to bring all officers forward to him in Tebourba. Reaching there we found it a community showing much evidence of recent hot fighting. Saw a number of destroyed German tanks in the streets which had been knocked by Br. Anti-tank crews. These tanks had the desert color on them and were new, the guns still having shipping paper on them.

Guide took us through olive orchard to base of hill just north of Tebourba which we climbed. Found Bruss there with Br. Inf. Col. Plans made for an attack on [Djedeida].[13] While we were on hill Stukkas heavily bombed Br. Artillery positions in outskirts of Tebourba. Impressive toy like sight. Native while buildings standing out of surrounding green olive orchard. Bombs brought batteries continue firing shortly thereafter. German fighter swooped down and strafed us. We saw long German column streaming up the valley towards Mateur.

My mission was to coordinate the loading of Br. Infantry, the Northamptons, on our tanks.[14] It added up to thirteen men per tank and I reported that as impractical. Bruss ordered it to be done anyway. Tanks took off at one o'clock loaded with infantry. I followed H/T but was soon outdistanced because the rough road made it impossible for us to keep up with the tanks. Caught up to the tanks just as they came back over a low hill. Bruss was buried well down in his and the Br. Inf. Col. was clinging to the back of it trying to flatten himself out as best he could to avoid being hit.

Our tanks which had charged across a little flat between two hills with the infantry still riding on the tanks had suddenly been engaged by

13    Djedeida Airfield is an airfield in Tunisia, located approximately 10 km east-northeast of El Battan, and 30 km west of Tunis. The airfield was built prior to 1942 and used by the German Luftwaffe. It was raided by elements of the US 1st Battalion of the 1st Armored Regiment on November 25, 1942, but the U.S. forces were forced to withdraw due to lack of infantry support. *Armor Command*, pp. 74–75.

14    The 5th (Huntingdonshire) Battalion of the Northhamptonshire Regiment was assigned to the 143rd Infantry Brigade, part of the 48th (South Midland) Infantry Division. W. J. Jervois, *The History of the Northhamptonshire Regiment: 1934–1948*, (The Northhamptonshire Regiment Committee, Northampton, 1953), p. 259.

enemy anti-tank guns and four knocked out and set on fire. The rest of our tanks withdrew back over the ridge into defiladed positions. I went up to take a look and could see the four tanks burning with a dense black column of smoke pouring out of the turrets of each of them.

Much confusion. There were men lying all around the tanks, most of them apparently dead. We could observe a few crawling and could hear some cries for help. I asked the Bn. Med. Sgt. what he thought about going out to try and pick some of them up. He said he was ready, so we got a Med. H/T and a driver and drove over the ridge down the hill and out on the flat where we came under heavy small arms fire. We drove out to the tanks, opened up the back of the door of one and dragged a boy in who was horribly wounded, having a huge chunk torn out his back and the back of his shoulder. The bullets were rattling off the H/T like hail on a tin roof and several other men whom we started to go to waved us away and withdrew, being fired at all the way back over the ridge.

We really didn't profit much by that trip for both the Sgt. And the H/T driver were wounded in the process, the driver rather badly.

Two tanks were ordered to try and work down along a railroad track. One tank came back and part of the crew from another. They ran into the anti-tank gun. Lt. Jehlik one of our best officers and finest men, had his head shot off.[15] We laid him down back over the hill and I put a shell case upright at both ends of his body to keep him from being run over and so we could find him in the dark.

We could see the enemy on the other hill across a little flat beyond our burning tanks. Just before dusk our tanks laid a heavy barrage on it and the infantry, the remainder of the Northamptons, attacked and took it.

It was then dark, and I went out into the battlefield and with two Br. Medics started taking inventory. There were many dead men and lots of severely wounded and some lightly wounded who had laid quietly until dark. They helped us locate the more seriously wounded. Went back for

15    First Lieutenant Eugene Franklin Jehlik, University of Illinois Veteran's Memorial Project, retrieved on February 9, 2020, from http://chiuiaaweb1.admin.uillinois.edu/illinois/veterans/display_veteran.asp?id=348

our Med. H/T's but didn't dare bring them up to where they would be illuminated by the tanks which were still burning briskly. We carried the men to the H/T's which we parked out of the immediate circle of light. Two of the H/T's went back fully loaded and I remained behind so as to guide the men in for the next batch.

Sat down and ate a "D" bar. Could still hear some of the wounded moaning and smell the odor of burnt flesh from the tanks that had served as crematories for some of the crews. Evacuated two more groups which cleaned out all of our boys that we could find alive and some of the Br.

Impressed by the cheerful and hard-working attitude of the Br. Aid men and stretcher bearers. Went back to our aid station and was swamped. Reports that our Dr. was not much help becoming completely unnerved at the approach of hostile planes. A grim scene in the shadows of wounded men on stretchers to be evacuated and a row of those who no longer moved or groaned off at one side. Helped load Jehlik into a H/T for removal to a burying point. Searched around in the dark for another body that was supposed to be laid out in that vicinity, but we couldn't find it.

Bruss went back to some H.Q.'s just before dark. During afternoon we spotted a small anti-tank gun in open and had difficulty in driving one man away from it who continued to serve it with shells landing all around him. Ammunition and gas came up during night.

### November ?, 1942

Br. Col. asked me to put tanks in position to fire in Djedeida at daylight and to use all the smoke we could to assist the Northamptons which were attacking shortly after dawn, with the very light forces they have. Bruss showed up just before attack. Very resentful that I had anything to do in his absence about making plans for the attack. We fired but infantry ran into intense fire and not only were driven back but were counterattacked and had to leave the hill they captured last night and fall back to our positions.

Saw three German prisoners, one badly wounded. We drew considerable mortar fire. Balance of F Co. arrived and went directly into line. Before I got to speak to the officers, one of them was wounded by a mortar shell. Through a mix-up they had not dropped their bags off in Souk-el-Arba where we stored ours as we came through so dumped theirs off in a pile at a little railroad station.[16] A few minutes later, Stukkas came over there, dive-bombed that spot and all of the barracks bags and officers' luggage was destroyed or burned. Bruss away after mid-morning. I "borrowed" a tank and went from tank to tank of ours that were in position along the ridge line. Tanks pulled down into cover along railroad for the night. The "Hampshires", a guard's regiment, started coming in to take over from the weary and badly beaten Northamptons.

At daybreak the tanks again moved up on ridge but pulled back down when fire became heavy. They were still under fire at the base of the hill, so I went out to them to order them back a short distance. Got on the outside of a tank to speak to the tank commander when a flight of Stukkas came diving down on us. Shifted around to the side of the turret away from the direction from which they were diving. They threw dirt all over us, but no tanks were hit, and no one was hurt. Sent out a message for all of the tanks to displace 300 yards so as to get out from under fire. The first tank to move failed to stop and all of the rest kept following like a bunch of sheep. Took after them in command H/T and after a wild ride, got them headed off, turned around and started back up again. The tanks moved into hull down positions and did some firing on targets that the infantry asked us to engage.

Just at dusk, we started to move back to an area about two miles toward Tebourba. The Germans had slipped an "88" in just across the river from us and it opened fire on the column and hit the lead tank. It continued to fire apparently at the exhaust flashes and with its screaming

16    There were two airfields located on Souk-el-Arba. The original airfield, which pre-dates Operation Torch, was located immediately to the southeast of the town and was captured by paratroops of the British 1st Parachute Brigade on November 16, 1942. Franz Kurowski, *Endkampf in Afrika: Der Opfergang der Heeresgruppe Rommel in Tunesien 1942/43*, (Druffel-Verlag, 1982), p.54.

sound and flaming tracer it was a scary affair. The rest of the tanks kept swinging wide of the one that was hit. I was in a tank and waited until they had all gone and the firing was stopped before I made a run for it and wasn't fired on. The tank that was hit was only damaged in the suspension system and that was repaired, and the tank was brought in during the night.

Tanks moved back in the morning but increased enemy artillery and mortar fire kept them from getting up to former positions. Stukkas caught our four S.P.'s out in the open and bombed them, killing half of the men and horribly wounding the rest. I helped give first-aid to the wounded and doped them up with morphine. I am sure that two of them wouldn't live. We again pulled back towards Tebourba. Enemy plane received hit in air above us breaking into pieces and falling all around us. Bruss called an officers' meeting when he came in tonight. Was particularly ugly and just about as much as accused me of being yellow.

We didn't move out but began to receive artillery fire in our area so did some displacing and set up tanks for all around defense. Br. Artillery continued to move forward. Saw an ammunition truck near us and hit and burn. Enemy air about all day and almost a constant series of bombing raids took place. Received word early in afternoon that enemy tanks were approaching from N. and was ordered to attack them. Ordered F Co. to proceed to edge of olive grove on N. and having heard that they were in position and could observe nothing, I started up through the olive orchard with H.Q.'s units. Reached edge of grove just as what was left of three crews from F Co. came straggling back. They were an awful sight being terribly burned. Their tanks had been caught in the rear as they were turning them around by anti-tank guns and set on fire. Sent them to an aid station with recon. peeps.

Had become separated from D Co. tanks in olive grove and communications broke down. Rounded up remainder of F Co. tanks and started out of grove into open flat to see if we could locate enemy tanks.

Gave both my 75- and 37-mm gunners instructions to fire at all buildings and haystacks and anything that might conceal an anti-tank gun and we moved out with the guns blazing. Soon found that there was only one tank with me and after about a mile it dropped behind. Shortly after that I spotted six enemy tanks moving slowly across abandoned airfield at a distance of about two miles. Thought I'd stuck my neck out far enough and turned around. Had my 37 mm gunner keep firing on the way back. Drew no fire. Rounded up D and F Co. tanks that were left.

It was reported that the enemy had crossed the river and were now in vicinity of our last night's bivouac, so I decided to move into groves west of Tebourba. As we started over, we saw a number of tanks advancing towards that same area from the opposite direction. We watched them for a long while before we identified them and believing they were British we cautiously approached them and were relieved to find on getting closer that they were friendly. Took a deployed position in the hills S.W. of Tebourba for the night.

More of our casualties came in including Lt. Thompson who had been wounded and badly burned. We were now evacuating to a Br. Clearing station back down the line towards Medjez-el-Bab. Learned of some of the maintenance personnel being killed during the day by shelling.[17]

## December 3, 1942

Didn't like our positions because I felt we were too close to the river and, therefore, within range of enemy mortar fire so moved over hills on to slopes running into Tebourba at dawn.

The men were just getting breakfast when a major from the 1st Armored Regt came up and said that Bruss wanted to talk to me over his radio. He had his light tank up on the hill and I walked up there with him. CCB had now come up with artillery and infantry and he said that the plan was to have us attack from one side and E Co. which was now back

---

17    Lieutenant William D. Thompson, *Armor Command,* p. 80.

with the CCB was to come on from the other flank and we were to "destroy" the enemy in this area. The Bn. that this major was with had been operating with a Br. tank group known as the Blade Force and had been in a number of actions against German tanks and they had been driven south from the vicinity of Mateur.

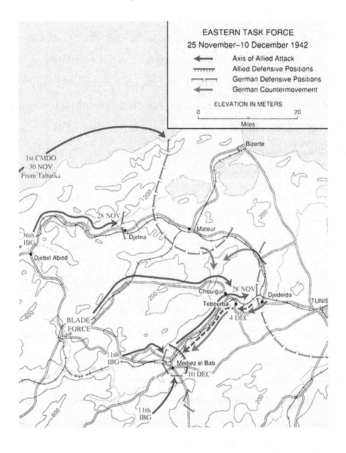

Figure 17: Map of Eastern Task Force in Tunisia, November 25–December 10, 1942 ("Historical Resources About the Second World War," retrieved on February 16, 2020)

While we were trying to get through to Bruss who was back at CCB, an officer rushed up to say that his company (he belonged to the same Bn. as this major) was being attacked. The major told me that his light tanks couldn't stand up against the heavier German ones, that he would try to maneuver around behind them and that he felt my mission was such that I should attack them. Before separating we walked out on the point of the hill where we could barely see a large number of German tanks scattered about in the valley below us and between us and where CCB was located.

I ran back down to where our tanks were and told them we were moving out immediately. Talked to the officers of D and F Co. and gave them a hasty plan. Piled into my tank and took off with all tanks starting to move. What I intended to do was to proceed up the valley floor and then cut back so as to catch the enemy tanks that I had seen in the flank. When we reached the edge of the olive grove, I waited a moment and then started up the flat. Immediately came under fire but they weren't hitting close. When I checked I found to my dismay that Phil Cocke was with me in the other H.Q.'s tank but none of the rest had left the olive garden.

Was unable to reach anyone on the radio. Elected to keep going, however, until we could reach some cover. We reached the base of some hills and pulled into an olive grove.

The next thing I saw was a column of dust and checking found it was kicked up by tanks which I thought were enemy judging from the direction they were coming. Ordered my 75 gunner to fire an A.P. at the first one to cross his sights down the line of olive trees that we were facing. Recognized them as friendly tanks too late to stop his firing. Fortunately, he missed. The tanks were light Bn. who Ex. Officer had brought me the word about the proposed attack. Talked to him again. He said he was going to make a swing around back of the enemy in an effort to rejoin CCB.

Cocke and I decided to return and see what had happened to the rest of our force. We again drew fire while we were proceeding across the flat and his tank was hit and burned but everyone escaped without injury. There were no tanks in the olive grove when we reached it, but they had all pulled back to the vicinity of Tebourba, many of them having taken shelter in and around the buildings. Some shells were coming in and most everyone had taken cover.

After some difficulty I got them out of the various positions they had taken and deployed them into line, and we started out over the broad hill between Tebourba and the enemy. We drew some fire. As tanks began to appear in the distance, I ordered ours to fire on them. Our tanks showed a hesitancy to advance and a movement forward was largely accomplished by my moving ahead fifty or one hundred yards and then their coming parallel to me.

On one such move I suddenly discovered a German tank below me at a distance of about 300 yards. Since I had used up all of my 75, I ordered my 37 gunner to fire an A.P. and he scored a hit on the first shot. Had him put in another and then the crew started to crawl out and run away from hit, whereupon I ordered him to cut loose with his machinegun. This caused them to turn around and run back so as to secure the protection of their tank.

Figure 18: Lieutenant Colonel Henry Gardiner stands before his M4A1 Sherman 'Henry III' Tank (Photograph from the Patricia Issel Collection)[18]

18      Gardiner's previous two tanks were knocked out in earlier fighting in Tunisia, and this particular vehicle was destroyed by a German anti-tank gun near Mateur, with the loss of two crewmen. The geometric insignia identifies this vehicle as being with the HQ, Co., 2nd Medium Tank Battalion, 13th Armored Regiment, 1st Armored

Just then we were hit. There was a blinding flash in the tank, a scream and I realized I had been hurt. I jumped out of the tank and ran back a short distance and crouched. There had been seven of us in the tank and I saw four get out. Other shells aimed at my tank started coming in, so I moved to one side so as to be out of the line of fire and walked on down the hill to a draw where I took stock of my injury. There was a cut in my left elbow that didn't amount to much and a slight one on my right wrist. The one on my elbow was bleeding quite freely so I got out my first aid kit, put some powder on it and tried to bandage it. Felt very weak and thought I was going to faint. Must have been the combination of fatigue and loss of blood. A tank was going by at that time and I hailed it when the tank commander got out and helped me fix the bandage on my elbow. Then I swallowed some of the sulfanilamide pills we carried. That was quite a job for I didn't have a canteen. Feeling all right and the enemy fire having slackened off, I went back up on the crest of the hill to take stock of the situation. When my tank had been hit, the others had halted and backed up a short distance, but they were well deployed and in position to handle anything that might approach from the front.

In the valley where E Co. was supposed to attack, we could see about six of our tanks burning and others that seemed to be disabled. The enemy was still where they were when I spotted them first thing this morning. Could see enemy mortar fire falling on the high hill N.E. of Tebourba on which the Br. artillery O.P.'s was located. We received a message saying we were charged with keeping the main road from Tebourba open.

A report came back that someone could hear voices calling from our tank. I went to investigate. Looked in and could see two dead men. They were the radio operator and the 75 mm gunner. Was just about to climb in the tank to recover my helmet and pistol when apparently the enemy saw me and start to shell the place, so I beat it. The hit that had knocked us out was on the right front and from the hole looked like an 88 mm.

Division. Col. Gardiner went on to command the 13th Tank Battalion in Italy but named his subsequent tank 'Ballykinler'.

During the shelling, one other tank that was in the group strung along the hill was hit and burned.

When nite fell, I left the tanks on the hill covering the road but moved them in closer together for mutual protection. Bunched all of the H/T's up in a little grove in a hollow to the rear. After dark, Br. traffic started moving thru our area into Tebourba. Guns and ammunition went up and a string of loaded ambulances came out. Our gas and ammo trucks came up and I sent them out to service the tanks on the hill. While this was in process an enemy plane came over and dropped flares. Thought that they had spotted us but the bombers that followed plastered Tebourba. Sent word to CCB that I felt our position would be untenable by daylight with the enemy apparently advancing steadily on both sides.

### December 4, 1942

About two o'clock we received orders to join CC B back down the Medjez road. Had the H/T's leave first so that the movement of the tanks wouldn't tip off the enemy as to what was going on before the soft-shelled vehicles could clear. The tanks followed us out. We only went about five miles and closed in at our new spot just at daylight. Bruss was there to meet us and placed the tanks in an orchard on either side of the road facing the enemy. Learned that E Co. in its attack had met with very heavy losses. The only officer left was the maintenance officer. By our pulling back there was nothing to prevent the enemy from cutting Tebourba off completely. This they proceeded to do, and we watched a group of their tanks work around the hills on which we had been sitting yesterday afternoon.

The 27th F.A. which had come up shelled them, but they were too far away to do any accurate shooting and they didn't seem to be bothered. I felt very badly to think of all of our stout-hearted Br. friends in Tebourba who were still holding out. We could hear them firing and there was a regular procession of bombers unloading on them.

Made a trip around to check the positions of the companies. We were receiving intermittent shell fire that we thought was coming from the enemy tanks. A fragment from one shell that hit near me passed between my legs, tearing a hole out of my trench coat. Another shell killed one of our H.Q.'s Maintenance Co. boys who was working on a H/T about twenty feet from me. My elbow was giving me considerable trouble, so I had one of the doctors look at it. It had swollen up somewhat, so he dressed it and had me put it in a sling.

Bruss who was holed up in a H/T had me go see the 6th Infantry about a plan for going out tonite and try to recover one of our disabled tanks which was out beyond our positions about a mile. As darkness fell two Br. ambulances passed thru us in a gallant attempt to reach Tebourba. They had been gone for only a few minutes when there was a burst of German machinegun fire and one of them burst into flames.

I told Bruss that I didn't think it wise for me to stick around with an arm in a sling and thought I'd better go back, and have it looked after. He agreed and it was decided that I would return with the trains when they came up. The kitchen trucks which was hadn't seen since we landed had come up with the trains and the magical news that they had hot cakes already prepared soon spread throughout the bivouac areas. Just as the trucks were ready to serve, Bruss received word that the enemy infantry had broken thru (later proven to be entirely false) and he ordered them to leave immediately. I piled in a peep driven by Tom Hargis of Ser. Co. and we started back.

The sky above Tebourba was all aglow and there was the constant rumble of firing. The Tommies were shooting it out to the last man. On the way back down the road we passed considerable Br. artillery which was badly disorganized and moving to the rear. Somewhat further back, we came to a point where it was all being directed off to one side of the road apparently for reorganization.

When we reached the Ser. Co. area, Tom took me to the D Co. kitchen, and I had some of the hot cakes the boys had lost out on. John Ford and one of his camera men came in and visited with me while I ate. Had my bedroll with me and Tom helped me spread it out between two straw stacks. Some pigs that were lying there moved, but not far.

## Evacuation to Field Hospital and Return to Front

**December 5, 1942**

Slept till broad daylight. Tom then drove me to where his group was camped, south of Beja, where we had breakfast, the main item being fresh eggs. Inquiry had disclosed that there was a Br. hospital not far down the road, so we set out to find it. Just before reaching Souk-el-Khemis, we turned to the right and followed a side road back up into the mountains. The hospital was in a small French hotel which served a lead mining community.[19] It was more in the nature of an evacuation hospital in that the cases that were being brought in there did not seem particularly serious.

A Br. non-com took a pair of tweezers and retrieved a piece of shrapnel out of the hole in my elbow, large enough to have made the trip worthwhile. A nice Medical Leftenant took a look at my elbow, said an X-ray would be advisable and that in any event I'd better stick around for a few days, so Tom left.

Was invited to lunch with two Br. Med. Officers. They had a portable X-ray machine and took some pictures of my elbow after lunch. I just loafed around during the afternoon and watched the ambulances as they unloaded to see if there was anyone I knew. About a third of the patients were Americans, the rest British. Found that I had been assigned to a room with two other walking patients. These were two very pleasant English officers who both had sustained gun-shot wounds in their arms while fighting on the big hill just N. of Tebourba. All of the medical personnel

19    Beja has two identified mines. The most commonly listed primary commodities are lead and zinc. *Mining in Beja*, retrieved on February 17, 2020, from https://thediggings.com/tun/beja-tun4084

were Br. soldiers and they were most considerate and helpful. We three seemed to be the only ones who rated beds, everyone else sleeping on the stretchers. There were electric lights, but they were blacked out at nine o'clock. We were all asleep before then, however, and I never slept as solidly as I did that first night.

**December 6, 1942**

My little medical officer was around first thing this morning with his pictures. They showed one pretty fair piece of shrapnel just under the skin and several small pieces more deeply imbedded. He removed the larger one and said that I could keep the others as souvenirs. We are on Br. compo. ration. My two Br. friends and I just can't get enough tea and crackers.

The Padre had been so solicitous since I came in that I felt bound to attend his services when he announced that he was holding them this afternoon. The hotel evidently had, also, been a sort of community center and there was a sort of theatre and ball-room attached. The floor of this large room was covered with rows of men lying on stretchers. The chaplain held his services in this room passing out hymn books as far as they would go to those who wanted them. It was a moving sight to see this group of men trying to prop themselves up to better be able to follow the Padre as he led the singing.

I wandered about afterwards and visited with some of the men. Found several boys from the 1st Bn. of the 1st Armor who had been with the group that we milled around with in the olive orchards the morning before I was hurt. They had run into trouble rather later and evidently suffered rather heavy losses. Had a copy of "Rhymes of a Red-Cross Man" in my [musette] bag which I gave to the Padre to add to his circulating library. Also had some cigarettes which I rationed out as far as they would go.

Everyone asks for information from the front, but we hear none. The Guards Brigade has come into the line around Medjez which so far as the

Br. boys are concerned is an assurance that everything is under control. Another nite of solid sleep.

## December 7, 1942

Dressing on arm changed. Not causing any trouble but my physician advising continuing to keep it in a sling. I beat my two English friends up this morning and walked over to the mine and watched what I suppose was part of a shift being lowered. Seemed strange to see bare-footed natives wearing turbans stepping aboard a cage. About the only thing that made them look like miners was the carbide lamps that they were carrying.

They have decided to make this a hospital to care for the more seriously wounded so my two friends and I were ordered to pack up. We were loaded into one of these comfortable appointed Br. ambulances late in the afternoon with our destination a field hospital near Bone. Couldn't see very much to start with and it soon became dark.

After a long drive we arrived at our destination which was a tent hospital in a very muddy field. The three of us were assigned to an officers' tent. Will never forget the sight that greeted us when we wormed our way thru the black-out curtains into our new home. We had arrived in the presence of the really seriously wounded.

It was a long tent and every cot seemed to be taken and not by walking patients. The place was illuminated by candlelight and shadows were long and grotesque. Two men in adjoining cots particularly, gave me a start. They were completely swathed in bandages except for one small hole which was where their mouths should have been. There arms and heads were a mass of gauze and cotton and from time to time they would feebly paw in the air with them and with the pale yellow light flickering on them and with the weird shadows that they cast on the tent wall, I was reminded of the "Dance Macabre". There were a lot of unpleasant odors in the tent and the worst which seemed like that of decaying flesh came from these two men. Found myself assigned to the cot next to them.

All conversation was in subdued tones, so I was indeed startled when one bandaged figure in a somewhat quavering voice said, "Is that you, Major Gardiner?" It was Tommy Thompson of D Co., who had been badly burned when his tank was hit and destroyed by fire the day before I was hurt. He was hungry for news of the Bn. and I gave him what little I had. As to his condition I picked that up from his doctors and others. Everyone, it developed, knew Tommy, and his cheerfulness and courage were always commented upon. The doctor felt that his eyes would be all right, but he said his face was terribly burned particularly about his mouth and that one ear was in bad shape. The other burned man was an English pilot and he was in a more serious condition than Tommy, his burns extending more generally over his body. Someone had located a long cigarette-holder for Tommy, and this enabled him to smoke, since the cigarette was kept just beyond range of the gauze. I started a cigarette for him and placed it in his mouth which was just a raw hole with hardly any evidence of lips. The stench that came from Tommy and the other burned soldier seemed to be from the ointment that had been used to cover their burns.

I didn't sleep well for there was nothing peaceful about this ward. There were so many men in distress, there was lots of coming and going, the smell was worse as the night wore on, and I began to feel pretty much of a gold brick with the minor injury that I had.

### December 7, 1942
*A letter to his mother*

"First off" as my English friends would say, all reports to the contrary, I am fine. You may have received word from the War Department that I was wounded or if they haven't gotten around to it, you may still receive such information. Don't let that concern you for it was only a nick that I received and am receiving excellent care. In a tank battle a few days ago my tank was knocked out by a heavy gun. I received a few small steel splinters in my left arm, which a very nice little English medical officer removed just as easily as taking a cinder out of your eye. He has promised to let me keep the X-ray picture as a souvenir.

Have written you several notes and cards since we landed but, in view of the general confusion, they may not have made it thru. This is a special "Christmas letter" quota and I'm only allowed one. We were constantly on the go from the time we got all our equipment on shore until I was laid up. In our advance eastward, we climbed over one high mountain ranges after another. The country has been much like parts of Arizona and California. Instead of Mexicans and Indians one sees dirty Arabs.

Every meal I've had since we landed has come out of a tin can, but the British have a special one they call "compo" ration which we have been receiving that has a great variety and most satisfactory. Up until three days ago, I had been preparing my own meals which normally consisted of putting a can of stew on the exhaust pipe of the motor to heat. In the valleys, we were able to secure some oranges and most every place we have been able to barter old clothes with the natives for eggs. Until I came to this clearing station, I was on the ground and in the open every night and I've been in excellent health. I wrote you that Director Ford of "How Green was my Valley" was with us, along with a group of cameramen for a couple of weeks. I doubt if I show up in any of his picture for he wasn't up at the front except at nites. However, he said that he got some wonderful bombing shots of the rear areas so watch for any movies billed "American Forces in North Africa" or words to that effect.

### December 8, 1942

The few Br. orderlies that are charged with the care of this tent are swamped with work. Found that even those patients with crutches have been helping with the feeding. My two friends and I, therefore, represented a considerable acquisition since we could be of material assistance. I took over the job of feeding Tommy which had been looked after by a fine looking, big Br. Col. who had a foot in a case and was getting about on crutches. It is a messy job feeding him because it has to be done with a spoon and it's hard to get at his mouth because of the bandages and gauze that surround it and anything that slops over gets underneath the bandages. The food is Br. compo. Oranges are plentiful, however, the area being full of native vendors.

This camp couldn't be in a messier area. The hospital was bombed when it was in Bone and lost a number of their staff so moved out into the country and set up in this plowed field. The stretcher bearers have a particularly difficult time of it and there seems to be a never ending stream of them entering the operating tent. My two English friends and I decided we needed a change in atmosphere so took a walk after lunch. We wandered down the road to a little nearby community, watched some French butcher a hog, bought some oranges, and came back.

**December 9, 1942**

The Medico who looked at my elbow this noon said there was no reason why I shouldn't rejoin my unit, so I made arrangements to go into Bone with several other officers who were being discharged.

Teamed up with a Capt. from the Coldstream Guards who was out to rejoin his unit. We dropped our luggage at a transient camp just on the outskirts of town.[20] I tagged along with my big newly acquired friend who suggested we go look up the Movement Control officer. It proved to be quite a long walk.

The town was teaming with soldiers and we passed a lot of fine looking Br. units from an armored outfit who had just unloaded marching out of the city. The downtown parts of the city were pretty well wrecked by bombs. Our Q Movement man proved to be a little captain whom we both knew. He gave us a lead as to where we could get a ride and invited us to supper.

20    When the Second World War began, the 1st and 2nd battalions of The Coldstream Guards were part of the British Expeditionary Force (BEF) in France while the 3rd Battalion was on overseas-service in the Middle East.

My friend was in need of some clothing having had his cut up when he went to the hospital, so we went around to a Br. supply dump where we were both outfitted and I acquired battle dress of theirs which is more practical than anything we had. Then to supper at the former residence of the Italian Consul who had left hurriedly. The meal was compo plus native bread and champagne, of which I had too much. Our host provided us with a chauffeur afterwards to take us home. We would never have made it otherwise.

We dropped in at a Br. Med unit which was moving up tomorrow and whom he suggested would provide us transportation. It was all arranged, and we had a round of drinks with our Medical friends who were having a party. Spent the night on the floor of the office of the officer in charge of the rest camp. Too much high living all of a change and I lost my supper. From the number of troops that were milling around the area after dark many of whom were drunk, I'll be a check would flush out a lot of A.W.O.L's.

## The Battalion Re-Organizes and Re-Equips in "Stukka Valley"

### December 10, 1942

We were given an excellent breakfast by our Medico friends and then loaded into the back of one of their lorries which was moving personnel forward to where they were establishing a new dressing station. The road we took was the Tabarka route and for miles out of Bone there were stocks of ammunition and gas on both sides of the road.[21] This was my first trip over this road in daylight and it proved to be an interesting one being most scenic. Saw a total of five Br. trucks that had recently gone off the road and taken varying drops.

Additional 4th and 5th battalions were also formed for the duration of the war. They fought extensively, as part of the Guards Armored Division, in North Africa and Europe as dismounted infantry.

21 There were two main routes leading out of Tebessa. The most direct led just inside the Tunisian border through Le Kef, a main British transportation center, to Souk-el-Arba and Tabarka. The other ran inside Algeria through Souk Ahras and eastward to Tabarka. Erna Risch, *The Quartermaster Corps: Organization, Supply, and Services. Vols. 1–2. United States Army in World War II: The Technical Services*, (Washington, D.C.: Center for Military History, 1952), p. 63.

We had oranges and crackers for lunch. The truck halted at a hospital area short of Souk-el-Arba. There we secured a ride in a Br. ambulance that was going into that community. Passed great quantities of ammunition and motor fuel store alongside the road. We went to the Town Major and thru him learned that CCB had a H.Q.'s in town. I borrowed a peep there and we were driven to the 78th Div. H.Q.'s which was set up in a group of farm buildings north of Souk-el-Khemis.[22] There my friend found where his outfit is and arranged a ride up tonite.

Was told that the American elements were coming out of the line now and were to camp along the main road. Drove on up the Beja road a few miles until I reached some guides who had been dropped off by a billeting party and found one for the 2nd Bn. 13th.

It commenced to rain and before long a straggling column of vehicles began to come by belonging to various units of the Armored Division. It was a pretty sorry sight for it was a beaten bunch of troops who knew they had been licked and were tired, wet, dirty, miserable and hungry. It was dark by the time the 2nd Bn. came along. H.Q.'s Co. was pretty much intact, but the rest of the outfit was a shell for there were only fourteen tanks that rolled in on their own power.

The outfit had been in action since I left up until last nite when they pulled out. The Guards Brigade now held the sector with a company of new M-4 tanks of the 2nd Armored Division that had come up from Casablanca. Found Jim Simmerman now a major and in command of the Bn., Bruss having been relieved. Gen. Oliver had taken exception to Bruss's handling of the Bn. and sent him back to Oran to start new equipment and supplies moving forward.[23]

While the Bn. had been in action and lost a few tanks, the casualties, since I left, had been light. That had not been true of the other outfits, however. The 27th F.A. which went into the area just across the road from

22    The 78th Infantry Division was a British Division.

23    James S. Simmerman went on to command the 2nd Battalion, 13th Armored Regiment though North Africa and onto and up the Italian Peninsula.

us had had a battery overrun, lost all their guns and a good share of the personnel from that battery.

One Bn. of the 6th Infantry had in what sounds like a serious error on the part of the commander abandoned all of its vehicles thinking the road was blocked when in fact it wasn't. CCB had lost its tank platoon and all personnel.

Everyone was so tired that they didn't stay up and do much talking but turned in immediately. I slept in the open. Was awake a good share of the time and had an uneasy feeling when I saw a long column of lights moving down a mountain road on the other side of the valley. Thought what a nice trick it would have been for the Germans to have mounted up in our vehicles and have boldly turned on the lights and come driving right on thru our lines.

### December 11, 1942 thru December 21, 1942

Gen. Oliver addressed all units and was unable to finish talking to ours because he was so overcome with emotion and cried. He said he just felt so sorry for the poor men. At first the dope was that we were going back to Algeria some place to rest and refit. However, that soon was given up and all efforts were made to equip us on the spot. When the Bn. and other units first pulled in, there was a great shortage of personal equipment so much having been lost. Blankets were a most important item because of the cold weather. CCB was down the road a few miles and I was called there regularly for conferences on re-equipping and supplying.

The Inf. Bn. C.O. who had lost all of his vehicles was relieved. The artillery had lost all guns from one battery and the T.D.'s were even worse off. A deal was made whereby we received twenty M-4 tanks belonging to the 2nd Armored which had come up to help in the Medjez fight. The first time they went into action they had four tanks knocked out so they can't run over "88's" either. We also picked up some M-3's so by the 22nd we had almost a complete Bn. of tanks. Secured a training area and did some test firing on all new weapons.

Made a lot of changes in the Bn. organization appointing three new Company commanders. We are short of personnel, particularly officers. Commissioned one from the ranks and secured some replacements.

There were frequent bombing and strafing attacks and this area became known as "Stukka Valley". Frequently at nite we could see the ack-ack fire and hear the bombs fall. Everyone had a good deep slit trench. The anti-aircraft discipline was bad throughout the valley, however, and friendly planes were fired on regularly and several hit and brought down.

I was asked by Gen. Oliver who was now a Maj. Gen. to tell my version of Bruss's activities during the time that Bn. was pretty much on its own. The Adjutant requested statements to bear out my story of which plenty were readily forthcoming and a number of which were really devastating. Was formally, i.e., matter of record, given command of the Bn.

Some of the boys made contact with the Monastery at the Thibar and secured wine.[24] We played "Hearts" in the C.P. tent using a drop light from the peeps. My elbow developed a slight infection but cleared after a short time. Got rid of two officers who had failed to stand up in combat, one being our medical captain and the other the lieutenant who had a tank platoon whose nerves just went all to pieces during the fighting. Mail, magazines, and some packages began to arrive. We received a number of new M-4 tanks, and I had one earmarked for me.

Every morning Jim and I would make a visit around the Bn. on foot. Had it pretty well dispersed and the 50-calibres rigged up for anti-aircraft defense. Filled D Co. up with M-4's and started on E, leaving M-3's only in F Co. Three of us, Jim, Captain Van Zant, a newly assigned officer, and I sleep in the C.P. tent rolling up our bedrolls every morning and stacking

---

24    In 1895, the White Fathers set up a farm (Saint-Joseph De Tibār farm) and monastery in Thibar on the road south of Beja heading towards Téboursouk. *Christian Missionaries in Tunisia*, retrieved on February 19, 2020, from http://www.tunisia.com/community/threads/christian-missionaries-in-tunisia.7117/

them in one end. Held a sort of staff and Company commanders' meeting every nite.[25]

Had a job of it keeping the men away from the native landowners' buildings because they all wanted to sleep in the barns, and I didn't approve of being near the buildings because they were likely a target. Rains made the roads very slippery and traffic had a difficult time of it. A constant flow of Br. troops moving up but no word of any progress being made.

The 1st Bn. of the 1st A.R. turned what equipment they had left and some personnel over to fill out our 1st Bn. and returned to Oran to refit and re-organize. We were able to secure oranges and eggs without much difficulty and they were a most welcome addition to our regular diet of Br. compo ration. We secured and tried out a new weapon known as the bazooka gun which has been designed to use against tanks. Put a couple of them in Recon platoon. Was able to secure promotions for all of the second lieutenants in the Bn. and two captains for the newly appointed Company commanders. The regular bombing raids are resulting in some casualties.

## Téboursouk

### December 22, 1942

We made a nite march over a very mountainous road to a bivouac site in the vicinity of Téboursouk. Our move was tied in with some Counter-Intelligence camouflage people who set up dummy tanks in the area that we vacated. Our new camp is in an extensive olive grove which spreads over some rough terrain. We seem to be back under the British again. They are supposed to have a lot of tanks in this area.

### December 23, 1942 to January 4, 1943

With the exception of F Co., the Bn. remained in concealed bivouacs during this period. Enemy planes were sighted daily but if they discovered

25    Captain Robert E. Van Zant, Robert E. Van Zant Collection.

us, they never bothered us although they continued to bomb "Stukka Valley" and took a crack at some of the dummies that had been erected in our place when we pulled out. The weather was miserable, it being cold and wet most of the time.

The day before Christmas I was ordered to report to the old CCB C.P. in the valley, the operating one having been moved into Téboursouk. It was raining as usual and the road was a mess, so I arrived plastered in mud. When I found out the reason for the summons, I procured a pan and washed up. All of the unit commanders had been rounded up to meet Gen. Eisenhower and Gen. Anderson. Gen. Oliver introduced them to us. Their remarks were brief and in the manner of a pep talk more than anything else. It seems that a big attack had been planned with the hope of our driving thru to Tunis. The weather has made the ground so bad, however, that it has been postponed. Gen. Eisenhower was concerned lest there be a let-up in the spirit of the troops.

Would have felt that the trip had been pretty much a waste of effort if it had not been for the fact that I found more mail for the Bn. at the rear echelon that I could carry in the peep. Sent transportation back for the rest of it. I felt somewhat like Santa Claus on my return late in the evening for most of it was Christmas mail.

On Christmas day I was invited up to CCB H.Q.'s. Gen. Robinett has one bottle of Scotch which didn't quite make the round of the staff and the unit commanders.

F Co. went up to Medjez-el-Bab to relieve a company from the 2nd Armored which was holding a defensive position there with the Guards Brigade. They were there a week and suffered no casualties although they had some close ones. I went down the morning of the evening that we took over and then alternated with Jim each morning in paying the boys a visit. We kept a platoon in the railroad station north of Medjez and they worked there with the Coldstream Guards and the Argyles.[26] The enemy

26    The Argyll and Sutherland Highlanders (Princess Louise's) was a line infantry regiment of the British Army. The 1st Battalion saw action in Northern Africa and then in the Allied Invasion of Sicily and through the Italian

used to drop a few shells in on them every day. The balance of F Co. was kept in reserve.

Learned that the Br. officer who was a captain and the Rt. Hon. somebody or other, who was evacuated from the hospital with me, was missing in action following an unsuccessful attack that the Br. and our boys made on Longstop hill on Christmas day.[27]

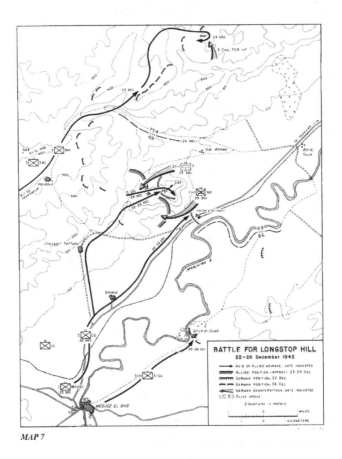

*MAP 7*

Figure 19: The Battle for Longstop Hill (Center of Military History/Public Domain)

Mainland. *The Wartime Memories Project—1st Battalion, Argyll and Sutherland Highlanders during Second World War,* retrieved on February 20, 2020, from https://wartimememoriesproject.com/ww2/allied/battalion.php?pid=790

27    The name "Longstop Gap" was derived from Longstop Hill, the British designation for Djebel el Ahmera, east of which the Allies were not again to pass for a long period. George F. Howe, *United States Army in World War II Mediterranean Theater of Operations Northwest Africa: Seizing the Initiative in the West,* (Washington, D.C.: Office of the Chief of Military History, 1957), pp. 340 and 345, retrieved on February 20, 2020, from https://www.ibiblio.org/hyperwar/USA/USA-MTO-NWA/index.html

We ran a sort of school from some Br. tankers to show them how to operate our tanks and then we turned five over to them. Some deal was supposed to be in the wind where they were going to secure our M-3's and we were to get all M-4's.

The company of the 1st Bn. was sent down to [Siliana] and placed under the French where they saw considerable action and suffered about as many casualties, however, from the French as when they were fired on by the enemy.

The Bn. commander, John Todd, while going up to an O.P. was hit by shrapnel and killed.[28] He was a most capable officer, quite a character and extremely popular. A simple military funeral was held for him in Beja which I attended. While I had become quite inured to seeing dead men, I must confess something of a feeling of shock to arrive at the grave and find that the body was only wrapped in a blanket which left the legs uncovered from the knees down. It seemed for some reason a little rough to see them throwing dirt in on top of John's uncovered feet.

We had a number of ranking visitors call on us while we were in the olive grove, most of whom were in a hurry. Took my tank out and fired it. I have a good crew being the boys out of the tank that used to be Bruss's.

Called up to CCB to be told that the Bn. was going south and that we would be joined shortly by the balance of the combat command.

*{Letter on December 23, 1942, describing the efforts to put together the means for a Christmas dinner is omitted.}*

**December 26, 1942**

*An extract from a letter to his mother*

Christmas dinner consisted of British canned stew, augmented by the contents of Elizabeth's Christmas package. [29] Our general called just

---

28    Lieutenant Colonel John Todd lost his life assisting 1st Infantry Division at Longstop Hill, but was posthumously awarded the Distinguished Service Cross. Steven Thomas Barry, "Battle-Scared and Dirty: US Army Tactical Leadership in the Mediterranean Theater, 1942-1943", retrieved on January 20, 2020, from https://etd.ohiolink.edu/!etd.send_file?accession=osu1313541748&disposition=inline

29    Elizabeth, or Libo to those closest, was Gardiner's sister. She married Dr. Gail R. Soper and lived in Evanston, Illinois. They had three children: Bob, Tom, and Sally Soper Gray of Davis, California. Gardiner's youngest sister

before noon and I took him on a tour of the area. The boys were in good spirits. They, of course, were all sorry not to be home but we have so much to be thankful for when we think of our friends who were killed and wounded that we don't mind the present inconveniences.

Last night we listened to a Christmas program from the States and then a group of the officers gathered in my tent and we had a little song feast. What we miss as much as anything right now is news of what is going on at the fighting fronts. So far as our operations is concerned, it is of necessity clothed with secrecy, so we hear little that is authentic and all sorts of wild rumors. Winston Churchill has a son who is a captain in the British Army and seems to be a sort of a free-lance and we see him from time to time.

**January 1, 1943**

Dear Dad:

The biggest morale builder for the soldier overseas is the mail he receives from home. Bullets, blood, mud and short rations are forgotten when the mail comes in. Some boys are always left out and that is tough. I overheard an unusual torrent of profanity the other day and on investigating the source found a boy with a card from the postmaster at Ft. Knox saying that if he would forward him 3 cents a letter which they were holding for postage due would be sent along. There is no snow here but it is cold enough for it. My tentmates are sound asleep and I am writing this standing up as I found it too cold sitting. I have my woolen cap on and my overcoat and have to blow on my fingers. (Continued January 2nd) Once again my tentmates are bedded down for the nite. The wind is whipping the sides of the tent about and it is a bit chillier than last night.

I had a very interesting experience and can no longer say I haven't been well fed since we landed. There is a monastery back over the first range of hills which operates a large modern farm. Our general was invited there for lunch today and since he knew I was interested in livestock he took me

was Alice Gardiner Sowerwine, Patricia Issel's mother. Interview with Patricia Issel on February 29, 2020.

along. We had a three-course meal consisting of head cheese, an [omelet] and roast lamb and American fried potatoes topped off with tangerines. There was also bread and butter. We get nothing but a biscuit out of a can in our regular fare for bread. In addition, there were three kinds of wine.

### January 1, 1943

Not many eggnog parties in this section today but up to the present moment we have no complaints. We are still drawing the British ration so were issued two ounces of rum per man for today. I was up front visiting one of our companies that is in the line when it was dispensed this noon so didn't get to sample it, but from all accounts two ounces is more than plenty and, if we get any more, the present feeling is that it could be diluted by an equal volume of water and still be very acceptable.

Every evening when we are in a stationary position, as we are at the moment, all of the officers of the battalion meet at the C.P. tent for a conference at six-thirty and then, if conditions permit and the reception will allow, we get the news over the radio in the command half-track. Last nite, just as our meeting was about to start, a delivery of mail arrived, and we overlooked the news broadcast and almost forgot about our meeting. With one's desk the straw covered floor of a tent, it isn't that easiest thing in the world to keep track of one's personal effects. Every morning when I get up, things are packed so that if the orders come to move, there is nothing left to be done but to throw my stuff on board.

Yesterday I saw about as colorful a sight as I've seen since I came over. The British have a group of officers headed by an officer of the Scots-Greys who is a famous jumper going through the country securing mules and horses for a pack company that is being organized to transport supplies in the mountains. The French have been assisting them and yesterday the natives in this area were ordered to bring in a certain number of animals to be examined for possible service. It practically amounted to their being requisitioned except that they were being paid for them at a price which seemed quite fair. The spot that was selected for this horse and mule market was the olive grove in which we are now camped.

All morning there were Arabs coming down out of the hills leading and riding the animals. Some of them were well mounted and decked out like the kind you see in the movies while others are badly down at the heel. I went over with our general who happened to be passing through and we watched the show for a while. The Scots-Greys officer turned out to be a man he knew against whom he had competed in the jumping in the 1921 Olympics.[30] The mules and horses were all being gone over very carefully and the percentage of them that were being taken was low.

Last evening after our business session, we used up a couple of bottles of Scotch which had been secured by higher authority and that constituted our New Year's party, with everyone getting to bed by nine o'clock. At the present time, breakfast is served at seven, so we are getting lots of sleep. Of course, one always thinks it is the other fellow that is going to get it, but one has to be practical in such matters. We've lost quite a few boys and their package mail continues to come in and the problem has come up of the disposal of their personal effects. A number of us have agreed that, if anything happens to us, we don't want anything sent home and that the contents of any incoming packages are to be distributed among the rest. While there is little you can do about certain types of fire or bombings, I think our chances of coming through are better than green troops because we've been in the thick of it for many days and learned something about keeping our heads down.

## Central Tunisia

### January 5, 1943

We pulled out of our bivouac area at 18:30 hours. And marched all night closing in the bivouac south of Thala just after daylight, having marched

30    It is unclear who this is as the Olympics were not held in 1921 but instead in 1920 in Antwerp. No British competed in individual horse jumping during that Olympic year.

100 miles. Our column followed that of the 601st T.D. Bn. under command of Lt. Col. Baker who, by virtue of seniority, was our commander also for the march. The 2nd Bn. had a Ser. Co. section along with an ample supply of gas and rations for several days' extended operations. Arrangements had been made to supply us with a number of tank transporters to carry those tanks that were the worse for wear. They failed to meet us at the appointed road junction, and we went on without them.

I lead the Bn. in the command H/T and Jim and I alternated in acting as car commander. It was cold but the road was fairly good. Most of the tanks made the march without having to re-gas although a number had to. The day was spent in necessary maintenance and resting.

**January 6, 1943**

The T.D.'s took off ahead of us and we pulled out from under cover just at dark. The head of the column hit the road at 1815. We marched 60 miles to a bivouac south of Tebessa, where we closed in at 0400 hrs. We had to negotiate one ford which gave several tanks trouble. Saw a number of bonfires along our line of march which caused us some concern as we wondered if they might not be signals by the natives to the enemy of our approach. The road was very difficult to follow at times for in the dark it appeared just the same as the rest of the surface.

**January 7, 1943**

On our outfit closing in, I went to Col. Baker's C.P. to check in.[31] His Bn. had made much better time than we and he was well set up with a very fancy C.P. tent. He said the Air Corps had reported yesterday having discovered some eighty German tanks out on the flat not many miles distant hidden under native Arab tents.

We got fairly well rested up by the afternoon when our liaison officer whom we had sent on ahead to Tebessa came into Camp with a Brig.

31 Lieutenant Colonel Herschel D. Baker was the battalion commander for the 601st Tank Destroyer Battalion. Victor Failmezger, *American Knights: The Untold Story of the Men of the Legendary 601st Tank Destroyer Battalion,*

General. This officer was the advance representative of Gen. Frendendall, who commands II Corps which is moving down to take charge in this sector.[32] All day we were treated to the sight of American transport planes passing overhead with an occasional flight of fighters.

This is grand country. It is very much like parts of southern Utah and northern Arizona with fine big fir trees, expanses of what looks like sage brush, and jagged mountings jutting out of the countryside at many points.

**January 8, 1943**

Col. Baker told me this morning that he had been charged with countering an enemy threat in this sector and he felt that couldn't be done from our present position. He was, therefore, recommending that we move to [Sbeitla] which he considered a vital point and asked me for my opinion, and I said I agreed. He recommendation was approved, and we dispatched a billeting party to look for a bivouac site.

The Bn. pulled out from Bou Chebka at 1900 and marched to Sbeitla where we closed in bivouac in an olive orchard several miles east of the town at 0600 hrs., after a march of sixty miles. There was a strong wind and it was a bitter cold march. Simpson, the Recon. Plat. Commander, who had gone ahead with the billeting party, met us on the outskirts of Sbeitla to guide us to our destination.[33] Sbeitla was a rather movie-setting type of place and showed considerable evidence of being shot up. We passed through several barricades and roadblocks manned by French native troops.

**January 9–18, 1943**

I was very much surprised on finding from the records that we were only in this area for ten days because so much happened, and we were so busy that I thought it was more like a month.

(Oxford, UK: Osprey Publishing Co., 2015), p. 25.

32    Major General Floyd D. Frendendall.

33    Lieutenant George H. Simpson. *Armor Command*, pp. 220–221.

Our bivouac was about two miles east of the town in a large olive orchard. The trees were not very big, and it wasn't a case of concealing yourself but rather of disguising the kind of vehicles. There were enemy airplanes over each day with a regular recon. flight of two planes every morning. They never bothered us in our orchard but traffic in the roads was regularly strafed and the only thing we moved in the daytime were peeps. We had a number of them shot up and several men killed and wounded.

One afternoon a single American fighter caught up to four JU-88's just over Sbeitla which were beating it back after a raid on the [Thelepte] airport and in a wild minute shot all four of them down in flames.[34] Two of them crashed near CCB H.Q.'s where I happened to be at the time and one right near our area. I went to the spot where the two had crashed. Have never seen such badly smashed up bodies. It was difficult to tell just how many men there were in the crews, they were so shattered and strewn about.

The railroad was operating to a point north of Sbeitla and trains running just at night. The Germans one evening landed some sort of a cub plane near one of the bridges, two men chased the guard away from the bridge and then they calmly proceeded to blow it up, jumped in their plane and took off.

Because of the constant air threat and the desire to keep the enemy from knowing just what our force consisted of, we went to considerable pains on our camouflaging. All vehicles were parked on the north side of the olive trees and camouflage nets were hung. The slit trenches were dug beneath the branches of the trees and the soil evenly distributed. All traffic was kept to a minimum in the area and confined to certain routes. We borrowed a harrow from the owner of the orchard and kept the area

34    Thelepte Airfield is an airfield in Tunisia, located about 20 km southwest of Kasserine. It currently is active and in use. It was used by the United States Army Air Force Twelfth Air Force in 1943 during the North African campaign against the German Afrika Korps. The first American units arrived in late December and the P-40s of the 33d Fighter Group arrived on January 7 from Telergma Airfield, Algeria. Andrew Knighton, "Life at Thélepte, a US Air Base in WWII North Africa in World War Two," War History Online, retrieved on February 21, 2020, from https://www.warhistoryonline.com/world-war-ii/life-thelepte-us-air-base.html

dragged so as to eliminate as many tracks as possible. Since our vehicles are all dark and stand out prominently in the semi-desert country, someone hit on the idea of smearing clay on our tanks. After a little experimenting a very satisfactory result was achieved and we pattern-camouflaged all of the vehicles with a light-colored clay. The boys' seemed to enjoy making their vehicles dirty.

CCB H.Q.'s and some other units followed us into this area several days later and took up a spot in the French barracks near the ruins on the other side of the town. We arranged so as to have a group of officers out on recon. every day and I was out almost daily.

Word came that we were to take part in an attack through Fondouk towards [Kairouan] so we shifted our recon. to that sector and made a study of that section insofar as we were able to without getting in the way of the French who were holding that zone. We loaned them our mortar platoon and a number of Tommy guns for an attack against a hill held by Germans. George Johnson and I observed the operation from a mountain across the valley.[35] It was quite a show, but nothing was accomplished for the French were driven back with considerable losses.

The wind blew a lot and sand swept through our area making things miserable. Showers were made available to the men at the French barracks on a schedule which allowed one shower per man during our stay. Kept the maintenance crews busy on the tanks pulling engines and changing tracks but never allowed one Company to have more than one inoperative tank at a time.

The T.D.'s and Infantry maintained certain outposts of the area and we had to set up and man a string of machinegun nests around our side of the general area. Each night after supper the Company commander and one officer from each Company along with the Bn. staff would meet in the C.P. tent. There we would listen to the BBC news over the command H/T radio and then each officer who had been on reconnaissance during

---

35    Captain George A. Johnson was one of Gardiner's company commanders who eventually was killed in action later in Italy. *Armor Command*, p. 243.

the day would tell what he had seen, and we would have a discussion on any and all matters affecting the Bn. After these meetings broke up those who were interested would stay on and read magazines for Jim and I had a very wide selection between us. A "trouble light" which we ran in from a peep would provide us with electric light in the tent.

In my recon. trips I saw some colorful French posts that looked like the ones you expected to see the "French Legion" manning. All of the French guards when they recognize that you are an American, say "O.K." and then ask you for a cigarette.

The T.D. H.Q's was set up in the buildings of the owner of this orchard just across the road from us. It was commanded by a Lt. Col who was quite a character and who certainly has a nose for liquor. The only time I moved my tank was one evening when I went out with it to experiment to see whether it could cross a broad sandy [wadi].[36] Had no trouble. Ser. Co. and Maint. Co., or rather those sections from these units servicing us, bivouacked back down the line some twenty miles where they had better cover.

The 2nd Bn. of the 6th Inf. had a new C.O. come in.[37] He is a young Lt. Col. and very much of a live wire. They are still getting equipment never having made up the losses they sustained at Medjez. We have to draw our water at night, and it isn't too plentiful although that is more because of limited facilities for handling it rather than supply for there is plenty of water at Sbeitla. Colored Q.M. troops brought in to work on ammo dump. CCB H.Q's was scattered about Sbeitla and out at the French barracks on the outside of town. A French ack-ack outfit near town could be expected to open up on enemy planes that came within view regardless of range. Got close to some enemy artillery fire when I visited a French outpost north of Hadjeb-el-Aioun. Saw the French batteries firing back at them.

Plans were made for an attack through the pass at Fondouk. Our Bn. was to go through being supported by the 27th F.A. and the 601st T.D's

36    In some Arabic speaking countries, a *wadi* is a valley, ravine, or channel that is dry except in the rainy season.
37    James D. Alger commanded 2nd Battalion, 6th Infantry Regiment. *Armor Command*, p. 157.

with the French artillery also giving fire support. The point that I didn't like was that no provisions was being made to clear the mines that were certain to be in that gap We constructed a model of the area in question which we kept covered with a C.P. tent. The plans were all drawn up and the date of the attack was fixed. However, the German with his usual alertness and ability to bear his opponent to the punch launched his own attack at a different spot than where we were planning to go just two days ahead of our own "D" day.

### January 13, 1943

While it is easy digging slit trenches in the sand, they aren't satisfactory as they were in our last olive grove because the sides have a tendency to cave in. We have our C.P. tent pitched in a rather open spot and last night I was afraid that it was going to blow down, the wind was so strong, but it didn't although a number of the pup tents were blown away. Some of the boys have pitched their tents right over their slit trench. If it should rain, it would be sort of unpleasant but at the same moment the only things coming from the sky are a considerably heavier nature than rain.

Someday it is going to be interesting to read the history of this country. There are a lot of ancient ruins where we are now, with some structures still well outlines. The road we travel goes right by a big arch which was evidently the gate to the original city and looks not unlike the Arc de Triumph. I shave and wash in what amounts to a large glass of water. One of the officers secured me some bread the other day from a French outfit which was something of a treat after the crackers that we have all the time.

The sunsets have been as beautiful here on the edge of the desert as any I have ever seen. Where we are now, we have a jagged mountain range to our west of Salt Lake City. Despite the discomforts there is no complaining. Everyone is glad to be alive and able to be eating food that is available. What we would like most right now would be an opportunity to bathe and do some laundry.

# Ousseltia Valley Campaign

**January 19, 1943**

I had gone to bed when I received word to alert the Bn. and to report to CC B. Sent out word to pack and for the Company C.O's to assemble at the C.P. pending my return. Two tanks had their tracks broken but the crews got busy and they rolled out with the rest of the Bn.

There wasn't much news at the meeting except that the Germans had made a breakthrough the French position at the north and overrun some of our T.D's that were in there and had been attached to the French for the purpose of meeting this threat. We sent a billeting party on ahead and our column pulled out at 2330 with our destination given as a point in the vicinity of Maktar.

**January 20, 1943**

A short distance out of Sbeitla we took a road running due north which was the only road radiating out of there that I wasn't familiar with since the enemy was not in that direction. It proved to be an excellent road with the exception of the by-passes around the bridges that had been blown. As always, we, of course, moved blacked out and there were times when it was difficult to follow the road because it was white as was the country on either side.

I always scheduled halts on either the odd or even hour depending on what time we started, the halts to be of fifteen minutes' length. Since the tanks were marched at the tail of the column, they didn't hold up anyone behind us. I, also, consolidated the kitchen trucks at the head of the column as a normal procedure so that there would be a minimum of delay in feeding the men on their arrival to the bivouac. While we were usually allowed forty-five minutes, the Bn. column would be strung out for more than an hour due to vehicles falling out for minor repairs.

I am giving here the Bn. marching S.O.P. throughout the campaign and not for this one particular move. This was the normal march set-up for moving the whole Bn. at night when there was no contact with the enemy. Our march on this particular move from Sbeitla to Maktar covered sixty miles, the last third of which was over a tortuous and difficult mountain road. We closed in a heavily wooded area which had been selected as a bivouac just as daylight, regassed, ate breakfast and everyone turned in for some sleep. I told the empty gas trucks to wait until dark before returning to Sbeitla to refill but the S-4 for the regiment countermanded my order and sent them back. On the way they were strafed by enemy planes and three of them burned up.

An officer from CC B which had set up shop in Maktar came out in the afternoon to say that the situation apparently wasn't so bad after all and that we could expect to spend the night in this area. We accordingly dug our slit trenches a little deeper and put up the C.P. tent. Another S.O.P. that I followed was to have all the company C.O's sleep at the Bn. C.P. so as to be immediately available in case any orders came in during the night.

### January 21, 1943

About two o'clock in the morning I was awakened with orders to alert the Bn. for immediate movement prepared for combat and to report to the C.G. at a point down the road for orders. As soon as I could get dressed, I took off taking another officer and a peep with me to come back to the Bn. with any messages. Emergency messages such as this one always reach you about the time you are supposed to be somewhere else. The General wasn't at the appointed rendezvous, his C.P. group having gone on ahead but the C.O. of the 27th Artillery was there acting on his behalf.

It seemed that the Germans, late yesterday, made a breakthrough into the Ousseltia Valley thereby threatening all of the French positions in this sector, so we are being thrown in to restore the situation. It was not a long march to the valley, but it was reported to be over a bad road and one which would be a poor one to be caught on by the enemy air. No plans had been developed except that we were to go into an assembly area in the valley to cover the artillery pending the launching of an attack.

In view of the delay I sent word back to feed breakfast and to leave the kitchen, gas, and ammo trucks in the bivouac area. We had to wait for the 601st T.D.'s, 27th artillery, and 2nd Bn. of the 6th infantry, because they could march faster than we could, so we went on ahead and we didn't get on the highway until 0600 hrs. The road was all that it was said to be, and the tanks had to back up in two places before they could complete their turns. We passed a lot of French horse cavalry bivouacked in the timber alongside the road and the pass the road went through was defended by French Bofors.[38]

The valley which spread out before us when we cleared the pass looked calm and peaceful. Out in the flat we could see the H.T's of the T.D's and the infantry spread right out in the open. The artillery had gone into position in fair cover at the bottom of a hill. We deployed out in front of them and had a smattering of cover which was well suited to our mud dobbed camouflage and the tanks really blended in beautifully.

Sent the Recon. Plat. out to look over the country to our immediate front to see if there were any obstructions to our movement. The T.D. C.O. sent word up for me to come down to his C.P. from which he reported he could see a number of enemy tanks milling about. However, since he wasn't my C.O., I declined to go feeling I should remain with the Bn. Early in the afternoon, I received word to report to C.P. of CCB which was back on the other side of the pass for orders. There at a meeting of the unit C.O's the plan was given, and we were assigned a mission which was very far from definite. It was to attack at once up the valley and at a point several miles north of Ousseltia, to swing to the east and drive

---

38    The Bofors 40 mm gun is an anti-aircraft autocannon designed in the 1930s by the Swedish arms manufacturer A. B. Bofors. It was one of the most popular medium-weight anti-aircraft systems during World War II. Elizabeth-Anne Wheal, Stephan Pope, and James Taylor, *A Dictionary of the Second World War*, (New York, New York: Peter Bedrick Books, 1989), p. 64.

through the mountains. One company was ordered to be placed in the CCB reserve.

When asked how long it would take me to get rolling, I said the tanks would be moving forty-five minutes after I left to C.P., and they were. Driving back to the Bn. a flight of friendly fighters swept up the valley and toward the upper end a heavy concentration of light ack-ack was thrown up so there was no doubt about the enemy being in the valley and in considerable numbers. We moved out in a line of companies in column. There was a crosswind and the Bn. made a brave sight as we rolled forward with the three tank companies churning up the dust and the H.Q.'s Co. all contributing their share. The country was perfectly level on the way to Ousseltia.

There, per our plan of attack, H.Q.'s Co. and E Co. dropped out and D and F Co's continued on without halting. Jim stayed with the Bn. H/T with that group under his control and I went with the two assault companies in my tank. Jim had communication with CCB, and I was in contact with him by radio. The maps we had of the area were 1/50,000 and our Recon. had not had time to go beyond Ousseltia.

At that point I had to make a split second decision which almost resulted in serious consequences. There was a wadi between us and the village of Ousseltia which could be crossed on the road, but I did not want to canalize our group and it meant swinging east earlier than it had been planned. I, therefore, continued on down the wadi on the west side watching for a suitable crossing point. The further I went, the more the terrain forced the two companies together and water showed up on the wadi and it became softer as we moved down it. There was no turning back and I had a bad few minutes when I finally picked a crossing and thought the tank was going to become mired down. However, we made it and the rest of the force succeeded in crossing at various points.

If we learned nothing else in Tebourba it was the hazard of rushing into an unknown situation. I was determined that we would not get ourselves in a position of being surprised to the point that it would be too late to defend ourselves. We reformed on the other side and I put D Co. on the left so that with their M-4's they could engage any targets which appeared on that flank since that was the side the enemy were supposed to be on. We moved north to the point that I estimated we were supposed to proceed and then swung to the east. We were able to take advantage of a trough which ran in an easterly westerly direction and moved up it for several miles without incident.

It was just getting dusk when suddenly several guns opened up on us from our left front. The D Co. boys replied immediately, their turrets all swinging around to the left which gave me the impression of a group of battleships steaming into action. The tank next to mine in with the D Co. commander was riding was hit and disabled but no one was hurt. I gave orders to our group to veer to the right and we moved over a hill firing at the direction of the enemy guns as we moved. Finding a sort of horseshoe of rocks, I placed the tanks around it in a defensive position, it now having become dark. Posted the men from the disabled tank as a listening post to our front and set up an all-around defensive position for night. The moon was not long in coming up and while it was cloudy, we felt a little more secure from surprise because we could see some little distance beyond our perimeter.

Having reported what we were doing, I received order to "continue the attack." Since I estimated that we didn't have more than two hours' operation of gasoline left I knew it was suicide to move on to enemy anti-tank guns without any reconnaissance. I elected to put on my own interpretation on "attack" and held our position.

We knew a main road lay off somewhere to our right and we weren't long in learning its exact position when we saw to our surprise the headlights of a car moving rapidly in the direction of the enemy. It was taken under fire by the enemy and burst into flames. Learned later this its occupant, who escaped with minor injuries, was William Stoneman, of the Chicago Daily News, who was going out to cover a tank battle which he understood was in progress.[39]

The C.O. of the 2nd Bn. of the 6th and the commander of F Co. came up to our position and informed me that they were going to attack up the road. We told them about the car that had been knocked out and the approximate position from where the firing had come. A short time later we heard a bunch of H/T's whining up the road. They were some distance from us when streaks of tracers tore across in their direction and fires broke out and we knew some of the H/T's had been knocked out. In short order our infantry boys were firing back at them, but they didn't have as much volume and it soon died out and the enemy ceased firing. We weren't within machinegun range of the enemy and to fire at an unseen target in the dark with our 75's would not have been effective and would have only disclosed our own position which was vulnerable to an infantry attack. Our liaison officer came up during the night to say that there had been some sort of mix-up and that there would be no gasoline available until mid-morning so that we were to move out to a certain cross road at dawn and after "demonstrating" return to the vicinity of Ousseltia where we would refuel.

## January 22, 1943

Just before dawn we moved out in battle formation and waited for it to become light. We then moved on to the road without incident. Saw what we thought was an anti-tank gun and took it under fire. Gave instructions for the move back to Ousseltia and ordered one platoon forward to cover us. The platoon leader misunderstood the Company C.O's order and went beyond where he was supposed to. Before we could get him halted, he ran into enemy fire and his tank was knocked out, but he and his crew

39    During World War II, Stoneman was with the British forces in France and was evacuated along with British troops at Dunkirk. In 1942, while covering the fighting in Tunisia, he was wounded as per Gardiner's account. After his recovery, he returned to London and covered the invasion of Normandy and the subsequent war in Europe. Retrieved on February 23, 2020, from https://www.nytimes.com/1987/04/14/obituaries/william-stoneman-83-foreign-correspondent.html

escaped. I decided to take a little different route back than that used by the rest of the group to check for any stray vehicles. Came on to a company of 6th Infantry in the midst of a hasty and disorganized move from a position that they had occupied during the night. They suddenly found themselves under mortar fire the source of which was unknown. Several men were killed, and they were right where they fell as the Company sought safety in a new position.

The Bn. rendezvous in the open near Ousseltia late in the morning but no gas was to be had. The enemy artillery did some firing on the village, but we were off to one side and while they were close, no one was hurt. The gas trucks came up shortly after noon and on completion of refueling and filling up with ammunition, we moved out.

This time I was given a platoon of T.D's and a company of engineers. My orders simply were to proceed up the valley driving the enemy before us. There was a road which moved in the direction we were supposed to go for several miles. E was still in Combat Command reserve and we moved out with F Co. on the left of the road and D on the right. I moved initially in the middle. Had a platoon of F. Co and the T.D's stay on the left flank with the mission to swing west after the road turned in that direction and securing our flank while we moved due north.

We knew the enemy was not far off, but we didn't know just where we would run into his first position. Our advance was by bounds, one company over-watching the other. Each point of cover was sprayed with m.g. fire as we advanced. One tank sergeant reported to me that he had spotted some tanks, so I went on without flushing anything to where the road turned west. Just beyond that there was a long ridge running at right angles to our front. From the crest of it there was about 1200 yards to another ridge which ran parallel to the first one and on which there was considerable cover. The intervening ground was rolling and without cover.

We moved over the first ridge and down into the shallow draw between the two hills with the two companies pretty much on line. By this time, I had worked fairly well over to the right flank. As we started up on the slopes of the 2nd ridge, the enemy opened fire on F Co. Fortunately, as it later developed, they just had the one strong point and D Company continued to advance without drawing any fire.

I had gotten somewhat ahead and as I came up over the ridge, I spotted the enemy guns on my left firing at E Co. An enemy tank was just backing off and I ordered my gunner to fire an H.E. at an estimated 600 yards. It was a hit, so I ordered an A.P. next and the tank burst into flames. It gave me a wonderful thrill. Saw some enemy troops running away from their positions and continued to fire into them. By that time the rest of D Co. had gotten up to where they could engage the enemy guns and they put in a withering fire and the enemy fire ceased.

It was growing dusk by this time and I didn't know how badly F Co. had fared and not wishing to spend the night on a covered ridge without infantry that still might be occupied by some enemy positions, I ordered the companies to rendezvous at the ridge over which we had come before hitting the enemy. It was dark before we were all closed in. D Co. had not suffered any casualties and all tanks were operative. F Co. had lost three tanks, one of which we could see burning along with the tank my gunner got and two other vehicles which later proved to be enemy trucks. The platoon of tanks that had left us to protect our left flank had run into soft ground and bogged down. I ordered the engineers to come up and outpost us.

During the night we received a company of 6th infantry but they were down to less than seventy effectives and tired, so I had them bed down with the tanks. I spent considerable time sitting out in front of our harbor watching the fires of the knocked out vehicles which burned well into the night. For a long time, I could hear quite distinctly the whine of enemy motors as their tanks moved about and I couldn't determine whether they were coming into the valley or leaving it. Was the enemy withdrawing or reinforcing?

## January 23, 1943

Didn't get much sleep during the night although I curled up in the turret of my tank for a few hours. At daylight a platoon from Recon. Company came up and said that they had been ordered to reconnoiter the country to our direct front. At daylight all tanks had moved out to where they could bring fire to bear upon the ridge across from us and I had the assault gunners stand by to engage any targets that might develop.

The Recon. Plat. headed right for the spot where the fight took place the day before and moved in almost a road march order except that they moved slowly. A short distance after they started to pass thru the shrub trees a gun opened on them. Our assault gunners were on it immediately, however, and it was put out of action. It had made good its first round though, hitting one of the peeps and killing the officer that was in it and wounding the driver. The rest of the platoon never stopped to investigate and came roaring back to us.

The remaining officer asked me what he should do. I suggested that rather than take his whole platoon he try and work over to the other ridge where the peep staying well to the right since I didn't think the enemy line extended that far and he should then be able to look down in the valley. I was standing on the back of my tank a short time after he moved out when I saw an enemy tank come crawling thru the brush to our front. I suspected it might be trying to get into position to fire on the peep so engaged it immediately. Buckovitz, who was my gunner, is a good man and he got a hit the first round. Several other of our tanks joined in and the enemy decided it was too warm for him and backed down over the hill. During the course of the morning several other enemy tanks poked their snouts over the ridge only to retire when we opened fire on them.

About noon the enemy artillery took us under fire. F Co., although in firing position, was pretty well concealed in a cactus patch. D Company on the other hand was sitting out in the open and apparently in view of the enemy observer for the rounds began to come in too close for comfort. One tank took a direct hit on the front which while it hurt no one knocked out a m.g. and started an oil leak in the final drive housing. I, therefore, had D Company back up a little to where they had some defilade and firing soon stopped.

During the day there were no orders but with less than an hour's daylight I received orders to send a Recon. in force up the valley but on the west side. At the time we were located practically in the center of the valley. I grabbed a platoon of D Co. and secured a platoon of Infantry in their H/T's and after showing them on the map where they were supposed to go started them on their way. After about a half an hour we lost radio contact with them. We heard no sign of firing, however, so hoped for the best.

Early in the evening I was astonished to receive instructions for us to pull back down the valley and join up with the reserve company. We were at the time occupying a piece of ground which if the enemy held it, the rest of the valley was untenable for us and we would have had to fall clear back to the base of the mountain over which we came the first morning.

I, therefore, decided to go to the Combat Command C.P. and find out just what the reason for our move was. I talked to the Exec. and S-3 and they told me that the General was expecting a counter-attack and because we were pretty much out by ourselves, felt that we might be cut off so wanted us to back up where we could get more support from the artillery. I said I was confident that we could take care of ourselves but if we did withdraw and the enemy occupied the ridge we now held, I was satisfied that the whole command would be in serious danger of having to move back. They agreed with me, so we had a talk with the General. He really was pretty jittery and he said if I felt secure where we were to stay and so the order to pull back was revoked.

It was late by the time I got back to our position. While I had been away our maintenance boys went out and retrieved two of our tanks that were disabled the afternoon of the fight and brought back the Recon. peep. A wrecker brought the peep out. While it was towing it apparently the brakes were stuck, and it caught fire. The body of the officer who was killed was in the peep. This wrecker which was out in no man's land was thereby illuminated but the driver just stepped on the gas and raced for our position with a regular comet trailing behind him.

During the nite our platoon which had gone out on the Recon. in force returned. They made a mistake and took the wrong turn shortly after leaving us. Just at dusk an anti-tank gun opened on the lead tank and secured a penetration thru the final drive housing. The crew successfully bailed out thru the escape hatch. According to their story the gun crew on the tank that was behind them did an excellent job pumping several rounds into the position where the gun flash came from and silenced it. Feeling that they couldn't accomplish anything in the dark they returned to our position. Failed to mention that just before dusk the tanks, mortars and assault guns lay a creeping barrage down on what we thought might be the enemy positions.

**January 24, 1943**

All of this firing and our Recon. in force must have had some effect for when Recon. elements moved out in the morning, the enemy was gone from our ridge. The first recon. this time we made with a platoon of tanks. We had some interesting discoveries and signs on the ride they had been vacated by the enemy. The most exciting of all was to find tank tracks of a size way beyond anything we had ever seen before. We had heard some G-2 reports to the effect that the Germans had a new tank in this theatre mounting an "88" known as the Mark VI. We now knew that we had engaged one and were very happy that it had decided to withdraw.

We found four light anti-tank guns that we had knocked out and quantities of ammunition much of it for 88's. They had been well dug in. There were three fresh graves near their knocked out vehicles and one empty grave about which were scattered some bloody bandages. With the enemy having withdrawn to the mountains on the east side of the valley and a large infantry force of ours moving up to renew the engagement with them, we were pulled back a few miles and went into a bivouac with the artillery.

**January 28, 1943**

Everyone was disappointed not to have any acknowledgement of our Christmas cables or letters because we were sure that at least the cables would get thru. I signed mine the way I did so that you would know that I was a Major, a rank which I had been carrying since October 23. If I were to send you a cable today, I would be able to sign it Lieutenant-Colonel, having been promoted to that grade yesterday. Have been holding down a job that called for that grade since December 12. Commanding Generals are authorized to make what are known as battlefield promotions and that was the basis of the last one.

We are now sitting in reserve a few miles back of the lines after a three-day fight in which the Germans took much heavier losses than we did and were forced to withdraw. As I write however, I can hear the rumble of artillery and last nite we could see the gun flashes quite plainly. This is as colorful a spot as we've camped in. We are buried in a big cactus patch in the floor of a long valley with mountains rising abruptly on either side. As I look up, I can see two camels standing alongside of an Arab hut at a distance no greater than just across a narrow street. There are five Arabs all swathed in dirty, torn blankets, squatted alongside a path of cactus, guarding the entrance to their little establishment, taking in our activities.

We were alerted during the nite for an immediate move so are just sitting. All movements in these areas, except those in actual battle, are made at nite and we moved in here after dark. The medics had a busy time of it the next morning pulling cactus spines out of the boys. The camels, a third one has moved into view, are kept hobbled when they aren't in use. They have mean dispositions and have put the run on several boys who have tried to approach them despite their hobbles.

It has been very cold at nite the past week and chilly during the daytime. Last nite I spread a newly arrived "New York Times" on the ground under my bedroll, which materially improved the situation. Have our C.P. tent set up but the wind in this area blows almost continuously which doesn't make it much different than if you were out of doors.

For some time, ours was the only medium tank outfit in this operation but there are now several although I don't believe any of them have been committed as of yet. During this past battle, I was in or on my tank most of the time. You use a throat microphone on the interphone and radio. In the excitement at one point I forgot to switch from interphone to radio and learned later that all of my fire directions to the 75 mm gunner to fire on some of the tanks were going out over the air. My radio is tied into units back of the lines, so they were getting a play-by-play description of what was going on.

May have to stop this as there is a lot of aerial activity which has just broken out nearby and may be on top of us any minute. There are now five camels edging across my front yard. They each have a big straw mat spread over their humps presumably to keep them warm. In our last battle the enemy abandoned large amounts of anti-tank ammunition when we drove them from their positions, but it is too big to carry home. The Germans have excellent equipment and seem to have ample supplies of all metals. A lot of their stuff is superior to ours.

We are still eating the British compo ration, which means that it's steak and kidney stew with hard biscuits and tea three times a day. I still like the biscuits. Now have plenty of soap again, Aunt Annie having come thru with a fine big box of practical and luxury items. One of the boys remarked that I should try to get someone to send me a jug of water. Had fresh eggs for breakfast the other morning, being the gift of a grateful French farmer whose place we had retaken from the enemy. This outfit hasn't been lacking for candy for the past week since there have been lots of packages. There is an added interest now in the magazines and papers containing as they do accounts of our own outfit although never mentioned by name. One story you may have read about was the kitchen truck that took the wrong road in the dark and drove almost into Tunis before they realized their mistake. That was one of our kitchens.

## A Period of Alerts, Shifting of Positions, and Waiting

While we aren't out in the semi-desert like we were at the last stop, we are still in the camel country and a couple of Arabs went riding by a short time ago on camels. This bivouac is up in the mountains at an elevation of around five thousand feet and we are camped in a heavy pine forest not unlike some of the country on the way over to Helena.[40] It has frozen ice each nite we've been here, and indications are that it will be frosty again tonite. This particular camp gives the impression of a little duration in that shortly after our arrival a field telephone was connected with my tent.

We had a three-days' engagement with the enemy last week which was very successful from our standpoint. The more engagements we have, the more effective fighting unit we are because of the added experience. I have one of the new General Sherman tanks as distinguished from the old General Grant tank and it did a fine job in this last show.[41] There is three inches of armor plate on the front so you can withstand a pretty severe hit.

Our kitchen crew went out on a foraging expedition this morning and seem to have succeeded in purchasing a couple of calves which they plan to have butchered tomorrow. At our last stop, a French farmer presented one company with a live pig. They had to move before they had an opportunity to kill it and put it in a sack on the back of a tank. Some place along the line of march the pig got out of the sack and escaped. When we aren't fighting or marching, we get about nine to ten hours of sleep a nite. Breakfast is always just before daylight so

40    He is referencing Helena, Montana, about 112 miles northwest of Bozeman.

41    For more on the M4 Tank and Gardiner's combat experience cited, see George Forty, *M4 Sherman*, (New

there won't be a concentration of men that would make a target for enemy planes. In an action such aas we had last week, there is very little opportunity for sleep.

### January 31, 1943

This has been a warm sunshiny afternoon and I've been following the sun around a tree and writing letters. We have a new boy who speaks French and yesterday we sent him out armed with a couple of cakes of soap and some dirty clothes in search of a laundress. He was successful so we are looking forward to some clean clothes tomorrow.

You would be tremendously interested to see the camels over here and the way the Arabs ride their little donkeys. The favorite way is to sit on top of a load with both feet hanging over one side and continuously beating a tattoo with their heels on the ribs of the poor little donkey. Last nite I heard what I imagine is the African equivalent of the coyote howling near our camp. Understand they have a sort of jackal around here.

### February 4, 1943

We have moved every nite since I wrote except last nite when we got badly needed rest. These all nite marches are trying on the drivers because the roads are rough and hazardous, and the dust has been very bad. This shuttling back and forth has been out into the desert and back into the mountains. At the present writing, we are in the mountain country again and, while it is midmorning, I have to stop from time to time to blow on my fingers and warm them up. I am sitting on a large fallen pine tree, looking out across a series of rugged hills covered with patches of pine trees and brush, much like the Big Horn country in Wyoming. Our kitchen trucks rejoined us during the nite, and we had our first warm meal this morning in four days. It consisted of bacon, gravy, crackers and tea which is considered a very satisfactory meal as we feed these days.

York, New York: Blandford Press, 1987), p. 63.

We got into this area yesterday morning just in time to take cover before the sun came up. Everyone was dead tired so as soon as the vehicles were camouflaged, we all curled up except the necessary guards. We were rudely awakened just at noon by a low level strafing and bombing attack, which, while apparently aimed at vehicles on the road alongside of which we were camped, included us in the line of fire. Fortunately, none of our men were hurt. Bombing attacks while unnerving are generally quite ineffective but there is much more to be feared from strafing which is altogether too accurate.

Just before we pulled out of our last stay a list of awards came out that had been made, based on some of our previous activities. I received the Purple Heart, which is automatic if you are wounded in action, and the Silver Star, which is based on an alleged minor degree of gallantry, there being two other which are more important and much more difficult to secure. Am enclosing a copy of the wording of the award, which I hope the censor doesn't object to. While bravery on the battlefield is all relative and probably unnoticed and unrewarded in most cases, I do believe as of the moment I can make one claim that can't be successfully disputed. That is being the tank commander who has seen more action than any other American tank commander in the fighting in this way to date.

It is now early afternoon and has warmed up to the point that I have shed some clothes, but I still have on my stocking cap. My standard clothing equipment for evening wear and nite marches consists of the following: shorts, one part of light socks and a sweater, sleeveless sweater, combat jacket (a rather heavy woolen jacket with a zipper front), pair of British wool trousers and gaiters, coveralls and a trench coat. With all of that to break the wind, I can stand in an open vehicle at nite and face the average wind without discomfort.

Today we are skipping the noon day meal so that we won't have any congestion of men during daylight if we receive a return visit from the boys that were over yesterday. Interruptions have brought this line to dusk and there is no alert for any projected move so we should be here thru the nite although it's not uncommon to be ordered to move immediately without any warning other than the word to go.

**February 6, 1943**[42]

We've moved again since I wrote you last and are better hidden than we were before. It snowed last nite on an adjoining mountain range at what appears to be at just about this same elevation.

All of our kitchen trucks which number five are equipped with big empty German artillery shell cases, which they use at times for dinner gongs. We picked them up after our last battle from a position where the enemy had been firing on us before we ran them out.

The General came around the other evening and in a little ceremony present the medals that had been awarded the members of this battalion to those who were here. Most of the men were absent, still being in the hospital. I received the Purple Heart and the Silver Star with an Oak Leaf Cluster. The latter is given when there are two separate acts which merit the same medal. Am not certain what the basis was for the Oak Leaf Cluster since I haven't seen any other order other than the one that I sent to you, but believe it was based on something during our last action.[43] Don't have any use for the medals here and would like to send them home but I think it might be better to carry them around with me.

Writing a letter in my present job is almost impossible. It is just one interruption after another. At the moment I'm sitting in the doorway of the C.P. tent trying to keep warm, the wind having sprung up. During the nite we were ordered to be prepared to move at dawn. Since it would have been a fighting move and certain equipment would have gone forward, I left the C.P. tent up. Everyone else, however, was required to strike their

42    On 5 February 1943, CCB was placed under the command of General Louis M. Koelz, French XIX Corps. *Armor Command*, p. 152.

43    Gardiner's official military records have him earning his first Silver Star but offers no date. Ironically, and in step with this passage, all other awards have dates associated with them to include his second Silver Star awarded on April 12, 1943.

tents and, if the word comes to go, all we have to do is step aboard and turn over the motors. It is now late afternoon, and nothing has happened, so we are guessing that this was just another false alarm although so far, we have not been alerted.

Don't know how the Arabs manage to keep warm at this time of year. They go barelegged and barefooted for the most part and their robes are all tattered and torn. On a cold day you see them squatted alongside a wall with their backs to it. The French are using a large number of them in these areas to work on the roads. Saw a group the other day with small blacksmith hammers, making crushed rock out of bigger rocks just by hanging away on it.

February 7, 1943

Dear Harold:[44]

The Christmas issue of Esquire arrived a couple of days ago, but Movie Start Parade hasn't reached the reviewing stand as yet. Many thanks, old dear, no one from myself but from about twenty-five officers who likewise haven't seen a female since we left England except for the occasional veiled native. Was keenly disappointed to learn of the circulation difficulties of the Police Gazette. I don't know but what Varga and his associates just about provide all that type of entertainment that a solider on "C" rations can stand anyhow.

Not long ago I saw a heavily bearded individual at our headquarters in a rather odd uniform and thought he might be a French officer who had just come out of the hills and hadn't had an opportunity to get cleaned up. He turned out to be a correspondent for the Tribune, a Jack Thompson by name, and we had a short visit.[45]

44    Harold is Harold Turner, a WGN (Chicago Radio Station) Staff pianist. He married Barbara Reed, daughter of a Chicago socialite, on February 6, 1943. Undated newspaper clipping of unknown origin courtesy of Patricia Issel.

45    Keith Heise, (December 15, 1995) "Tribune Writer John Thompson," retrieved on February 26 2020, from http://articles.chicagotribune.com/1995-12-15/news/9512150109_1_cuban-missile-crisis-mr-thompson-troops

*{The entries from February 11–14, 1943, include the struggle against the weather, which included cold nights, rain, and snowstorms.}*

## February 15, 1943

This has been a grand sunshiny day without any wind and the birds are singing so spring must be close at hand. We are alerted again, and it looks as though we really would move tonight so I'm going to turn in and try to get a little sleep before the order comes in to actually move.

## Kasserine Pass

On May 16th, 1943, the Tunisian campaign having been concluded, [I wrote my father a letter] part of which follows:

There shouldn't be any reason now why the censor should object to a little personal history since it can be of no value to the enemy. We sat at a point between Maktar and Ousseltia for about ten days and were yanked out on a few minutes' notice and ordered to Sbeitla where we were in the two-day action covering the withdrawal of the division which came in for quite a little publicity. We marched from there to Kasserine to Thala to Tebessa to a point about 30 miles southeast of there in one nite and a half day. After being there not quite two days, we made the same trip back to meet the Germans who had broken thru into the Kasserine valley. It was an emergency trip started without any warning late one afternoon. We had to march most of the nite and found ourselves in action shortly after daylight the next morning. That engagement lasted for four days following which we had a good rest.[46]

---

46    Many notable articles and books have been written about the battles at the Kasserine Pass. These include world-renowned author and historian Martin Blumenson, who authored *Kasserine Pass: The Epic Battle Where Patton met Rommel in the African Desert*, (New York, New York: Tower Publications, Inc., 1966), and an often-referenced article written by Gardiner in the *Armored Cavalry Journal* titled "We Fought at Kasserine," March–April, 1948.

Dear Dad:

This stationery or rather note paper is part of the loot we picked up when we ran the Italians and Germans out of this valley two days ago. They broke thru a mountain pass and moved a substantial force thru only to find that our tank outfit plus a lot of artillery had been rushed up from another sector and they had a substantial force to contend with. After two days of heavy fighting they decided that they were in danger of being cut off and made a break for it which at times was a regular stampede. We have our bags and vehicles bulging with souvenirs and I have a cute little sand colored German convertible coupe formerly belonging to some staff member of the Afrika Korps that our General said I could keep. Its usefulness will be limited, however, because it might draw fire from our own troops.

Just at dusk the other nite we captured some two hundred and fifty prisoners most of whom were Italians of supposedly one of their crack mountain outfits. We didn't have any infantry with us so herded them back to the rear with a tank in the lead and one in the rear and one on the other side. It has been raining a lot lately and the roads behind us are a mess, so it was nice to have a labor pool to draw from. They are also used as grave diggers and there has been plenty of that particularly for their own outfit.

I am sorry that the War Department's announcement to you was worded as it was because I certainly was not seriously wounded although I might well have been since two of the boys in my tank were killed and two seriously wounded. When you get a hit on a tank that knocks it out the results are apt to be pretty serious for the occupants. If they don't get you in the tank, they do their best as you are leaving it. Had another tank knocked out about ten days ago in which one of the crew was killed and another seriously wounded. Those of us who got away did so under a perfect hail of bullets. We ran a short distance but concluded it was too hot so fell down and crawled for about three hundred yards before we decided we could get on our feet again. I was helping a wounded boy and the enemy tanks caught up to us and I had to leave him and make another break for it which was also under fire. Formed a very poor opinion of their marksmanship that day.

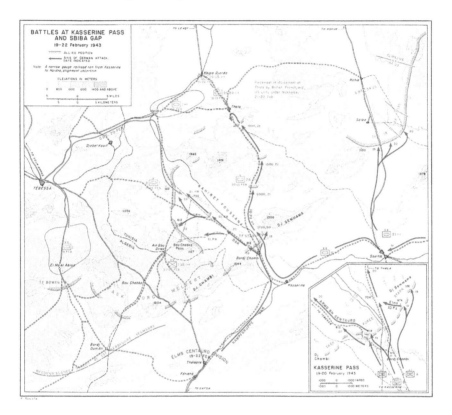

Figure 20: Kasserine Pass Area of Operations (Wikimedia Commons/Public Domain)

Had quite an experience since I lay in an exposed position with enemy tanks passing on both sides of me until darkness fell which was the longest hour of my life to date. I then made a wide circuit thru the hills and hiked between thirty and thirty-five miles back to our own lines. That experience seemed to have interested some of the gentlemen of the press so you may have heard of some version of it. I always give them Chicago as my address since that is where my military records list me as coming from.

The 75 m gunner that I have has been with me in two tanks and is a particularly good shot. In this last action, which was a three-day affair, we came under fire of what I thought was a heavy German tank in what we call a hull down position. I gave him a range of two thousand yards and an order to fire on a round of H.E. It looked like a hit, so we put in another and then one round of A.P. The next day when we took that position, we found we had been firing on a 75 mm anti-tank gun, had hit it squarely near the shield, wrecking it completely and scattering three members of the crew about the immediate vicinity. The photographers were around taking pictures so you may see something of it and a write-up about the gunner, Buckovitz.

You would be tremendously interested in this section of the country. There are Roman ruins everywhere and, in this section, the camels are bigger and better-looking animals than the other places we've been. I have a very warm spot in my heart for a little Arab family who took me in the morning I was hiking back along with the two native French soldiers that I had joined up with and fed us. When we came upon them, we didn't know but what we might have another day's hike over the mountains ahead of us, so I tried to buy some eggs. They didn't have any but produced a chicken and then insisted that we come into their tent where we sat on a mat while the old Arab's wife put some sort of meat in a pot, poured a little water into it, backed up a goat and added some fresh milk and after it was well warmed up gave us each a spoon and we all dived in. Am glad to report that nothing unpleasant developed although things were certainly far from clean. To date the command has been remarkably free from any sort of intestinal disorders. If we are here into the warm weather, however, I am afraid we can expect all sorts of trouble.

We are laid up in a big cactus patch at the mouth of a pass that has been much in the news the past couple of days since it's the one the Germans broke thru and which they ran back out of when we put the pressure on them. They have mined the roads heavily several miles from here and we are just sort of standing by until the engineers can get us a clear path thru. We were shelled in this operation by the biggest gun we've yet encountered. It was a 210 mm piece and we picked up a number of empty cases when we passed by some of the positions that it had been fired from.[47] This outfit continues to add more battle streamers to its record and has seen much more combat action than any other American unit on this Continent.

Met General Teddy Roosevelt, Jr., who has a command in this area, the other day. He is very affable pleasant person. His son is with a combat unit in Africa and was seriously wounded recently but is now reported as going to make it. We are again beginning to see quite a bit of our English friends and less of the French. The latter haven't been much good except in the high mountains because the Germans had taken most of their equipment away from them.

Figure 21: Kasserine Pass (Photograph from the Patricia Issel Collection)

**February 28, 1943**

Dear Dad:

The natives raise cactus and the patch we are in now takes all of the

---

47    The gun was most likely an Obice Da 210/22 Modello 35, an Italian howitzer. Ian Hogg, *Twentieth-Century Artillery*, New York: Barnes & Nobles, 2000.

battalion without congestion and offers considerable concealment. We have just over a hundred vehicles in the outfit and we represent the fire power of three battalions of 75 mm artillery.

Ten days ago, we had the mission of covering a withdrawal of our division and we found ourselves facing more tanks than we had in our outfit with a lot of artillery supporting the enemy. We had the satisfaction of stopping the attack cold and could have been sitting there yet if our flanks had been properly protected. We made a daylight attack the last morning of this present operation which had me very uneasy for some time. Had the two companies that were to lead the assault buried away in wadis out of range of direct fire during the nite. Had to move them two miles to a predetermined jump off line in the dark over ground that we had not been able to reconnoiter because of hostile fire. The problem was to affect a junction between two companies, get them on the line headed in the proper direction and out of where our artillery barrage was to start. Normally that wouldn't have been so difficult but when we started moving at five A.M., we found ourselves enshrouded in a heavy fog which didn't lift until after the artillery cut loose. Fortunately, we had kept our direction well and when we could see, found that we were practically on the desired spot.

I haven't seen anything of the American hospital units in action, but I have the highest regard for the British. The big danger in fighting such as we do is that the injured may not be evacuated in time. Tanks range about the battlefield and when one is knocked out it is usually in no man's land and it is generally nite before it can be reached. That has meant that badly injured men have laid for hours before anyone could reach them. We have a medical detachment in the battalion consisting of two officers and twelve men. They don't do much more than patch things up and then start the injured to the rear. The big factor in our kind of an outside is the matter of supply. The quantities of fuel and ammunition that are needed when we are fighting is staggering and all such items, of course, have a long way to come to us. For the most part the roads in this country have been good and the bridges capable of carrying our loads. In fact, this current operation is the only one we've been in when the condition of the roads has caused any real concern.

My elbow where it was hit last December is causing a little trouble at the moment having developed a slight infection. Apparently, some of the small pieces of shrapnel that weren't removed have started travelling around and are working towards the surface. The medics are watching it closely and it is coming along all right. At the first opportunity I will have another X-ray taken of it.

**February 28, 1943**

Dear Harold,

So, you decided that since I couldn't be around to look after you that you would get someone else who would. I must congratulate you, old fellow, on your excellent judgement and your salesmanship. As you know, I haven't seen Barbara more than a couple of times but that was more than enough to classify her as of the "one in a million" variety and I am delighted that she has reciprocated your view as to an alliance. If it's to be a flat, an apartment or a cottage, you can expect a candidate for the guest room when we get this thing finished and they send us home. After four months sleeping on the ground and in the open about all you will have to fix up for me is a spot on the sidewalk. Your letter of January 14 reached me about ten days ago just before we jumped off on our last shooting scrape.

My guardian angel has been sticking pretty close the past two weeks for I've ducked a lot of steel in these recent engagements and by all rights should have been killed, injured, or captured a number of times. Lost another tank, one of the crew being killed and another wounded. In my other tank that was knocked out, two boys were killed and two seriously wounded. It's a rough game, but if I get back, I'll have some stories to tell.

## Immobilized by Mines, Rain, and Higher Headquarters

**March 1, 1943**

Don't know how our weather maxims apply in Africa but this month is certainly starting out like a lamb. This has been a delightful sunshiny warm day and no wind for a change. In this whole sector the ground is covered with snail shells and I notice the live or occupied ones are beginning to crawl now. While there has been a scarcity of water, the water until this stop has been good. Can't say so much for it here, there being an abundance of mineral material in it. We are going on our third day in this particular cactus patch. One has to be careful walking around at nite for there are deep holes which the natives dig in which to store grain.

Just at this point I looked up and saw a big camel caravan passing by on the road about a half mile distant. The Arabs are all afoot and each one seems to have about two camels and a donkey. My guess is that they are on their way back into the mountains after having spent the winter in the desert. It would be interesting after the war to make a trip thru this country and see what use the natives have made of the equipment that was left behind by the troops when they passed thru here. They won't lack for containers because there has been considerable laxity in picking up empty gasoline cans. The only colored troops of our own that have seen in this theatre have been truck drivers. The French have a lot of black boys, however, and they are supposed to be particularly tough, kill their own wounded, and supply themselves generally from what they capture from the enemy. The camels are still coming and there is now an almost unbroken line of them for several miles.

*{Entries from March 4–7, 1943, discuss the waiting, powdered eggs, and the challenges with the weather.}*

Figure 22: 1st Armored Division tankers in defliade. Note the 1st Armored Division shoulder patch.
(Photograph from the Patricia Issel Collection)

### March 11, 1943

We had two treats last nite, one was a serving of tomato juice, which was the first we had since we left the Durban Castle, the other was a concert from the regimental band which was temporarily relieved of its labor detail and is making the rounds of the various units in this area. I have a new tank and the crew have named it "Henry III" since I've lost two in action. That is written on it in rather small letters on both sides. The tank no longer looks new however for it has been smeared with mud to make it look more like the countryside that we expect to be operating in shortly.

### March 13, 1943

Won't waste any time in getting this stationery headed back towards you for the way things are shaping up it may be some little time before we will be able to do any letter writing. After a fight each side sort of backs off to lick their wounds and rest up and then it is just a question of which one thinks he is ready first before things really flare up again.

Had carried the X-ray picture of the shrapnel in my arm around in my dispatch case as a souvenir but lost it with the other things that were in it when my last tank turned.

The rainy season is still with us. Started out yesterday on a little reconnaissance trip with two peeps. The one that I wasn't riding in got stuck in a mud hole and we were there two hours getting it out. At that it was finally pulled out by a caterpillar which had to be sent out because two other peeps and a truck were also in the same bog hole.

In the course of our trip, which was a forty-four-mile trip one way, with a one-way walk of an hour and a half, we got up to and examined Henry II. It was burning when we abandoned it and apparently the enemy had decided to finish off the job with a demolition charge for the inside was completely destroyed. When conditions permit, there are some of the exterior heavier parts that can be salvaged. We receive a free issue of cigarettes and a few Life-Savers about once a week. It is often enough to keep the boys well supplied with cigarettes. Someone certainly sold the Government a bill of goods for which each issue there is at least one tube of Barbasol per man and a few of us use it and for those that do the issue is about four time what it need be. Some little use is now being made of it since we discovered that rubbing in on your ears and face gives some relief from sunburn.

Don't know the reason but there has been a light delay in the kickoff. The weather may have been a factor for it continues to rain and because of the heavy traffic the roads have become quite a problem.

## Attacks Against Flank of Afrika Korps

**March 30, 1943**

The nicest thing about getting one's name in the paper is the way it has stimulated by mail. Am afraid it will be impossible, however, to answer all the letters I have received so long as conditions continue as at present. This is hardly a letter writing period for, as I write, the shells are sailing back and forth over our heads.

We are sitting in a desert valley floor with nothing between us and the enemy who are hiding in the hills to our direct front. The artillery from both sides is engaged in counter battery fire right now, which means that they are trying to shoot each other up. That normally takes the heat off of us except when we close in to protect the artillery as we will be tonite. While they will be in a different position than they were firing from today, the enemy knows that and if they guess right, we won't get much sleep and will have to climb into our tanks if things get too warm.

Artillery fire is hard on green troops but once you have experienced some of it, it isn't bad because you find out that on the whole it is really very ineffective if you stay properly dispersed. In the last action we were in that you read about we had a very uncomfortable time of it on two days when we were accurately and heavily shelled by a 210 mm battery, which is the biggest we've run up against. I have one of the empty shell cases which will make a grand wastepaper basket if I can get it home with me.

When the ration trucks came in last nite, they brought some mail and I received nineteen letters and then picked up five more today. Most of them were inspired by the newspaper articles that you have been seeing. You must not lose sight of the fact that newspaper reports never play down the news. We have been very much amused by some of the articles that we have seen about boys in the battalion. Whenever the reports come around, I turn them loose on those individuals who will make a good story because I know how much it means to their families to hear about them. You want to remember that I was underlined>recommended</underlined> for the D.S.C. So far as I know no action has been taken on that matter. We aren't interested in the awards we get. All we ask is that we get home safely. I am, of course, careful and the longer one is in the game the harder you are to knock out but, of course, anything can happen but then again you might get hurt in a bombing raid hundreds of miles from the front.

If things go as scheduled there ought to be a lot in the papers about the American forces in this theatre in the next couple of weeks and it should be good news. We have a rather important role to play and this battalion with the experience it has had will be called upon to head one of the missions. If it goes thru it would wind up with us dangling our feet in the water and that is quite an incentive in itself since we have been eating dust on the edge of the desert for a couple of weeks now.

I haven't had my clothes off with the exception of my shoes and coat in better than two weeks now, so it is just as well that we are living outdoors. We have given Henry III another daubing of clay so that it appears almost white now. When the battalion is on the move it is just one tremendous cloud of dust and it isn't the most pleasant situation under which to operate. Aunt Annie's camphor ice which I am using on my lips and nose is one of the most valuable assets at the moment.

### April 1, 1943

We were in a position today much like you might find in some sections of Salt Lake Valley. This getting up and arriving in a new position before daylight calls for a considerably advanced reveille now that the nites have become much shorter.

As I write this my tank crew are heating up a can of hash for me and there will be the inevitable biscuits and coffee. We liked the crackers that we received in the British compo ration much more than the American canned biscuits. Today our tanks are backed up into a series of gullies that run out from the case of a mountain that rises sharply to our rear. They are what we call in a hull-down position so that all that is exposed in the direction of the enemy is the turret containing the gun.

We spent yesterday morning in about the same position and in the late afternoon I took a company of tanks on a sort of reconnaissance in force out into the valley in the direction of the hills that are held by the enemy. We hadn't gone more than a mile when we came under artillery fire which developed into as heavy and as accurate a concentration as I've been in and if I do say so that means something. After continuing for short distance, we made a loop and came back. The dust which has become terrific gave us quite a bit of protection and we fortunately came back in without anything worse than a few gray hairs and some dents. It is just about as hot now as it gets in the summertime in Salt Lake City. The nites lately haven't been quite as cold as they were. So far, we have been able to keep our water containers pretty well filled up most of the time, but the allowance is tighter each day.

We camp near an oasis at nite and you can hear the frogs croaking away. The Arabs had some grain planted around this oasis, but we have pretty well ruined it with our tanks.

Have seen a number of articles in the home magazines and papers about a general whom I recently met who is now our big boss, most of which refer to him as "Blood and Guts".[48] So far as those of us who do the blood shedding are concerned, its "Blood and Bull" – and we don't like his movie newspaper complex.

Our associates on the other flank seem to be doing the feeling out this afternoon and the firing sounds just like a constant roll of thunder. We can see the burst of the shells, but the guns are concealed from view. If things continue to warm up, I may have to sign off for the shells have started to go over our heads so maybe the German is getting ready to feel us out. The way we're set up at the moment we'd like nothing better than to have him send a bunch of tanks at us.

---

48    The general is George S. Patton.

Figure 23: German "convertible" confiscated by Gardiner (Photograph from the Patricia Issel Collection)

Am enclosing a picture which I hope the censor won't take exception to if he bothers to open this letter. It is this year's convertible that the Germans so kindly presented to me when they departed thru the Kasserine pass, which is the low point in the mountains just over the top of the car. The star and white markers were added by us to blot out enemy markings. Just now the car is back with the service elements in the rear. When we get this present campaign wound up, I hope to be able to make some use of it. Yesterday we had some officers sent up to us from a sister outfit in the rear to get a little combat experience.

There is a regular movie set oasis about a mile from here and another a few miles back up the valley where we have been spending the nite. The closest one is a heavy grove of palm trees about a flowing spring which sinks in the sand a short distance after it leaves the trees.

The poor natives have been driven away from there and back into the hills by the fighting.

## April 1, 1943

Whew – it is hot! This is the warmest day we've had, and I suppose only an introduction to what will follow. The only shade that we have today is that cast by our tanks for we are sitting out in the middle of the floor of a valley which is probably classified as semi-desert. There is a town off to our right, shimmering in the haze which we took a few days ago that has been much in the news of late.[49] The dust becomes worse every day and you can't move without kicking up a cloud of it.

Am wondering how much my old friend Worthington had to do with the "Tribune's" request for my picture. It is no false modesty to say that my activities to date are not deserving of such publicity and, if they do run it, I will feel rather embarrassed, particularly with regard to my Chicago associates in the battalion who have been contributing just as much but who haven't gotten into the limelight.

The nites continue cold and last nite I slept with practically all of my clothes on. In fact, since the start of this campaign, which is now almost three weeks old, I really haven't had my clothes off. That isn't literally true since I have made one change of socks and underwear. We haven't had a chance to pitch our tent since March 16th and I don't know when we will have another opportunity. The reason should be in every day's paper.

## April 7, 1943

Am having a difficult time getting this letter started. All day there has been a stream of our bombers accompanied by large numbers of our fighters passing overhead in the direction of the enemy. A little while ago a particularly large number of fighters went overhead. They must have gotten into a pretty warm fight because they are now coming back, singly, in parts

---

49    He is most likely referencing the Battle of El Guettar and Maknassy Pass, March 16–25, 1943.

and at different elevations. Most of them are low, just skimming the ground, indicating that they are out of ammunition or low on gas and anxious to avoid combat. Sometimes when they come in this way there are enemy planes following them and then we get to see someone else do the fighting for a change. We've had a ringside seat for a number of dogfights lately.[50]

We took up a battle position before daylight as usual but contrary to the routine of late, we have received no orders so far today for any sort of action this afternoon. On four of the last five days, we have made sorties out to our front in the direction of the hills held by the enemy. These were ordered, we were told, for the purpose of creating a diversion, seeking a weak point and locating enemy positions. I don't know how much diversion it has given the enemy, but he has certainly had a lot of live target practice and I am beginning to feel like a tin duck in the shooting gallery. If we continue to make no more progress than we have lately, I think we are soon going to be eating dust kicked up by our English cousins from the desert as they roar up the coast road while we sit and watch them go by.

*{The entries for April 9–18, 1943, include discussion on the constant moving, the hot weather, and camels wandering into minefields.}*

## Regrouping and Taking Positions for the Kill

**April 19, 1943**

Dear Rowlie,[51]

My what I wouldn't give for half an hour near a swimming hole in the Finger Lakes district just now. We are on the march, but something has held up the unit ahead of us, so we are just sitting baking in the sun. A day march is a novelty with us, but we haven't had to concern ourselves about the enemy air since he was driven up into the north. We are just leaving

---

50    The fighting he is referencing now is known as the Battle for Fondouk pass, 8-9 April 1943.

51    The Gardiner collection has a listing of letters sent from and to Rowlie Davis as well as to Judge and Mrs. Davis and to R. L. Davis, Jr. The relationship is unknown.

the edge of the desert country now and we're glad that the Eighth Army boys made it unnecessary for us to spend any time in the real desert.

While we had an active and important role in the recently completed phase of the campaign it was only a minor one compared to that of the British. As things are planned now, we are supposed to be in on the kill. However, I long since learned that the only certain thing in the army is the uncertainty.

### April 20, 1943

This may very well prove to be one of these installment letters since we are all packed up ready to move and only waiting until the unit ahead of us clears the road so we can get on it. After an all day and all nite march, we are back up in the country where we campaigned last winter. The change has meant no improvement so far as the mid-day temperatures are concerned because it is very hot and humid. There is plenty of shade, however, for a change which is a big help.

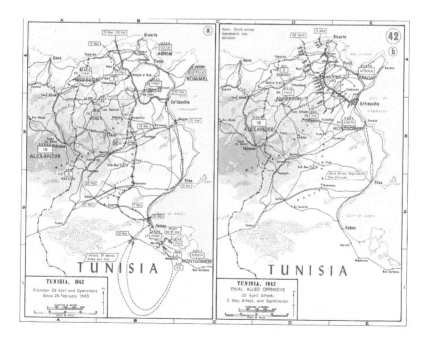

Figure 24: Final victory in Tunisia
("Historical Resources About the Second World War," retrieved on March 21, 2020)

Even allowing for an unusually rainy spring, I had no idea, based on what we saw last November and December, that this section was such a fine agricultural area. All of the valley floors seem to be in grain, and it is a bumper crop. In among the olive orchards, one finds either grain or clover. From the looks of things, the livestock must have to go back into the hills for pasture. Those hills seemed brown rather bare last winter but are rich green now. Am afraid we will have one of the pests that are common to moist areas over here and that is the mosquito.

We are still in woolens, which are fine at nite, but becoming most uncomfortable in the daytime. We have had a change in command up the scale a few notches and one edict that has resulted is that all members of the command will wear neckties! Unfortunately, I have one. In contrast, the British, particularly the Eighth Army seem to be able to fight pretty effectively and still be sensible about their dress. The desert troops' answer to the temperature extremes during a twenty-four-hour period is shorts and a sleeveless shirt, which they supplement with a heavy long overcoat when the evening chill begins to develop.

As to newspaper reporters and photographers: The only time I believe I have been in line of a new camera was a brief shot by a newsreel cameraman during the Kasserine operation. I was out on foot watching a group of tanks come back in from a little scouting expedition. Have never met Ernie Pyle nor do I know of any instance when he visited our particular section of the front. I have met [Kluchohn] of the "N. Y. Times", Thompson of the "Tribune", Coe of the "U.P." and Norgard of the "A.P."[52] Some of the photographers that are about, I used to see in Ireland.

### April 21, 1943

The boys spent the morning washing the clay off of their vehicles which we had smeared on them to make them blend in with the semi-desert background that we have been operating in for the past three

52    Frank Kluchohn of *The New York Times*; John Thompson of the *Chicago Tribune*; and Noland Nogard of the Associated Press.

months. They could just as well have been doing something else, however, for it clouded up right after lunch and about mid-afternoon started to pour and it's been coming down for an hour now with no sign of any let up. Fortunately, we had the C.P. tent up and the storm gave sufficient warning so that we had it well trenched. If this should keep up much longer, we will have a problem getting some vehicles out onto the road.

Last nite was the first one "Up North" since we left here early in January. It proved to be fairly warm and it has been hot again today, the rain only serving to make it steamy and sticky. Have accordingly shed my heavy undershirt for a light one. Some fool regulation has recently been ordered by those who are more concerned about appearance than our comfort is that we must wear ties and leggins when we aren't wearing coveralls. I wear the latter all the time and to date wear a pair of trousers and a wool shirt underneath them.

### May 3, 1943

There has been quite a little break between this and my last letter, but we've been ready to jump off any minute and I never expected to have time to finish a letter so didn't start one. Even though the battalion has continued to sit pretty much in the same place for the past week, I've been on the go. Each day a group of us have gone out on reconnaissance over and in the direction of the country where we expect to be employed. That involves a trip by peep and then walking and perhaps crawling where you get up to the enemy lines and try to see as far beyond as possible.

Dad would have a lot of fun driving in this country for the roads are just trails that we've made, and they are either about straight up and down or at an angle that makes you wonder whether you are going to wind up by rolling over. It isn't what we consider tank country and that is the reason we've been sitting back for the most part watching the artillery and the infantry do the work. They have been trying to make a hole thru the mountains for us so that we could get out on to the rolling country between here and the sea.

We were alerted during the nite to be ready to move at five this morning so had breakfast at four-thirty instead of five-thirty as is our usual schedule. However, it's just another case of being all packed up and no place to go for it is almost mid-morning and no further orders.

Am enclosing another citation. This makes the second Oak Leaf Cluster for the Silver Star. As I've told you before, an Oak Leaf Cluster is given where an action warrants an award of the type that has been previously given. The General some time ago received certain awards and decided that the action out of which I received a Purple Heart was also deserving of a Silver Star, hence this latest, which is sort of a repeat. That makes six decorations just in case you're not sure, D.S.C, Silver Star, Two Oak Leaf Clusters, Purple Heart and Croix de Guerre.

*The following is a further extract from the letter written to [my] father on May 16, 1943, a portion of which was previously quoted on [February 27, 1943].*

"Our next move was in conjunction with the offensive aimed at Gafsa and Maknassy. Our battalion was with the force that took Maknassy and we operated a little east and north of there, which was the most desert-like country we had been in. When the Eighth Army pushed up along the coast, we moved up to the Faid Pass and then marched up to Ghardimaou via La Kef. From there we moved north of Beja and then joined in the II Corps offensive. My tank was knocked out and I was wounded just north of Mateur. The battalion two days later was east of [Bizerte] on the sea with the tanks lined up on the shore blowing out of the water the few Germans who attempted to escape via barges and small boats."

# Hospitalized

**May 8, 1943**

Dear Elizabeth,

Am writing this in bed at a rather awkward angle since there isn't any backstop. This isn't the kind of bed I've been looking forward to because it's in a tent hospital and I'm a patient. Day before yesterday the battalion led off on a dusk attack against an enemy position in the hills just north of Mateur. I was with the leading company when it ran into a mine field. The tank next to me was wrecked by a mine and I ordered my tank to back up. As we were doing so it was hit by an anti-tank gun and set on fire. Only one other member of the crew and I got out.

We were right under the enemy positions and the infantry opened fire on us forcing us to lie flat. It was a sort of grim race for a ways because the tank was in gear and still moving slowly backwards which was the direction I wanted to go. That kept up for about fifty yards when it stopped. Every time I would start to move some sniper would open up on me, so I finally decided to stay put. All during that time there was a constant exchange of overhead fire and some shells bursting all around so all in all it was a kind of long drawn out and unpleasant day. I lay there with a battle roaring back and forth until dark which was just thirteen hours. Our battalion re-attacked in the late afternoon and drove through to our objectives. The German infantry popped up when they went through their positions and again opened fire when I tried to get out.

I came off extremely lucky, my injuries consisting only of small shrapnel fragments in my left leg most of them being below the knee and all along the front side. Went first to our battalion aid station, then to a clearing station and now I'm at an evacuation hospital. If no infection develops, I should be ready to rejoin my outfit in a few days. The day before I was hit, I was coming down the road when I saw an ambulance parked near General Robinette's peep that I recognized so I stopped.

Found that he had been injured in the leg by a shell fragment and his driver badly wounded. His injury, while not believed to be serious, will keep him out of things for a considerably longer time than will mine.

This hospital is staffed by American nurses. They wear coveralls. I am in a tent with fourteen officers which has one nurse and two orderlies during the daytime. At night one nurse looks after this and another tent and we have one orderly. They have a big surgical set-up here and during this recent push have been swamped with work.

Heard a little Arab boy one day playing a sort of a flute while he was looking after a bunch of cows. Have forgotten to mention in any of my letters that they made me turn in our little captured German car. Had hoped to have it to do a little running around in when we got to the end of the line. This is of course a disappointment not be in for the finish having been through it all to this point, but I'll never complain as to my luck in this war regardless of what the future may bring. I've had so many shells come close that could just as well have been a little closer which would have been too close.

### May 8, 1943

This is the first time I've tried out our medical set-up and to date it has been as follows: I went first to our battalion aid station which was set up in a grain elevator just outside of Mateur. Our doc daubed the spots with alcohol, dressed them and gave me a ticket for the next stop. It was then late at night and since I wasn't badly off, I went up to the combat command headquarters to tell them I'd be gone for a few days. After that I tried to find the battalion headquarters but was unable to do so, so the officer who was chauffeuring me and I bedded down in a small building since it was raining.

We were awakened by a peacock screeching and found that we were in an outhouse of a large estate. Took a run out on the battlefield to check my tank because I wanted to be certain whether anybody but the

75 gunner and I got out. There wasn't much left inside of it since it had burned completely. We did run across one of our boys who was badly wounded and who had been lying out since his tank was knocked out the morning before. Several men had been picked up in that area during the night and we thought we had them all. The search hadn't been continued at daylight because the area was under long range artillery fire. This boy was in no condition to move in a peep, so we sent an armored ambulance out to pick him up.

I then located the battalion headquarters, picked up a few personal things and had a peep run me down the line some seven miles to an evacuation hospital. There I was taken into a big tent where a doc again cleaned off the spots where I was nicked, poured some sulfa powder on the same and gave me a ticket to the next stop. This time I rode on a stretcher and in an ambulance, a distance of seventeen miles to the evacuation hospital, where I am now reposing.

This is a surgical hospital where any cases requiring operative treatment are looked after before they are sent any further to the rear. I made a trip to the operating tent where a doctor just took a peek at my few cuts, with the exception of one which he dug around in a little but didn't find anything. Was sent to a tent where they have the officers. Found two there from the regiment, one being from the battalion. He had been in a tank that was knocked out next to me and has a badly burned back. There are two medical officers on either side of me. One is in a pretty bad way as the result of his peep hitting a mine. The other has a cut foot and broken ankle as the result of being struck by a shell fragment.

There are fourteen officers in this tent, which is capacity. We have the standard army cot, with mattress, pillow and sheets. There is a nurse who looks after this tent in the daytime and the night nurse has two tents. Two soldiers do the orderly work in the daytime and one at night. Our meals are the same as we get when our kitchen trucks are drawing "B" rations.

While the battle seems to be pretty well over, they are still receiving a lot of patients. It rained hard last night, and ambulances couldn't make it through from the front. Our hospitals have been getting a stream of German wounded. They receive just the same treatment as our own men. It's just as well that I'm a good pill swallower because I'm getting two every two hours. It's some routine preventative treatment to head off infection. This last action, while short, was costly as had been predicted and the regiment had many officers killed. While I don't know what happened to the battalion yesterday, we had been very fortunate up until that time.

Don't worry about me because I'm fine and will get a good rest before I have to go back to work again.

### May 9, 1943

Had just gone to sleep last night when I was awakened by the nurse who told me to get dressed that I was being moved. There was a load of sitting up cases and we were brought to another tent hospital about twenty-five miles further to the rear. Strange to say, life isn't quite so soft here in that the cots are canvass and there are no sheets or pillowcases or electric lights as there were in the last stop. The nurses, however, wear skirts and I walked over to the officers' mess in this noon and had a piece of apple pie. Ran into a number of my friends here. It looks as though this would be as far back as I would go. Will probably spend two or three days here then rejoin the boys if I can find them.

This spot is just a few miles from where we spent most of December. At that time, we were being bombed so regularly that this valley became known as "Stukka Valley." We had a lot of attention form the enemy air the last few days of this operation but, for the most part, of late we've definitely had control of the air. The last time they bombed our tanks, I was caught outside and spent a very uncomfortable few minutes underneath my tank for after they bombed, they came back and strafed us several times.

The country we have been operating in these past few weeks has been very beautiful. It has all been a deep green and some of the hilly sections reminded us of parts of Ireland and Scotland. The livestock, in particular the work animals, have been having a wonderful time in that, since their owners have taken to the hills, they wander about in the grain fields eating to their hearts' content. This country produces a lot of grain and one sees a number of big grain elevators, such as are found at home along the railroad.

Am sitting outside of our tent, near the main road, which is teeming with activity. Despite the fact that except for a few isolated pointes the war in Northern Africa is over, there is one American Division still moving up. It had been started before we finished off the job, so I guess is going on up to do the police work. There are quite a few civilian cars on the road which is a strange sight. I imagine they are some of the refugees from Tunis and Bizerte rushing back to see what is left of their homes. Everyone is guessing, of course, what point, or points have been selected to attempt the long promised invasion. Am satisfied that the bulk of our force will get into that operation at an early date.

## Back to Duty but as Regimental Executive Officer

**May 13, 1943**

I persuaded them at the hospital that I could do just as well back with my outfit as there, so they released me a couple of days ago. Never did get back to the battalion, however, for when I reported into the colonel of the regiment, he said he had placed another lieutenant-colonel in command of the battalion and had a new job for me.

I am now the executive of the regiment, which means second in command. There is no change in rank, but it is in effect a promotion since there are three battalions in a regiment of this kind, plus three separate companies. It corresponds to the job I had in the battalion before I was given command there. However, it would be sometime before I would be in line for the regiment since there is already a successor for the colonel earmarked when he leaves us as he is expected to do shortly.[53] The present dope is that he is to be made a general. In a regular army regiment such as this, it will be a long time before they put a national guard officer in command so long as they have the regular army boys to draw from and there are a couple of them of the right grade available in the regiment now.

To come to the present setting. The tent that they gave me is made from a big German fly that was captured along with a lot of canvas the other day. It has been set up so that it is like a low roofed room, the top being perfectly flat. The floor is matted grain since we are camped in a grain field. I am sitting on my bed, which is on the ground, as I write this, and the light is being furnished by two candles that I have set up on a German shell container which also serves as a set. It is really very cozy.

The regimental headquarters is camped on a hill-side overlooking the valley in which the battle was fought when my tank was knocked out a week ago. Today a very impressive ceremony was held where the boys are buried who were killed in this last fight. From this hillside, we look across a broad valley, which is surrounded by rugged mountains. We face the west and there was a beautiful sunset tonite. This seems to be the snail season and when I woke up this morning, they were all over the sides of my tent. They are of the type that have a curved white shell, being, at the longest, as broad as the length of the first join of your thumb.

I have only one part of my leg bandaged now, it being just above the calf where there was the biggest cut. Am taking things easy and should be a hundred percent before long. This last accumulation of metal that I have gives me an Oak Leaf Cluster for my Purple Heart which I have been awarded. The D.S.C. was given to me in a little regimental ceremony last nite. I hated to leave the battalion because one develops as strong a

53    Colonel Clarence C. (CC) Benson commanded the 13th Armored Regiment at the time. He took command from Colonel Hamilton H. Howze, who commanded it during the battle at Kasserine.

tie with a group of men as you can when you associated with them as intimately as I did with those boys and when you do so on a life and death basis.

The day after I returned from the hospital I drove into Tunis with the colonel and some others. We were there during the middle of the day. It was impossible to get anything to eat but I had one package of Hershey's along, which carried us over until the evening meal. We ate them while inspecting the complete havoc that the bombers had done to the Tunis docks. The city itself had only been hit in one spot I saw.

It gets quite chilly where we are nites now and there is always a heavy dew. My trench coat, which was ready for the ragpile, burned up with my tank.

**May 16, 1943**

This isn't turning out to be much of a rest period for me after all so I will have to still wait for an opportunity to really do some letter writing. The next move that we make will find me riding in a peep so I'm trimming my belongings so as to fit into the limited capacity of such a vehicle. We haven't been able to turn in any of our winter clothes, so I still have quite a few items of clothing that are excess. My leg is coming along fine, and I should soon be able to dispense with the bandage which is just over one spot on the shin and calf.

**May 19, 1943**

Dear Elizabeth,

The conveniences of the rear areas are beginning to reach us, and I now have a bottle of ink. Had been without since last year but had managed to borrow a pen-full here and there from various headquarters up until about two months ago when everyone's supply ran out.

There is some improvement in our rations since the shooting stopped but it is spotty. We haven't had any sugar now for about five days but have been enjoying such luxuries as grapefruit, tomato juice and nice canned cherries.

Henry III was knocked out by an anti-tank gun on the morning of May 6th in a big tank battle just north of Mateur in the smash that broke through to Bizerte. It was hit by what is known as an A.P.H.E. shell meaning an armor piercing high explosive.

The "D" Co. kitchen, some place along the line, acquired hen and a brood of chickens. They kept the old hen and her family in a box when they were in camp. The boys insist that as soon as the word is passed out that the outfit is to move that the old girl rounds up her family and loads them into the box. The have grown now to the point where they require several boxes now, but the boys haven't any thought of eating them. They are now regarded as part of the family. Had lunch at Service Company the other day and discovered that they had a pet rabbit. The rabbit's normal hang out is under the serving table alongside of the kitchen truck. It is tame to the point of being affectionate and seems to enjoy being picked up and petted. There is an order out which prohibits the acquisition of dogs or we would have a pack of them.

They go in for winter wheat and grains in this area in a big way harvesting is in full swing at the moment. Am beginning to see shorn sheep among the flocks that are everywhere. The camels are also shedding now, and they are homelier than ever. While most of the young ones that I've seen have been of greyish color. In one area where we were a few weeks ago every house seemed to have a family of storks on the roof. There are some snakes and when we were in the desert country, we saw lots of lizards. The flies are becoming a nuisance now and we are experiencing lots of wind to the point where it is difficult to keep tents up. They say in this area that if the wind doesn't stop after three days, it will blow for six and if it doesn't stop then it will blow for nine. We just passed six. Fortunately, we won't be here to see what happens after the ninth day.

## Victory Parade in Tunis

**May 20, 1943**

Today will mark one of the highlights in my experience in Africa. There was an allied victory parade in Tunis and the colonel was given a pass, which was the only one issued to the regiment. He didn't care to go and gave it to me, and I had a fine place from which to see the parade, and it was a sight of a lifetime. Do hope you get to see it in the newsreel and also that it is in color. It will take a letter in itself to describe it and I'll jump to some other things and then come back to that if I have time.

*{This section of Victory Parade in Tunis has been truncated to focus the reader on Gardiner's combat experiences; much of what has been not included is details of the parade. One highlight was a brief discussion of the Moroccan Goumiers; further information on the Goumiers can found at https://www.warhistoryonline.com/world-war-ii/mountain-warriors-wwii-goumiers.html}*

## The Division Marches Overland to Morocco

**May 23, 1943**

No tent over my head at the moment nor will there be tonight. We made 142 miles today which is a pretty good jump when you consider that there were 840 vehicles in our column and the road was very mountainous. It was one we had marched over last November. Quite a contrast in conditions then and now.

**May 25, 1943**

Yesterday we rolled only 124 miles but today made 171 and it was again over the mountains. Our trip so far has just been routine.

**May 30, 1943**

We didn't have as long a march today as usual (just under a hundred miles) so are in camp with the afternoon before us. The head of the column has been pulling out each morning at five o'clock which in view of our continued movement westward with no change so far in time has meant that we've been eating breakfast and breaking camp in the dark. Our outfit starts out at a slightly different time each morning since the order of march is rotated one place daily so that everyone gets a crack at being first, second, etc., out and in of the bivouac sites.

While it has been dusty in some places, the roads have generally been good, and the scenery has been grand. For the past two days I have been observing new country and now we are seeing new types of people. Our bivouac sites haven't been so pleasant, being normally alongside of the main road in some open dusty area. At each stop a small tent is put up which I share with the regimental commander. It is always put in the center of things, which means that we may have the dust of over eight hundred vehicles blowing through our home. About all the tent really does is keep the direct sun off when we close in camp while it's still up. It hasn't rained on us nor will it on anyone traveling these roads between now and November since they say that there won't be a drop of rain between now and then.

The censor permitting the following are some of the highlights since I last wrote to you. The day before we left Mateur I drove up to Bizerte and went for a swim in the beach that fronts the city proper. There were many soldiers in swimming. Bizerte must have been a beautiful city at one time, but it is certainly a wreck now. I have seen many war torn communities, but Bizerte has been hit the hardest of the lot. Some of it may come from shelling from the sea but the big end was the result of bombing.

When we were camped for the night near Constantine [Algeria], I went into the city with some of the officers. There are many airfields around Constantine and the city is filled with American troops. There is an officers' club in town, and we went there and had the treat of some ice cold beer. At several of our stops since we have gotten into the rear areas, we have been able to secure ice and last evening for the first time since we landed, I had a good big healthy helping of chocolate ice cream! We were camped near a town that has been occupied by American troops for some time and they have educated the place to ice cream and we were able to secure enough for the officers' mess.

The night we spent near Algiers I took two officers in town with me and we spent the evening with Ted Ryan. He has some super-secret civilian job and, while he has been abroad and in Africa for months, he had only been in Algiers for two weeks. We first went to his apartment for a drink. The place he is living in is a home on the hill that overlooks the Algiers harbor which has a magnificent view. There was a balcony where we had our drinks and then we went to a French restaurant, well outside of the city. It was quite a ride, but worth it. I believe the principal reason Ted selected that place was because it apparently didn't come with the military ban which closes all bars at nine o'clock. I went up to Ted's apartment after we left the restaurant and the other officers had gone back to camp and visited a couple hours. Algiers is a city on a hill with twisty streets and I had quite a time in the blackout finding my way down to the harbor road that lead out of the city.

Probably the most interesting stop we have made was at [Sidi-bel-Abbes], which is the home of the French Foreign Legion. The night we were there we (the other two officers who had dinner with Ted and me) had two officers of the Legion who spoke English to dinner at camp. They, in turn, invited us into their officers' club in town for a drink. Am afraid it would disillusion most of the Hollywood followers of the Foreign Legion. It is just off of a garden that is open to the wives and children of the officers of the Foreign Legion and a number of women came in for a drink at the bar while we were in there and the children were running in and out of the place.

The Legion barracks are impressive but have no desert atmosphere about them and Sidi-bel-Abbes is a modern appearing city and very green. Our first night out of there however wouldn't have required much of a rearrangement to make a fitting backdrop for a Legion movie. We were camped near a walled Arab village and the surrounding country was just as barren and bleak as you will find. The camp was overrun with Arabs who had onions and dates for sale. Don't know where the onions came from since the surrounding countryside appeared burned out.

We are still wearing woolen uniforms but all of the American troops we've seen on our trip are wearing cottons. We certainly envy the French and British in their shorts.

### June 2, 1943

Yesterday we ended our march in the early afternoon and today has been given over to sort of setting up camp. There was no dew last night which may be explained by the fact that there is almost a constant breeze blowing in from the ocean. While we are several miles inland, we are on the edge of a forest towards the water so get the full benefit of the breeze. Mosquitoes are said to be a problem here and everyone has been ordered to sleep under mosquito bars, but I didn't notice any last night. Perhaps they don't give trouble except further inland.

You can forget about me not being as well fed as you think I should be. We now are receiving the benefits of the rationing program at home. It looks as though we would get the "A" ration until further notice, which is just about the same as we had in the camps at home, with the exception that the milk is canned, and the eggs are powdered. What comes as the biggest luxury in our diet is fresh meat two times a day. The natives in this country are great hands at raising onions and we have nice fresh onions on the table for the noon and evening meal, along with tomatoes and lettuce. Wine is also showing up on the supper table.

Nature has had considerable foresight in arranging to have, in addition to the tremendous amounts of grapes that are produced in this area, large quantities of cord grown hereabouts also. The forest we are in is a cork forest. Haven't found out yet how often the bark can be taken from a tree but all of those in this forest, which extends for miles and miles, have been completely removed from the ground up to a uniform height of four feet. This doesn't seem to in any way adversely affect the tree and it just gets busy and grows that bark back again. I wouldn't be surprised to run into the native expression of "corkin' one's shins."

When we started our recently completed march a new "acting regimental commander" took over and he is still the boss and all indications are that the "acting" part will be dropped before long and he will be elevated from lieutenant-colonel to colonel. He is a regular army officer and is the fourth generation to make the army a career. He is three years younger than I am.

*{Sections of the diaries and letters are omitted in this version of Gardiner's account to focus on the actions Gardiner experienced in combat. Therefore, the sections titled "The Regiment Trains Near Barat" (starting on June 6, 1943) to the end of Part I (on October 27, 1943) have been omitted.*

*Highlights during this period include the acquisition of Gardiner's fourth tank in the war, "Henry IV" (July 19, 1943), the introduction of Ernie Pyle's column in the Stars and Stripes (August 2, 1943), the movement of his unit back to Algiers (August 13, 1943), the "training and relaxing" (August 31, 1943), and the third hundred and seventieth letter he wrote (October 11, 1943)*

*After victory in North Africa, the 13th Armored parent unit, the 1st Armored Division, began training for its next operation. It was moved across the desert west to French-Morocco and was quartered in and around the city of Rabat where it underwent a major reorganization. General Ernest N. Harmon, commander of the 1st Armored Division, placed Colonel Hamilton*

*H. Howze in command of the 13th Armored Regiment, and he quickly saw fit to rearm the Regiment with more modern equipment. The M3 Stuart light tanks were replaced by M5 Stuart light tanks, and the M3 Lee tanks were replaced by the M4 Sherman.*[54] *While 1st Armored Division was refitting in Morocco, other Allied forces invaded Sicily. In September 1943, General Harmon reported to the Fifth Army commander, General Mark W. Clark, that the 1st Armored Division had completed rigorous training and was ready for combat operations once again. The 13th Armor landed in Italy near Naples in November 1943, where Allied units had already carved out a beachhead. After assembling in Capua, the Regiment waited in reserve. Their mission was to attack through the Liri Valley once infantry units had seized the surrounding heights.}*

---

54    George Howe, *The Battle History of the First Armored Division*, (Washington, D.C.: Combat Forces Press, 1954).

# 3 | Italy
## November 1, 1943–May 31, 1945

### Crossing the Mediterranean

The following letter is the only record covering the period of the move from Africa to Italy. A convoy of four LST's lead the headquarters units of the regiment and tanks and personnel of the line companies at Oran. After an uneventful crossing in which this unescorted group passed within sight of Sicily, [I] along with the other members of the 13th who made the trip were unloaded near Naples.

**November 1, 1943**

While a lot has happened since I wrote to you last, I haven't time to write about it now. Last nite I played "Hearts" with three other officers and just broke even. When we made the trip down on the boat from England, it cost me quite a little money to learn how to play. This time I should be able to do better. Our meals are all out of cans these days with the exception that the cooks are able to do some baking. The service of the officers' meals, however, is considerably improved over that we had had for some months.

## The Regiment Assembles Near Naples

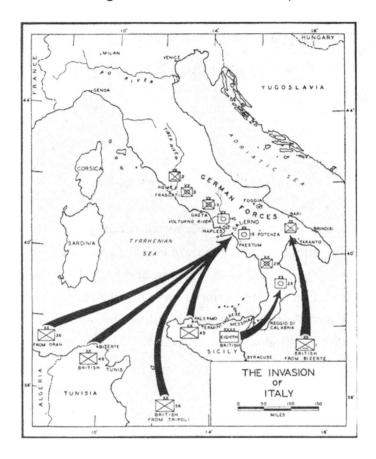

Figure 25: Across the Mediterranean to Italy (Wikimedia Commons/Public Domain)

**November 5, 1943**

Am sitting on the ground with my back against a nice big tree soaking up some southern Italy's warm sunshine. Our camp is scattered about thru a large wineyard. The wineyards that we have seen so far differ from those of Africa in that the vines are trained between trees and sufficiently above the ground so that vehicles can pass underneath them. This permits them to cultivate most of the ground and the section we are in now is in grain. Instead of Arab peddlers, we have Italian ones. Their principal wares are apples and walnuts both of which are excellent quality. There are also peanuts, onions, peppers and persimmons to be had. In order to keep them out of camp, we have established a market along the main road that runs by camp. They aren't interested in money but want cigarettes or candy. There are "vino" vendors at every turn and I'm afraid we are in for some trouble in that respect. In Africa, the natives did not traffic in liquor, it being against their religious principles. That which the boys secured, they got thru the French.

### November 7, 1943

Any soap that is sent to me should be laundry soap. We are able to get sufficient face soap thru our P.X. issue but laundry soap is at a premium. It isn't difficult to secure laundry service around here and so far, the rates have been cheaper than in Africa, but one must supply his own soap.

Everyone is in pup tents except the colonel and me, although ours is a very small one and doesn't much more than accommodate our bedroll and valpacs. My valpac is pretty much the worse for wear. We have a layer of straw under our bedrolls so have a nice comfortable place to sleep.

Everyone goes to bed early since it becomes dark shortly after five o'clock and there are only a few places such as the command half-tracks that are close in where you can show a light at nite. Breakfast is at six-thirty, lunch at eleven thirty and dinner at four-thirty. The past two nites, six of us have jammed into on half-track and played "Hearts" until eight o'clock. I'm money ahead on those two nites, which about makes me even with my losses on the boar. During those sessions we have listened to the BBC evening news and the German propaganda stations and "Lord Haw Haw".[1] The German reports as to their activities, while distorted, are nothing as compared with the stories they tell of the Japs' successes. According to the report last nite, the Japs had just about cleaned the Navy out of airplane carriers and fighter planes in the South Pacific.

---

1    Lord Haw-Haw was a nickname applied to the U.S.-born Briton William Joyce, who broadcast Nazi propaganda to the UK from Germany during the Second World War. Colin Holmes, *Searching for Lord Haw-Haw: The Political Lives of William Joyce,* (New York, New York: Routledge, 2016).

*{The passages that follow, the remainder of November 7 to early December 1943, provide accounts of Gardiner and his soldiers's daily experiences settling into the Italian environment and can be found in the original diaries and letters. During this period, Gardiner offers a contrasting view of the Arab-Italian cultures and native interactions and provides a backdrop of the dichotomous nature of war where there are periods of intense combat interwoven into the human capacity to strive to live life as normal as possible. Concerts, shopping, and exploring restaurants were not uncommon activities during any era of conflict, and they hold true in Gardiner's initial experiences on the Italian Mainland. We resume with the "Visit to the Front" section in early December 1943.}*

## Visits to the Front

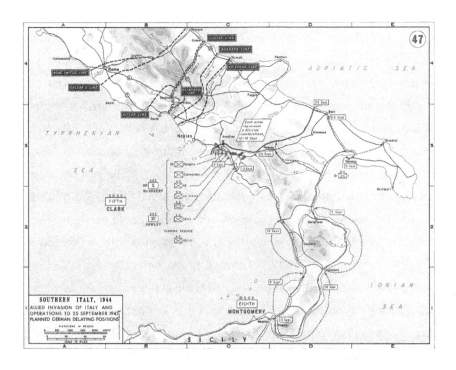

Figure 26: Italian Battlefield, September 1943 to June 1944 (U.S. Military Academy/Public Domain)

## December 7, 1943

Trip to front and to a point considerably in advance of any previous visit. Our artillery has moved up preparatory to attack tomorrow during which Italian motorized brigade has important objective.

## December 8, 1943

Those who visited the front today reported the Italian attack failed. Watched a crossing of the Volturno at night by the 6th Infantry.

## December 10, 1943

Meeting called by C.G. at Division to discuss probable employment included statement by C.G., G-2, G-3 and a British Captain who was an expert in aerial photographs.

## December 11, 1943

Took a walk this afternoon. Chanced upon some Teller mines.

*{Omitted entries for December 12–14, 1943, that entailed letters home assuring of his safety; restrictions on censoring information in correspondence; and descriptions of internal inspections.}*

## December 15, 1943

George Johnson and I visited [the] front climbing the recently captured Mt. Maggiore.[2] Passed bodies of three Germans and one American on way up. Saw lots of abandoned German equipment and rations. We had a ringside seat although somewhat removed for an attack on San Pietro which was spearheaded by a company of our tanks. Attack failed and we saw two of our tanks burn. Our artillery fired a terrific preparation.

---

2    On December 2, 1943, 600 American and British guns put on a huge, synchronized artillery barrage on Mt. Maggiore in preparation for what became a successful attack by the 36th Division's 142nd Regiment. Mt. Maggiore became known as the "million dollar mountain" because of the huge amount of ammunition expended, and artillerymen called the barrage the "Serenade to Mussolini and Hitler". 443rd Antiaircraft Artillery Battalion in World War II Italian Campaign Battle for Mt. Maggiore, retrieved on March 1, 2020, from http://www.texasmilitaryforcesmuseum.org/36division/archives/443/44363.htm

Much enemy air activity and we had ack-ack shrapnel failing all around us several times. Saw our planes drop propaganda leaflets written in German which were poorly gauged for they all drifted back into our lines. Back to camp after dark.

### December 16, 1943

Last night I returned to camp long after supper time. I heated up some water in the C.P. truck and poured in three packages of Hemo.[3] That, plus part of an envelope of fish, one has just arrived, and some very nice cookies that came out of a Christmas package made up my evening meal. Lunch had been eaten away up on the side of a steep mountain where another officer and I had gone to secure a ringside seat for certain activities that were going below us.

Waterproofing starting. Spent morning with Col. and Bn. commanders going over proposed plans. Our Recon., to front, reports continued lack of progress and heavy infantry losses. Arty. fired all night and again all day. You could feel the vibration of the guns at times.

### December 17, 1943

Accompanied Col. On inspection of progress of waterproofing and watched mine removal training. Steady stream of bombers heading toward enemy lines. Reports that we have seized some additional ground on Fifth Army front.

### December 18, 1943

With representatives of three Bns., I made a trip to the front and hiked out to a place on the northernmost point of Mt. Maggiore. It was a three-hour climb to our objective, but we returned to our jeeps in two hours. Visibility was poor but we had a fair view of the Rapido and the Liri Rivers and the country south of Cassino. Very little enemy fire and ours

---

3    Hemo was a nutrient drink made by Borden's.

was all on new objectives several miles in advance of where it was falling on my last trip. The British have taken over on this mountain and the Col. commanding the Infantry Bn. that is in possession treated us to some tea. His headquarters had been shelled the day before, killing four men. We saw fresh graves of 17 Americans, two British, and four Germans. Saw an unburied German. Passed three groups of Italian refugees working back through the hills toward our lines. Much American equipment and supplies abandoned along trail.

### December 19, 1943

Our liaison officer came in about mid-morning to report that contact with the enemy had been lost all along the Fifth Army front. 'Twas a beautiful day, so Gabe and I took off to see just how close to Rome we could get.[4] Met an oncoming jeep on the way up bearing for stars and carrying General Eisenhower, followed by a flock of two-star Generals. The enemy had resumed contact before we reached Migano along much the same line that existed yesterday. We drove to where a tank company was in position just north of Mt. Rotunda and arrived there just in time to see eight ME-109's start peeling off. They looked like they were heading for us, so we took refuge under a tank. Their objective, however, was the village of San Pietro about 1,500 yards across the gulch which had been occupied by our troops yesterday. They hit it and the enemy artillery shelled it all the time we were up there. We wanted to examine some of our tanks that had been knocked out in the attack on San Pietro four days ago so taking shelter behind the rock walls that fill that sector went over. Came upon a very ripe German corpse. He had been badly torn up by a shell. Next, we came upon the bodies of eight Americans who had been killed within the past day or so. They lay just as they had fallen apparently having been caught by a concentration of mortar fire. Judging from their positions, two of them had lived for a short time. When we

---

4    Gabe is Lieutenant Gabe D. Anderson, *Armor Command,* p. 92.

reached the road leading down the mounting into San Pietro, we found the Medics about the only ones around and they were having to proceed on foot to evacuate the wounded who had been injured in the bombing and shelling. Saw one of our soldiers lying alongside the road who had been killed a few minutes before.

We examined four of our tanks that had hit mines and then been burned by the Germans. Didn't go up to the tanks that I saw burn the other day because they were in the area about 200 yards down the road that the enemy was shelling. Saw an artillery outfit getting positions ready that they would occupy tonight, only about a quarter of a mile out of San Pietro. On our way back to our jeep we took a different route. Passed by the bodies of three civilians who had apparently been killed by artillery, also a number of mules and cattle. Watched a formation of our bombers attack [Cassino] protected by our fighters. Heavy flack thrown up at them and one of our fighters didn't get out. Pass Bn. of infantry going forward to take up positions the other side of San Pietro. The enemy was laying a lot of mortar fire in their intended sector as we left. Saw many mules being trucked to the front.

*{Entries for December 19–23, 1943, omitted.}*

## Christmas and New Year

**December 24, 1943**

One of our officers whom I have regarded as a particular fiend, called me aside today and told me he had contracted venereal disease and was going to the hospital for treatment. Our regiment, for some reason or other, is considerably the worst of the Division from the standpoint of venereal disease. So far this month we have had 54 men go to the hospital with venereal disease. Turned over some candy to the chaplains for distribution to local orphanages.

### December 24, 1943

Our Christmas Eve party has come and just about gone. It is dying out pretty fast, however, judging from the feebleness of the singing as against a little while ago. All of the officers in the regimental headquarters gathered in a recently pitched mess tent early this evening. There was plenty of brandy and cognac and one bottle of Scotch, which, among something over 20 officers did not last very long. One officer had received a box of popping corn and we popped that. There was plenty of candy and nuts.

We sang all of the Christmas carols and then just whatever song anyone started. As I write, I can hear "Silent Night" floating in from where another group is gathered. I left the group to go to one of the halftracks to listen to the President's speech. It was just a year ago that I made a long drive over the mountain roads that were very muddy to rear C.P. for a meeting with General Eisenhower. It was a meeting of unit commanders along that front and he gave us a sort of pep talk.

### December 25, 1943

General Harmon came by for a little talk to the officers following which the band gave us a concert. General Eisenhower is to be the Allied Commander for the coming invasion of Europe with "Monty" to handle the British forces. While we won't be in the big show, the way things are moving at present there is no one I know who bemoans that fact. It is going to be mighty rough and bloody. Naples off limits. Typhus.

### December 25, 1943

This has been a very nice Christmas and a much better one than last year. The commanding general and the band both paid us a visit this morning. The general's call was a brief one, but the band stayed on and played us a nice Christmas program.

The colonel and I each visited eight of the kitchens of the regiment. They are too scattered out to get around to all of them in a reasonable time. There was a very generous issue of turkey for today's meal, the ratio being a hundred and eight pounds of turkey per a hundred men. One kitchen where I stopped was going to serve fruit cake, which had been made by their own mess sergeant. It was fine. I ate at the second battalion headquarters mess. There was plenty of turkey, dressing, gravy and potatoes. They also had some native olives. Those that I've run into before I haven't cared for, but these were really quite good. The dessert was a sort of pineapple cobbler. One thing that Dad wouldn't like about Thanksgiving or Christmas in the Army is that there is no cold turkey to be had afterwards. This should be our last Christmas away from home.

### December 27, 1943

George Johnson and I spent the day at the front climbing out on the nose of Mt. Maggiore. Saw a group of enemy fighter bombers protected by fighters, there being 23 planes in all, come in and bomb a road and some artillery positions. I couldn't tell whether they did any damage, but all of the planes got away despite heavy ack-ack. We took a new trail part of the way and passed three dead German soldiers in rather advanced stages of decay. Also saw five German graves to one American that I hadn't seen before on this trip. Witnessed several very heavy artillery preparations of ours but apparently with nothing behind them besides harassing the enemy. We were in the vicinity of some enemy artillery fire when we got back down in the valley and were returning to our vehicle. One round killed two men and wounded two others. The visibility was perfect today. Snow on all higher mountains and it was cold.

### December 29, 1943

In the H/T most of the day in connection with the C.P.X. CCB has been given some elements of the Division and some armor from the outside and is off to a fight.

While bad weather slows down the fighting, of course, it also slows the ending of it. The attitude of most of the men is the quicker we get going the better for it will be over just that much sooner. Am using a new scheme for sleeping. It consists of wrapping a bath towel around my neck and up to my ears when I go to bed, which takes care of the more tender part that projects outside of my bedroll.

### December 31, 1943

This is a wet New Year's Eve but not in the sense that one normally associates with that date. It has been pouring all afternoon and evening and, with the temperature as low as it falls and the direction from which the wind is blowing, we won't be surprised if there is snow on the ground in the morning.

There is a Division Officer's party tonight not far from here but no one from the regimental headquarters seems to be going. The reason is that you must have either a nurse or a Red Cross girl in uniform as a date in order to get in. No one seems to have been able to make the grade in that respect. While there are a number of hospitals in the vicinity, they are all very busy and those few girls that can getaway seem to have already been booked for the evening. Considering the weather, most of us are glad we aren't going out. I didn't realize there was a suitable building left standing in the town where the party is being held to accommodate such an affair. HAPPY NEW YEAR!!!!!!

Before the start of the year [I] acquired a small pocket diary for 1944. Each page which consisted of 17 lines was for three days. Daily entries were made in this diary until the end of April.

## Elements of the Division are Committed

### January 1, 1944

A gale and driving rainstorm developed at about 0500. All German tents blown down and many others and trees broken. Excellent turkey dinner.

## January 3, 1944

Have a touch of pleurisy so am beginning to think I am material for the Old Soldier's Home. A swarm of forts escorted by P-38's went by today.[5] I saw 78 forts, but others reported over a hundred.

**January 3, 1944**

Dear Elizabeth,

Several days ago, I sent you a package containing three leather cartridge cases of the kind that are worn by the German infantry. One of them is to be sent on to Davey.[6] The boys will be interested to know that I took them from dead German soldiers who were lying just where they had fallen. In answer to their first question—No, I didn't kill them.

There was also enclosed a part of the belt from a German machine gun. The boys may know that our .30 caliber belts are made out of webbing, but the Germans use metal. Their machine guns fire much faster than ours do and you can recognize them instantly by the sound they make. Our machine guns have a sort of a pop-pop-pop while theirs rip-rip.

The cartridge belts had some ammunition in them, but we aren't allowed to send that thru the mails.

## January 4, 1944

With three other officers I climbed Mt. Maggiore this afternoon, getting to an artillery O.P. just after dark. The 6th Infantry attacked at 1930 hours and we were above and looking down on them. Terrific artillery preparation. Saw Neblewerfers firing. Rained, blew. One blanket but warm.

## January 5, 1944

We were watching for a tank attack by G H.Q. Bn., but nothing developed. We saw tanks stuck and in defiladed positions. Enemy artillery

---

5    A B-17 Bomber was considered a "Flying Fort" because of its size.

6    Owen David "Davey" Sowerwine of Menlo Park, California., is Gardiner's nephew, the older brother of Patricia Issel. Correspondence with Patricia Issel on March 1, 2020.

fire very heavy. Saw German prisoners and five bombing attacks. Saw one dead German.

**January 6, 1944**

Reports of more progress by 6th Infantry and some tank action but being held up by bad ground conditions.

**January 7, 1944**

Wounded of 6th Infantry that have cleared Medics now total 250 who include our close friend Col. Ringsak, who is apparently out of the war. Saw more than one hundred forts bound for enemy targets.[7]

*{Entries from January 8–11, 1944, omitted.}*

**January 12, 1944**

"Stars and Stripes" reporters around again. Took them to the 6th Infantry. They lost 4-0, 68-EM killed, 270 wounded, 302 others evacuated. Word that our waterproofing goes over to 1st Armored. Allies acknowledge losing 60 forts yesterday over Germany. They claim 120.

**January 13, 1944**

Out to training area with Col. in armored car but came in for lunch and then out again for evening's program. Walked through the "enemy" lines twice. Things churning around with CCB coming out of the line and all sorts of rumors as to where other elements of the 1st are bound.

**January 14, 1944**

Saw some new German mines for rolling down hills. We are now told that we may send the "Stars and Stripes" home, so I will be sending you

---

7    Lieutenant Colonel Elton Woodrow Ringsak was the recipient of the DSC, the Commander of the 2nd Battalion, 6th Infantry on March 25, 1943. The Hall of Valor Project, retrieved on March 1, 2020, from https://valor.militarytimes.com/hero/23123

one from time to time. Our favorite cartoonist is a young fellow by the name of Mauldin, who does a series of entitled "Up Front."[8] He is a young fellow, who went straight out of Art School in Chicago into the Army. The reason we like his work is because he does such a realistic job. I have met him and spent about half a day with him. He was wounded not long ago but not seriously.

**January 15, 1944**

To CCB re pending plans. We are to consolidate with them. No one likes that idea in our staff because we lose our identity. Out to watch second Bn. problem. Stayed until after dark. Fried chicken for supper.

**January 16, 1944**

Lunch with 1st Armored. They are packing up ready for an amphibious move.[9] Stopped in CCB. Two of our officers moved up there today and more will follow. Orders tonight to establish an O.P. Trocchia. Things will soon be popping. Wonder what my job will be.

**January 17, 1944**

The Col. spent the day working on a scheme for the employment of the regiment which he took up to try and sell to the General tonight but without success. Cols. have an unhappy time of it in tank regiments because they don't get to fight their outfits as a rule.

**January 17, 1944**

Have the C.P. truck to myself tonight and it is still fairly early, so I hope to get several letters written. The boys in maintenance company rigged up a heater (gas) which works like a charm and keeps the place very comfortable. Until it was installed the floor was so cold that two

8    Bill Mauldin became a famous cartoonist. For more see, Bill Mauldin, *Up Front*, (New York, New York: W.W. Norton & Company, Inc., 2000).

9    This is in reference to the Anzio Landings.

men who had to work in here all the time developed trench foot. That, of course, wasn't the only reason.

There is a very sweet little girl who I judge to be about five years old, who is here at breakfast every morning with her bucket to get what scraps she can and then she comes back at noon and again in the evening. Her face is a mass of freckles and she always has a broad smile. I call her "Ginger" and manage to have a little something for her every day or so. She is the one who had first choice on the jewelry that I gave away.

Last week was something of a high water mark in the way of entertainment since we've been over here. Humphrey Bogart, who, of course, is one of the movie tough guys, put on a show in our area. He had two gag men with him and a peroxide blonde wife, who was in the first row of some chorus 15 or 20 years ago. She sang and Bogart put on a skit of "Youse guys and mugs," etc. The boys didn't think much of him and he was far from their idea of a tough guy.

There were some "Stars and Stripes" boys here the same day getting a few pictures for an article. Bogart has a picture entitled "Sahara" which is built around a tank so they thought a shot of him on a tank might make a good story.[10] I arranged it so he and his wife posed in the tank. Bogart was very pleasant and friendly, and I had quite a long visit with him. The picture "Sahara" was shown here last night, and it was roundly booed, largely because of many impossible and ridiculous things that it did (the tank and crew).

Then Joe E. Brown was here. He had a song writer with him, who played the piano and kidded with the boys. Everyone thoroughly enjoyed Brown. It was his last show for the day, and he was very generous in staying on. There is nothing artificial about him and he seems like a fine sort of a person. One thing noticeable was there were no off-color jokes,

10     *Sahara* was set in the Libyan desert in 1942, where a group of American soldiers become isolated in their tank during the retreat to El Alamein. As they drive across the desert they pick up a group of Allied stragglers, but with their supplies of fuel, food, and water running low, they try to reach a desert fortress, but a large German detachment is also heading there. Rosley Crowther "The Screen; ' Sahara,' an Exciting Picture of Desert War, With Humphrey Bogart as a Heroic Sergeant, Is New Feature at the Capitol," *New York Times*, November 12, 1943.

which sets it aside from all other entertainers that I've run into. You probably know that he lost a son in the war.[11] He wound up by having the boys sing "God Bless America" and it wasn't any flag-waving gesture. His performance was over in another unit's area and I didn't have occasion to meet him.

Don't believe I wrote to you about going to dinner a week ago Sunday. The papers have told you about the fact that some Italian units have been in action against the Germans in Italy. Some of their officers recently had lunch with us and they, in turn, invited us to come over to their mess.

Four of us went, including the Colonel and Dick Grandona. It was by far the best meal I've had since I've been in Italy. The mess was a private home. Most armies, except Americans Army, require the civilian population to provide accommodations for their troops. There weren't enough Italian officers, who spoke English, so we got along nicely. The officer who sat on my left had fought in Spain and Russia and in Sicily and Italy against us. I asked them how they were getting along with the French troops. They said they wanted to be friends, but that the French weren't of the same mind.

### January 18, 1944

British attacked on Fifth Army front and seemed to be making good progress. Meetings, plans, etc., re: move. Warning order tonight to move commencing day after tomorrow. It's not far off.

**January 18, 1944**

Dear Elizabeth,

Being wet as much as we are, you would expect to find a lot of colds, but there are very few. About the only disability that seems to be tied

---

11    Captain Don E. Brown was killed when his military plane crashed near Palm Springs, California.

directly with the weather and ground conditions is trench foot. So far, I've escaped it. This is being written in the C.P. truck under conditions which make the war seem far away.

My tent mate and I are the sole occupants of the truck. The sergeant who normally works in here has gone over to the command truck to tune the radio in on the seven o'clock news for us. We have a loudspeaker rigged up in here and there is a lovely program of music coming on over the BBC. After the seven o'clock news which is a fifteen-minute program, we will listen to Wrick Von Valk from Berlin who will give us the German official war communique from Der Fuhrer's headquarters and then a propaganda flavored newscast. We have a nice gasoline heater fixed up here which gives somewhat the same effect as a grate fire. Despite all of this, if one steps outside, you can hear the guns grumbling away and see their flashes in the sky.

The BBC announcer just said that with the exception of those troops serving in India, all men who had served more than six years overseas had been returned home. That doesn't sound so good for we are under the British now. All of the lost dogs in this section of Italy seem to have adopted us. Someone had proposed a dog show and if we are here much longer, we may hold one. You can tell Dr. Johnson that I went to the dentist no later than today. We have a nice young regimental dentist who calls Louisville, Kentucky his hometown. He cleaned my teeth and said that they were holding up well, but he expected if have a cavity next time I was in for periodic cleaning. Since the last time I was in to call on him he has picked up a salvage battery which he uses to power his drill instead of having it operated by the old foot method.

# Cassino[12]

**January 19, 1944**

Up to the CCB for final discussion of line-up of personnel. The 13th ceased to function as a unit at noon, the Bns. came under command of CCB. Moved up tonight and Col. Howze and I are still in the same tent. Swarms of bombers outward bound. Took a good hot shower.

This is being written near a woodstove, which is booming away to the point that I am just about to back out the other side of the tent. There are two dogs curled up by the stove. No one claims them but they just moved in to keep warm.

When we struck our tent on the last move, I gave all the odds and ends to my little friend Ginger. She has a perpetual grin. All those poor little children will miss us badly because we kept them from going hungry. The dogs will miss us also, and our laundress.

**January 20, 1944**

CCB headquarters moved to a point on Mt. Lungo in time to serve lunch there.[13] The Col. and I set up our tent in such a position as to get some defilade. The regiment closed up during the night. 36th Division jumped off at 2000 hrs. to secure bridgehead across Rapido.

**January 21, 1944**

From two in the morning until daylight the enemy whistled heavy shells overhead which landed in vicinity of the 36th Division headquarters. Made a recon towards where on bridgehead was being attempted. Two attempts to secure and hold crossings failed. Will be attempted again tonight.

12    By January 1944, Allied forces had become stalemated along the German Gustav Line, which was anchored around the strong fortifications of Monte Cassino. The mud, mountains, and rivers made an armored breakthrough impossible. In order to defeat this defensive line, the Allies launched Operation Shingle, the amphibious invasion of Anzio, behind the Gustav Line. Combat Command A (CCA) of the 1st Armored Division was part of the initial landings, but CCB, including the 13th Armored Regiment, remained in the Cassino area ready to exploit any German weakness and attack through the Liri Valley should the opportunity arise.

13    Mt. Lungo dominates Highway 6, overlooking San Pietro.

## January 22, 1944

Recon. to S. bridgehead. Visited C.P. of third Bn. 143rd Infantry.[14] Had to duck several times because of mortar and small arms fire. Saw soldiers streaming back from river reporting that most of their men had surrendered when they found themselves out in the open at daylight. Saw a battery of Bofors deserted and much abandoned equipment. All of our troops driven back across river. Landings near Rome.

## January 23, 1944

Another recon to N. bridge site and to center. Visited with infantry who had been driven back. Their morale low. Heard much "Screaming Mimmies" and small arms' fire. Picked up a few items from quantities of abandoned equipment. Starting to rain. We've missed our chance.

## January 23, 1944

Our situation is much the same as it was about a year ago this time but modified to the kind of war that is being fought in Italy as against Africa.

No, we aren't with the force that landed south of Rome yesterday morning. A great many of our close friends are with that group, however. We are, of course, glad to know that they are making satisfactory progress, but we do not consider that the real test of their success will come until tomorrow or the next day when the enemy will have begun to exert maximum pressure of the invaders.

Where we are now you are unable to dig slit trenches because everything is a rock. Instead of digging a hole, you build a wall of rocks. My tent mate and I are back together again, and we have our small tent pitched close to a rock ledge, which protects from that side which is the most important one since the enemy is that way. To take care of any

---

14    The Battalion would eventually be relieved of command for not following orders and Major Parks Bowden, the Operations Office, assumed command. Alex Bowlby, *Countdown to Cassino: The Battle of Mignano Gap, 1943*, (United Kingdom: Leo Cooper, 1995), p. 164.

shells, however, that might land on the other side of us, we have built a nice solid rock wall. It is an easy job for the rocks are just the right size and on the spot. There is really very little danger in our present location, however, from enemy shellfire for there is quite a substantial mountain in between us. Please don't be alarmed by such stories. In this spot there isn't any more danger of being hit by gunfire than there is of being struck by lightning at home. We don't do any calisthenics in the mornings, so I pile rock for exercise. It also gives me a place to rest my toilet articles when I shave. I have become a softy since I started living with the Colonel for he heats water in the morning for shaving. He is very generous in that he always includes me. Since we came to our present camp the water bucket has a thick layer of ice on it every morning.

There are no Italian natives around this camp although many of them used to live not far from here.

The other day I had an experience which was much like the setting of "Journey's End."[15] I was out on a recon and stopped in to visit at the command post of an infantry battalion that was in a hot fight. The way you are usually directed to an infantry or artillery C.P is to follow a particular wire line which is strung on the ground. This particular line led to a deep dugout which some poor Italian had constructed near his home when he was in no-mans-land and decided to try and stick it out. I found the mouth of the dugout closed off by a blanket. Inside it was cramped because the small group of officers and men who were in there were more tenants than the place had been designed to accommodate. The place was illuminated by one sputtering candle so there were more shadows than light. The men were tired and dirty, as is usually the case with front lines troops. While I was there the enemy mortar fire was particularly heavy and the ground would shake violently. You can be glad your soldier boy is not an infantryman for these boys have to sit and take everything the

15    Set in the trenches near Saint-Quentin, Aisne, towards the end of the First World War in 1918, *Journey's End* gives a glimpse into the experiences of the officers of a British Army infantry company. The story plays out in the officers' dugout over four days from March 18, 1918, to March 21, 1918, the last few days before Operation Michael.

enemy can throw at them. With us, we usually sit it out in relative quiet places. One of their favorite weapons, i.e., the enemy's, is what the soldiers call "Screaming Mimmies." The German name is "Nebelwerfer" and what it is is a multi-barreled mortar. The name comes from the noise that it makes when it takes off. There is no mistaking it and fortunately, you hear the noise in ample time before the shell lands so thereby are able to take cover. They are usually fired in volleys of six.

**January 24, 1944**

Went to C.P. of 135th Infantry to arrange for recon. parties to pass through their lines. Twenty-one members of enemy patrol captured. 34th Division attached tonight N. of Cassino after terrific artillery preparation. More progress reported from Rome landings. Am not much of a cog in this operation.

**January 24, 1944**

34th making little progress, mine fields being principal obstacle. Trip to rear areas and a good hot shower. Returned to find second Bn. had gone up to the front to fire. Went out to watch. They received no return fire. It now appears that we may be sent around to the landing operation.

**January 26, 1944**

All of our troops are now back across the Rapido. Certainly not much satisfaction can be derived from what this II Corps had to show for all the lives and ammunition that have been expended. Tried summary court cases.

**January 27, 1944**

Visited C.P. second Bn. who have positions forward of Trocchia. Climbed mountain in afternoon to watch second Bn. 13th fired. Looked right down on Cassino. Personnel mines bad. Shelled crossing bridge on Hy-6.

## January 28, 1944

Visited units in rear. Saw a 240 mm gun Howitzer of ours which has just come into this theatre. Col. tangles with CCB Exec. and S-3 [are] not keeping him posted as to what is going on. 34th Infantry still making no progress in its attack N. of Cassino.

## January 29, 1944

To second Bn. 6th Infantry and then walked well out on flat N.E. of Cassino. Homes full of natives. Visited platoon of tanks that were shelling Cassino. Attack of 34th making slight progress.

## January 29, 1944

I supposed you will worry certain amount regardless of what I can say to allay your fears. The reason I tell you some scarey things at time is because if I tell you just what I am doing then you won't be imagining worse things.

As I write my tentmate and I are listening to a "BBC" program, which is both touching and amusing. It is a regular feature and consists of messages from British soldiers' families. The messages are short and are spoken by the children and they all sound very small. Every once in a while, some youngster refuses at the last minute to talk and then the mother does the talking and prefaces her message by saying "Joey is here in the studio with me but he won't talk," etc. Nearly all of the kids start out by saying "Hello, Daddie." There was a little Scotch fellow a moment ago who had a brogue like Harry Lauder.[16] Saw an announcement of policy by the British Army the other day to bring men home after they had served six years overseas. We have little to complain about in the respect. Thousands of British soldiers in this theatre have been away from England more than twice as long as we have been away from the United States.

16    Harry Lauder was a Scottish singer and comedian popular in both music hall and vaudevillian theatre traditions.

Am enclosing the latest cartoon of the boy I wrote you about. Had a visit today with two of the reporters whom I saw a good bit of in Tunisia. One of them you may recall since he mentioned me in several stories. His name is Hal Boyle.[17] Am not expecting to break into print this campaign because a staff officer normally has to do with the making of plans which the units carry out. However, I do still have a tank of my own. We decided to name the regimental headquarters tanks after places in Ireland and mine is "Ballykinler". That is the name of the camp where I was stationed there.

Am also enclosing an article about Sgt. Odd, whom you should remember.[18] He is still holding down the job of communications sergeant in "D" Company. Some "Stars and Stripes" reporters visited us awhile back in search of some personal interest stories, so I took them over and showed them Odd's "home" which was something of a landmark. They took a lot of pictures of it and I supposed some of them may show up one of these days.

With communication lines more secure than they were in Africa and the enemy air less troublesome in the rear areas, the flow of supplies to the front is much better. Another result is that our rations are better. We had had fresh meat for one meal for three days running now. The present mess that I am eating at is better than the one I attended all of the time I've been in Italy up to a short time ago. To start with, there are so many officers that it is divided into two parts; I eat in the higher ranking one with the General. We have a Filipino boy who waits on us. He is a native of the Island but, before coming into the Army, was a table waiter in a Miami Hotel so he hands me my steel helmet as I leave after each meal for I hang it on the ground right back of where I sit.

---

17     Harold Vincent "Hal" Boyle was a prolific, Pulitzer Prize-winning journalist for the Associated Press. During thirty years with the AP, Boyle wrote 7,680 columns. He is best known for his work as a war correspondent during World War II.

18     Odd is a movie character from a 1949 film titled *Whisky Galore!*

### January 30, 1944

Again, out of N.E. of Cassino but this time drove further. Visited rear C.P. of third Bn. 168th Infantry which was in a hot fight. Some progress being made N. of Cassino.[19] G.H.Q tanks giving good support. 240 mm started shooting over our heads.

### January 30, 1944

I never cease to be impressed by the position of the Italian people in this war. This morning I made a tour of the front line area and found families still occupying most of the farms about which the fighting was raging. The natives in that particular area haven't yet learned the benefits of having American troops quartered around them. All of the soldiers in that section are busy fighting. They have no thoughts of laundry and there are no extra rations to be passed on. The children haven't learned to ask for candy yet nor the men to beg for cigarettes.

One doesn't see many able-bodied men but there are lots of women and children. The youngsters pay absolutely no attention to all of the shelling or firing unless a shell lands almost within their midst. It would certainly be the safer thing for them to evacuate. However, they have no means of transportation, their gardens do provide some food and so long as their homes remain standing, they stay on, hoping that the tide of war will pass on before they are further injured.

19    The 168th was part of the 34th Infantry Division at Cassino.

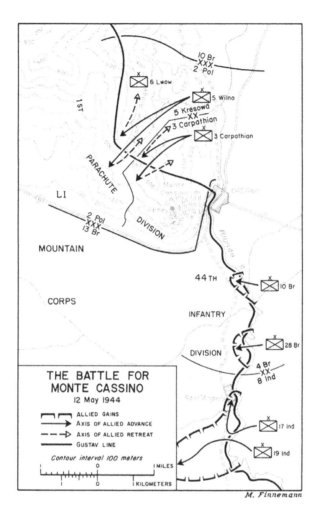

Figure 27: The battle for Monte Cassino (Center of Military History/Public Domain)

## January 31, 1944

Last night a Recon. Co. that was part of CCB was whisked away to the Rome operation and it was felt strongly for a while that we were going. Four more correspondents joined the H.Q.'s and two Brazilian observers.[20]

20    Brazilian Expeditionary Force, also known as Força Expedicionária Brasileira or FEB in Portuguese, consisted of about 25,700 men that fought alongside the Allied forces in the Mediterranean Theatre of World War II. Ruslan Budnik, May 7, 2019, "The Smoking Snakes: The Brazilian Expeditionary Force in WWII," *War History Online*, retrieved on March 6, 2020, from https://www.warhistoryonline.com/instant-articles/the-brazilian-expeditionary-force.html

## January 31, 1944

Haven't left camp all day. Which is not in keeping with my normal routine since we have been up here. Most everyone was waiting around so the General, who is quite athletic, suggested a game of volleyball. Somebody produced a ball and a camouflage net was rigged up and we played a couple of games. It was warm enough at that point so some of the men stripped to the waist. The ground was very rough, and I turned my ankle but not badly and kept on playing.

This headquarters continues to accumulate newspaper reporters and photographers. We have had a "Life" photographer here for some time. He is an English fellow, who took most of the pictures of the Sicily and Salerno landings that appeared in that magazine. Just a few minutes ago four newly arrived correspondents left this H/T after listening to the news. One of them was Frank Gervasi, a feature writer from "Collier's", another Sulzburger of the "New York Times", and then there was a reporter for the "Chicago Tribune" whose name I didn't catch.[21]

## February 1, 1944

This morning I took Bob Strand, which is the name of the "Chicago Tribune" reporter, who is now staying with us, on a little visit along one section of the front. Every soldier whom we met who looked like he might have a story worth reporting, Strand would ask him where he was from. If he came from Chicago, or close by, then he would take his name and a few notes about what he was doing, etc.

One officer said he lived in Michigan but had gone to school in Chicago. On being asked if he had attended the University of Chicago, he said no, an embalmer's school. This officer commands a company that is now in the front line, so he has plenty of business for burial parties.

21    Arthur Ochs "Punch" Sulzburger

**February 2, 1944**

Tanks reported on edge of Cassino, but enemy continues to fire from there. Reports from bridgehead of heavy losses among rangers.

**February 3, 1944**

We moved to new bivouac site at eastern base of Trocchia. Second Bn. 6th ordered to Rome beachhead. Four of our tanks reported to have gotten into Cassino last nite but to have been destroyed. We are right under the guns of a battery of 8 inchers and the effect is terrific. All our artillery firing and some counter battery coming in.

**February 3, 1944**

Yesterday for supper we had chocolate ice cream! The mess officer had saved up the ingredients over a period of weeks and gone well to the rear where there is some ice plant functioning, and had it made. There was enough to be able to give the boys seconds.

Tonight, we heard a news broadcast which struck us as being rather [novel]. We heard BBC relay a message from its Italian Correspondent on this front, in which sound effects supposedly recorded on the battlefield today were broadcast. Since the battle described was one to which we were party, we had heard the same sound only much closer up. The crash of the guns tonight is deafening and one big fellow (ours fortunately) almost jolts you off your seat every time it fires.

Our observation on the BBC German news broadcasts for the past two nites has been that, so far as sections that we know anything about, the German news has been more accurate. Sulzburger in commenting on the fact said that he had noticed that, while in Russia, the German accounts of the fighting on that front were quite reliable. He said, however, that their overall program is to tell the truth only where their listeners are in a position to know the facts.

## February 4, 1944

The CCB Exec. didn't like the firing over his head last nite so the whole H.Q.'s had to move about 300 yards. Rained all afternoon and things are already a mess. Apparently, the Hun still dominates Cassino. Artillery fire lighter.

## February 5, 1944

Some high-trajectory weapon put a few in on us this morning. Went down to help with a badly wounded man and found a cook in a kitchen with his head blown half off. Two others from the mess section had to be evacuated because of shell shock. New Zealanders moving in.[22]

## February 5, 1944

We have moved a couple of times since I wrote to you last and are no longer in a rock pile. Our present site is on the terraces of a hillside vineyard. It is a picturesque setting and to add to it the mountain tops all around us are covered with snow. I am now wearing overshoes as protection against the mud and wet.

Last night the radio reception was good, and we listened to a number of German propaganda stations. One of them involved a discussion of the four freedoms of the Atlantic Charter. The commentator announced that he was going to talk about the false doctrines known as "Freedom from Want", "Freedom from Fear" and "Freedom from Speech".[23]

I have my back to the wall of a small house, which is one of the few in the vicinity which has not been hit by shellfire. There are no natives remaining around here. Don't know what has become of them for it

---

22    The 2nd New Zealand Division or, the "DIV."

23    The Atlantic Charter, a joint declaration made by President Franklin D. Roosevelt and British Prime Minister Winston Churchill on August 14, 1941, that provided a framework for U.S. and British war, and post-war, goals. The Charter formed the basis for the charter of the modern United Nations. University of Minnesota Human Rights Library, "The Atlantic Charter, Joint Declaration by the President and The Prime Minister, Declaration of Principles, Known as the Atlantic Charter, Aug. 14, 1941, U.S.-U.K., 55 Stat. app. 1603," retrieved on March 6, 2020, from http://hrlibrary.umn.edu/education/FDRjointdec.html

certainly isn't shellfire that bothers them for I've seen them living in hotter sports than this.

### February 6, 1944

Seems to be a New Zealand Corps that is coming in and there were the elements of an Indian Infantry Division all around us.[24] There were two air raids by enemy fighters this morning and there were two yesterday afternoon. Our headquarters doesn't seem to like battle noises or shelling, and we moved back this afternoon to Mt. Lungo.

### February 6, 1944

This has been a case of "He marched up the hill and he marched down again". We are back camping in our rock pile again tonight. It is much quieter than it was in our last spot and not nearly as muddy.

In the headquarters sections where they work in their tents all day, they have wood stoves and some very novel little homemade oil and gas stoves. The officers in those sections sleep in those tents. Since the Colonel and I are normally out all day, we don't need a stove during the daytime and we, so far, have preferred not to bother with one for the night. It is a little bit unpleasant going to bed and getting up but once we are in bed, we are fine. On those cold nights, I wear bed socks, and my long underwear and put my coat and the clothes I take off on top of the bed. My hair has grown out far enough so that I can sleep with my head out.

### February 7, 1944

Germans continue counterattack on beachhead. More of our forces (2 T.D. companies) shipped here.

*{Letter dated February 7, 1944, omitted.}*

---

24    For more on the Indian Army in Italy see https://montecassinotours.com/index.php/page/id/19/the-indian-army-in-italy.html

### February 8, 1944

Our own planes bombed one of our artillery positions yesterday, killing eighteen men and wounding twenty-five. Our 8 in. guns shelled our own infantry in N. Cassino today. Made a trip to first and third Bns and H.Q.'s Company.

### February 9, 1944

Gabe and I visited Cairo walking doom Trocchia on in. Saw four dive-bombing missions of our planes in vicinity of Abbey.[25] Passed by fourteen dead American soldiers lying where they were killed. Saw fabricated shell German pill boxes, wire minefield, knocked-out tanks, and S.P. guns of the enemy.

### February 10, 1944

Back to rear areas for summary courts and a shower. Learned sergeant tank commander of F.O.'s tank with the 27th Field Artillery at beachhead K.I.A. Saw more 240's moving up.[26] Heavy rains, much enemy artillery fire.

{Entries for February 10–14, 1944, that discuss the techniques he used to stay warm, the mingling with the natives, and a climb by foot up Mount Lungo to get a view of the battlefield are omitted.}

### February 15, 1944

Watched from closeup wave after wave of four and two-motor bombers blast the famous Abbey above Cassino into a heap of rubble. Seemed really tragic but reports persisted that the enemy was using it. Walked over to Cairo passing many dead mules and four dead Indians.

25    Monte Cassino is best known for its abbey, a monastery established by Saint Benedict in 529. It is the site of one of the most tragic battles of the European theater of the war that Gardiner describes. The Allies mistakenly suspected that German troops were hiding inside the abbey and heavily bombarded the monastery, which actually housed many civilians who had sought refuge inside the building. Monte Cassino Abbey, retrieved on March 7, 2020, from https://www.atlasobscura.com/places/montecassino-abbey

26    240 mm Howitzer Motor Carriage T92 was a self-propelled howitzer.

Witnessed a heroic rescue of a New Zealander wounded alongside of ammo dump.

Figure 28: The ruins of Monte Cassino
(Wikimedia Commons/Public Domain)

### February 16, 1944

The Colonel and I took H.Q.'s tanks down to where third Bn. was practice-firing and fired. I directed fire, fired and loaded my 75 mm. Further bombing missions on Abbey and vicinity scheduled but cancelled because of having to direct all air to beachhead to meet heavy counterattacks.

### February 16, 1944

It is colder with us today than any time so far. That isn't entirely a matter of temperature, however, because it is the wind blowing off the snow that has us shivering today. Our friends from "Down Under" are really uncomfortable as are the dark-skinned boys who are with them. The most popular heating stove that has been devised is one made out of several empty brass shell cases that burns diesel oil. For those who have wood stoves, their fuel supply has been simplified by the wrecking of the railroad ties by the Germans and the blasting down of so many of the tress by shellfire.

The Quartermaster became all mixed-up somehow for we had turkey on St. Valentine's Day. We continue to have fresh meat once a day and hotcakes are a fairly common item on our breakfast menu. There is certainly a contrast between the way our troops eat and those of the enemy. He nevertheless continues to be a formidable fighter.

Yesterday I witnessed at close hand one of the most spectacular events of the war.[27] It was awesome and tragic as well and I am sorry they felt it was necessary. Don't believe the censor would approve of my telling you what it was since that would indicate where I am. However, the newsreels will be featuring that event at home shortly and pictures of it will be appearing in all the papers and magazines.

### February 17, 1944

The Combat Command S-3 went to the Hospital several days ago and since there is some doubt about his immediate return, the General today said he wanted me to start familiarizing myself with that job.[28] The New Zealanders are attacking tonight.

### February 18, 1944

The New Zealanders put two bridges across the Rapido on the railroad during the night and had a couple of companies in and around the railroad station of Cassino at daylight. Heavy fire prevented their reinforcement and they were counterattacked and had to withdraw. The ailing S-3 returned so I again seem to be out of a job.

### February 18, 1944

The "Stars and Stripes" has some sort of a deal with "The Reader's Digest" whereby they print and distribute with that paper the current issue of the "Digest". They print it on the same paper as the newspaper and you have to fold and cut it several times to get it into the proper shape to read. Right now, they are running off the February issue and they give you the complete "Digest" with the issues of the paper over a period of

27    The Allied bombing of the Abbey at Monte Cassino.

28    Major Frank J. Ryder, Jr.

a week. There is no charge for the paper, or this added service. In that connection all cigarettes and candies that are issued are free. The ration on cigarettes is a package per man per day.

**February 19, 1944**

The New Zealanders are just about back where they started from except that they have had some heavy losses. More disturbing news from the bridgehead with reports of our troops having to give ground. Enemy counter battery fire very effective on our 8-incher today.

**February 20, 1944**

We couldn't get Germany on the air last night or tonight. Hope it was for the same reason as last night which was a heavy raid on the Vaterland. It was the most costly one reported to date. The RAF knowledge the loss of seventy-nine planes. Enemy artillery continues active.

**February 21, 1944**

Up at six and out with the Colonel all day observing a problem of the second Bn. which was in a large measure one of negotiating difficult ground. The Colonel and I certainly get fed up with this H.Q.'s set-up. It is certainly a lame staff compared with the one they had in Africa. I really haven't anything to do but so far, it's a healthy spot.

**February 22, 1944**

Up early again and out this time with the first Bn. We spent some time experimenting with various expedients to get mediums across soft spots. Turkey for dinner.

**February 23, 1944**

It was the third Bn. this morning and they plowed up more Italian farmland and bogged their tanks down. There is a new plan of attack all drawn up for the Cassino assault, but an all-day pouring rain forced postponement.

**February 23, 1944**

Yesterday I wrote Dad that we had been enjoying dry weather to the point that the dust was bad on some roads. I hasten to report that there are no longer any complaints on that score. When we woke up this morning, it was raining, and it hasn't let up since. Was out in my jeep this morning and became stuck twice. This evening I received a call that some mail had arrived at the rear echelon. Normally, I would have sent my driver after it, but I didn't think he would be able to get through so told them to hold it unless someone was coming this way. Apparently, some good sailor did come by for we received quite a good mail a few minutes ago.

The Quartermaster must be running for reelection for yesterday we had turkey again and today pork chops. Last evening, we saw the Fred Astaire picture "Flying High" and were delighted with it. While the soundtrack was good, we missed some of the lines because of the noise of the big guns which were angry last night.

**February 24, 1944**

No rain but very high winds. The coming operation which bears the code name "Dickens" is again postponcd.[29] Back to the rear echelon and dropped in at a Q.M. "shower and clothes exchange unit". It's all class "B" clothing but I did very well.

---

29    Operation Dickens was the third Battle for Monte Cassino. Information on Operation Dickens retrieved on March 7, 2020, from https://codenames.info/operation/dickens-i/

Figure 29: Ruins of the Benedictine Monastery at Monte Cassino, May 1944, following the four battles. The battles included the Third Battle which Gardiner references as Operation Dickens. (Wikimedia Commons/Public Domain)

**February 25, 1944**

Am sure not doing anything towards helping win this war in my present status. Can take slight comfort in the fact that there are many others in my present inactive position. Climbed Lungo and got soaked as a heavy rainstorm came up while I was on top.

**February 25, 1944**

In the issue of "Life" that we received yesterday there are a number of Bill Mauldin's cartoons. Among them is my favorite entitled "Hit the Dirt". It is of the boys clinging' to the rocks of a steep mountainside as an enemy shell is heard coming in. I have escaped getting "trench foot" but that has been a lot of it. For the most part, those who come down with it are the men whose feet are cold and wet for long periods and who don't have the opportunity to exercise them. These are most often found among the infantrymen who are in frontline positions and ack-ack crews in the forward areas.

Yesterday I dropped in at one of the "Shower Clothing Exchange Units" that the quartermaster operates just out of gunshot. In addition to getting a good hot shower, you can have a complete exchange of clothes. You just swap the underwear, socks, shirts, trousers and coveralls that you take off for clean ones. The clothing that you receive in exchange for that which you turn in is known as Class "B" clothing. It has been used but it is clean, and all buttons have been sewn on, any tears repaired, etc. These units are ideal for troops just out of the line and those who may not have extra clothes or the opportunity to get their dirty ones washed. I traded everything yesterday except socks and coveralls. Towels are also furnished.

It has been raining again all day so here we sit and drip.

### February 26, 1944

More rain. Went for a walk and found myself in a minefield of Teller mines rigged up with a trip wire and pull igniters.

### February 26, 1944

Yesterday one of the editions of what is known as "The Front Line Follies" played in the second battalion area. These shows consist usually of a master of ceremonies, a comedian who winds up playing a mouth organ or yodeling, and two or three girls who tap dance and sing a little. It does take the boys' minds off the monotony of their present existence and they are very popular.

There are rest camps in the rear areas for both officers and men. Units receive allotments of so many officers and men to send to these places. The usual period allowed there is three days. The officers' rest camp is located at a fine hotel on the sea that was a popular prewar spot, and which escaped damage in the fighting. Those who have been there, in addition to real beds, linen and baths, report excellent food, complete relaxation and usually enough nurses also "resting" to properly take advantage of the dinner dance music.

This rainy weather (it poured again today) makes for plenty of time to write letters so I am pretty well caught up in my correspondence. This is my 121st letter since the first of the year.

Sulzburger dropped by to say hello today and in tow he had a J.G. from the Navy who was having a look at the front lines for the first time. This particular individual was a son of Willkie. He was about as dumb as they come. That is not just green but slow on the trigger and certainly not any reason why one should vote for his father.

### February 27, 1944

Back to Napoli stopping at all engineering dumps on route in search of matting suitable for use with tanks in crossing soft spots. No success. Amazed at tremendous quantities of bridging that is available. Visited Naples Airport which is jammed with all types of aircraft. No rain. Roads jammed with traffic.

### February 28, 1944

News from all fronts were meager. Indications are new attack on beachhead is shaping up. The 88th American Division is now taking over a sector on this front.[30] Also a fresh Moroccan Division has come in. Climbed my favorite mountain.

### February 29, 1944

Poured all night so the employment of armor in the Liri valley becomes progressively further away. Air attacks on Germany from England

---

30 The 88th Infantry Division was one of the first all-draftee divisions of the United States Army. It fought in North Africa and then at Monte Cassino on February 27, and the entire division relieved the battered British 46th Infantry Division along the Garigliano River in the Minturno area on March 5. John Sloan Brown. *Draftee Division: A Study of the 88th Infantry Division, First all Selective Service Division into Combat in World War II*, (Lexington, Kentucky: University Press of Kentucky, 2014).

renewed. Supper discussion: How much of an Army of occupation will America maintain abroad after the war.

## March 1, 1944

The Colonel and I took both our peeps and headed over the Apennines for a visit to the Eighth Army front. By nightfall we had travelled 186 miles most of which was over mountainous roads and driven slightly beyond Ortona where signs and the sound of firing indicated a halt. Prepared our own meals. Called on first Canadian Tank Brigade. Considerable fighting during night.

## March 2, 1944

We travelled to coast road back to Vasto and then followed the same road over the mountains.[31]

Mrs. Carlock is the mother of the boy who was the driver of my tank at Sbeitla.[32] He was killed when the tank was hit and burned in the tank. Officially, after that action he was carried as MIA, which means missing in action. They are very strict about the proof that is required before a man is listed as killed. Since the boys was sitting alongside of him was captured and the rest of us didn't see him after he was hit, we couldn't say that we saw him after he was killed. There wasn't any question in my mind he was dead, so I wrote his mother to that effect.

Letters of condolence are supposed to go "through channels". That means they are turned over to the War Department for forwarding so as to make sure that they won't arrive before the official notice reaches the family. What I have always done is wait a sufficient time for the word to be delivered and then write direct. Carlock's case was different, however, and since I was saying he was KIA as against MIA, I sent the letter in the prescribed manner. Late last summer I was told that letters were still

31    Ortona and Vasto are on the Italian Eastern Coast where the Canadians fought during their attack in December 1943.

32    Corporal Orvis Carlock, *Armor Command*, p. 174.

being received from Mrs. Carlock, addressed to [Orvis], so I wrote to her again "through channels". It is that letter which she acknowledged, apparently my first one never being delivered.

After we reached Italy, a letter came to the regiment asking if we could throw any light on the identity of a body that had been found in a burned-out tank at Sbeitla last Spring and buried. The tank number was given, and it was my tank, so I immediately answered to the effect that the boy was that of Carlock's. Apparently, on receiving that information, the Carlocks were informed that their son was KIA and my last letter to Mrs. Carlock was forwarded. Her letter is really very touching. Her son was a particularly fine boy and at that time regarded as the best driver in the battalion.

Drove for four hours yesterday and again today through now. The drifts on the road had been shoveled out in many places and it was much like going out to the Big Hole in the spring when the road was first opened. The banks in some places were as much as ten feet high. More about that jaunt later. Quite like spring on the other seacoast with the fruit trees in blossom.

**March 3, 1944**

The C.G. of the New Zealand Division stepped on a "Shoe Mine" on Trocchia yesterday and lost both feet and a leg.[33] Continued rain kept me in camp. Changes are in the making which cause me to believe we won't be used on this front. Save a movie in the Med. tent.

**March 4, 1944**

Third attack against beachhead seems to have petered out. Daylight bombing of Germany continues. Any D Day here grows more remote with rain continuing. Boys at beachhead must be getting fed up.

---

33    The Schu-mine 42 (Shoe-mine), also known as the Schützenmine 42, was a German anti-personnel mine used during the Second World War.

## March 4, 1944

Just returned from seeing a movie. It was Bob Hope in "Let's Face It" and very entertaining. The picture was taken from a musical comedy by that name which I saw in New York. This movie was held in a big tent about three miles to the rear of where we are camped, and the Colonel and I drove down. The seats are empty gas cans. Last night we saw a movie which was within walking distance or I should say slipping and sliding distance of here, the mud is so bad.

The show we saw last night was "Five Graves to Cairo", with Eric Von Stroheim playing Rommel. It was shown in a hospital tent in a first air station that is set up in an adjoining area. We found it worthwhile. There was a newsreel which showed scenes from the occupation of Naples and shots of the world series ball games between the Yankees and the Cardinals. That picture was set in the Libyan desert. When we stepped outside of the tent, we sloshed around in mud well above our ankles.

## March 5, 1944

Took a ride in a cub plane over enemy lines and had a good look at Cassino and Monastery.

## March 6, 1944

Rained all nite. There is a reorganization in progress on this front with a reshuffling of troops and it is my guess that the 13th won't be employed in the Liri valley. Climbed the mountain and watched our heavy artillery shell targets up the valley.

## March 7, 1944

Dropped in on a few elements of the regiment for a visit. The sending home of our first group of men to be rotated (one half of 1% per month) has been a boost to morale even though the chances of others are slim.

Played volley-ball this afternoon. Ice cream for supper. Enemy shelling close by this evening.

### March 7, 1944

This has been an extended Christmas. Today I received the package from you containing the toilet roll, candy, ink, pen, pencil, underwear, etc. There was only one mistake in the package and that was the candy. Apparently, this package has been sitting near a stove for the past three months for those candy toffy pieces had melted and run over everything else. No damage done, however, to anything but the candy.

### March 8, 1944

Two fresh eggs for breakfast, courtesy of the Q.M. Observed a test of track vehicles to determine ground conditions. Drying out very fast.

### March 9, 1944

Fresh eggs again this morning and a P.X. ration of three Coca-Colas and a movie tonight. A test again made of ground conditions and we understand attack was planned for tomorrow and now it's been postponed again. Wish they make up their minds.

### March 9, 1944

We all feel very fortunate at being in Italy as against the other theatres. No one has any desire to get tangled up in the jungles of the South Pacific and all the bugs that go with them. The climate in England wouldn't be any better than it is here, and if we were there, we would be lined up ready for the jump across to the continent when the whistle blows and we aren't interested in getting tangled up in the early phases of that campaign.

With the weather still holding up operations here and the supply situation being so good we are almost living in the same style as the boys at home. This morning we had two fresh fried eggs apiece for breakfast which marked the second morning running for such a treat. Those were the first we have had in Italy. In Africa we were able to buy eggs for the mess. You can't do that here and these were shipped in. I don't believe we've missed a day now in several weeks when we haven't had fresh meat for one meal. We always have whatever it is for dinner. Today it was beef and this evening we had "C" ration hash, but the mess sergeant had mixed some flour up in it and it tasted different than a straight hash and was quite good.

There was another first for today in that we were able to buy three bottles of Coca-Cola apiece. That is the first of that we have had since leaving Ireland. In order to get any at the next issue, the bottles have to be returned. We had a volleyball game this afternoon and I drank two of my three bottles afterwards. While they still shoot at you around here when you make yourself conspicuous, you can see that we are being wonderfully well taken care of at present. It is still quite cool, and the surrounding mountains are all covered with fresh snow.

### March 11, 1944

The weather here would have been ideal for an aerial attack which is supposed to pave the way for the assault on Cassino, but it had been postponed and was again tonight. There is considerable talk of reorganizing the Division. I wonder where I will wind up.

### March 12, 1944

The moon was shining when we went to bed last night, but we awakened this morning to find fresh snow on the mountains that surround us and a drizzle of rain falling. It is now mid-afternoon, and it is raining hard so any large scale activity on this front will be some time developing.

Since ground conditions were so bad that we knew nothing was going to break for some little while, my tentmate and I took off on a two-day trip recently. We took both our peeps, an Italian officer's tent that I have which is smaller than our present side wall but quite a bit larger than the regular pup tent, both of our drivers and rations for two days.

The weather forecast was for clearing weather or we might not have started out since it was raining hard the morning we left. My tentmate and I rode in the same peep, taking turns driving and our drivers followed us in the other peep. We didn't use chains although several times when we were crossing some of the higher mountains, I thought we would have to put them on to get through, but we made it all right.

One could have written a story just on the nationality of the various M.P.s that we encountered on our trip. We made a hundred and sixty-eight miles outbound and returned over the same route except for short distance where, because of military operations, the roads were one way. Successively, we were directed on our way by M.P.s of American, New Zealand, British, Indian, French, Polish and Canadian units.

The road we travelled took us over two divides and for almost four hours we drove through country that was covered with snow. There were groups of natives all along the way, working on the roads under the direction of soldiers. For the most part, they were shoveling snow and in many places the drifts that had been cut through were well above the top of the car. The road was a series of curves and switchback until we got well down out of the mountains. Unfortunately, it was either raining or snowing when we were well up in the high country, so we didn't have the opportunity to enjoy the scenic values of that section. All of the communities that we saw were perched right up on top of some mountain and several of them looked like illustrations out of a fairy story book. For the most part, the towns that we saw hadn't suffered as severely from the fighting as have those in this area. The country over there along the seashore seemed to be further along than on this side in that we saw a number of fruit trees in blossom.

We visited with the officers of a tank outfit the one evening we were away. Our trip was quite unofficial, just being prompted by a desire to get away and do a little sightseeing. It didn't rain on us on the other side. The Indian troops that we see are of all types and you see a wide variety of turbans and whiskers. Surprising to me they are always bathing regardless of how cold it may be. I'm inclined to believe that they are motivated by some religious principle rather than by reason of personal hygiene. It always strikes me as a little odd to see some bewhiskered and turbaned Indian come roaring down the road on a motorcycle. They seem to do everything the British soldiers do except fly. Feeding them in the hospitals other than their own present a problem because of so many don'ts in their diet.

**March 13, 1944**

A perfect day and every indication of fair weather again tomorrow yet the word was flashed this evening that the attack was still not set to go off. What the hell is the matter? Played volleyball this afternoon and have set aside my long woolen underwear that I've been wearing since shortly after we moved up here.

**March 14, 1944**

Another grand day and this evening we received word that tomorrow is D-Day at last.

**March 15, 1944**

From a position out on the flat in front of Cassino, I saw 355 four-motor and 213 two-motor bombers blast Cassino from 0830 until noon. A number of their bombs were prematurely dropped, and one formation bombed a friendly community. Our troops suffered considerable casualties as a result.

**March 16, 1944**

Went closer to Cassino than any time yet. They have had trouble getting tanks in because of the rubble and craters resulting from the bombing. A bridge was put across HY-6 during the night and tanks have crossed it. Monastery hill was smoked all day. Medium bombers (ours) bombed our positions. Climbed hill this afternoon.

**March 17, 1944**

Out on the flat towards Cassino again but this time on the other side of HY-6. Enemy mortar fire heavy but New Zealanders and Indians making progress. Whole area consistently smoked. Saw enemy dive bombers attack bridge. Sure, don't have anything to do.

**March 18, 1944**

Out along forward slopes of Trocchia. Close to a dive-bombing attack which hit the C.P. of G.H.Q. tank group. Three men from the 13th wounded and six from the group killed. Watched our fighters attempt to drop supplies to Indian troops on slopes of Mt. Cassino. Most of the parachutes floated beyond.

**March 19, 1944**

Enemy resistance in Cassino still strong and some counterattacking in progress. Only real encouraging development was report that the "Maoris" had captured some one hundred and fifty prisoners in town.[34]

**March 19, 1944**

Last night we had the movie shown here entitled, "This Is the Army". It was definitely <u>not</u> the Army as we know it. We thought there was a little too much flag waving in it and too much emphasis on hardships of that phase of Army existence which we all look back upon as a holiday. Our movies are, of course, seen on a small screen which means that many of the shots in "This Is the Army" lost the proper effect because the figures were so reduced. There were plenty of local sound effects last night for the artillery was particularly busy.

---

34    The Māori Battalion was an infantry battalion of the New Zealand Army.

You will again read of a particular record-breaking bombing attack. Was really too close to it to be comfortable and I don't think a camera would have worked so well just when the bombs hit because the ground shook so violently.

Have a new peep driver whose name is Householder, which seems rather fitting one to tie in with mine. My older driver I had inherited with my present job and, of course, have had for a long time. While I had no complaint about his driving, he was sort of a queer person and I think a little gun shy. He would get sullen spells and since one peep driver also serves as your striker, I finally gave up trying to figure him out and made this shift. My new driver has bushy red hair.

### March 20, 1944

Reshuffling of our units in Cassino in progress. We understand the New Zealanders lost seven tanks today by artillery fire.

### March 20, 1944

Our friend Sulzberger in the "N.Y. Times" had lunch with us today. He is a very pleasant person and most interesting. There are few places he hasn't been in Europe or Russia and, of course, he has met all of the big shots. His wife is in Cairo and he expects to spend some time with her soon.

Am afraid you still aren't finding much encouragement in the news from this theatre. The enemy continues to contest every foot of ground and to counterattack whenever he does lose a position.

### March 21, 1944

No advance being made in Cassino for enemy infiltrates just about as fast as they are cleaned up. Enemy artillery fire in Cassino very heavy. Have watched a New Zealand graveyard near here grow from nothing to eighty-three white crosses.

## March 22, 1944

Enemy air attack with fighters hedgehopping right up HY-6. Ack-ack engaged them but with difficulty because of their low flight tactics and only damage was to our own personnel. Subsequent flights of our own fighters shot at. General Clarke called General Allen to say saluting of first and second Bns. was very bad. General Allen very much provoked.

### March 22, 1944

Presume you will soon be seeing pictures of Vesuvius on the rampage.[35] Up until shortly after the first of the year we were camped within sight of its cone and at night when it was active the glow of the lava could be plainly seen. It makes an ideal landmark for the aviators both by day and night.

The boys are beginning to play baseball now that the ground has dried up to where that is possible. However, level places are at a premium in this mountainous country and some diamonds have the infield on one terrace and the outfield on another. Whenever you see British troops, you see football fields. The R.A.F. are the best off in that respect for they play right on their flying fields. We still play volley-ball when the weather and business at hand permits.

## March 23, 1944

Two shells fell in Second Bn. area last night killing one boy and wounding three others. High winds with rain and snow falling most every day. Vesuvius reported to be even more violent. No progress in Cassino and planes are still dropping food and ammunition to troops on certain heights.

---

35    On March 17, 1944, Mount Vesuvius began an eruption that, over the ensuing week and a half, rained down rocks the size of basketballs, covered some areas with up to a meter of ash, and released a slow-moving wall of volcanic rock, lava and debris that burned everything in its path. Nearby residents in the town of San Sebastiano had to evacuate. The 1944 eruption of Vesuvius was the worst eruption of the volcano since 1872, with the most famous eruption in the volcano's long history occurring in 79 A.D., when the aftermath of the eruption entombed Herculaneum and Pompeii, killing an estimated 30,000 people. Sara E. Pratt, (March 17, 2016) "Benchmarks: March 17, 1944: The most recent eruption of Mount Vesuvius," *Earth: The Science Behind the Headlines*, retrieved on March 7, 2020, from https://www.earthmagazine.org/article/benchmarks-march-17-1944-most-recent-eruption-mount-vesuvius

## March 24, 1944

Stopped in at the two American cemeteries that are to the rear. I should estimate that there are 3,000 of our boys buried in those two areas. That is a heavy price to pay for the little progress that can be shown on this front and this evening word comes that we are going back to the rear and the Indians are withdrawing from certain high points.

## March 24, 1944

For the first time in over two months we will be sleeping tonight beyond the range of enemy artillery fire. The first night we moved into our last area they sent shells over us all night and there has hardly been a night since then when some didn't land in our general area. We are now back in the same general area where we spent Christmas so, if we spend any time here, I should be seeing Ginger and my washerwoman.

The girl in the enclosed snapshot is one of the "doughnut" girls who is attached to the division.[36] Three of them joined us at our last stop in Africa. They came over here but there are only the two now. These two just make the rounds of the units passing out doughnuts, visiting with the boys, admiring their girls' pictures, etc. The girl in this picture showed me a clipping from the "N.Y. Times" yesterday in which both of our names were mentioned. It was Sulzberger's story about the day he took young Willkie to the front and he spoke of stopping in to get some doughnuts and meeting the girls and visiting with me at our headquarters.

## March 25, 1944

During the night the troops were withdrawn from the points they've been on where they have been supplying them from both sides. All American troops in this sector seem to be withdrawing and we set up in

36    These "girls" were voluntary American women who worked on the front in support of the troops. The Doughnut Girl moniker was first noted in World War I where women would volunteer to make doughnuts for the "doughboys" on the Western Front Sue Zeiger, *In Uncle Sam's Service: Women Workers with the American Expeditionary Force, 1917-1919,* (Philadelphia, Pennsylvania: University of Pennsylvania Press, 2004), p. 52.

a bivouac area near our Christmas area just at dusk. Could see Vesuvius which was pouring dust into the sky.

## Out of Reach of the Guns

**March 26, 1944**

We are camped just far enough up the slope of a hill so we can see out over the valley below us. There is a large village just below us which suffered considerable damage during the fighting through here but mostly in the center where a road intersection was heavily bombed. The community's Church escaped injury and this morning I was awakened at five o'clock by the ringing of its bells. It was a very pleasant way to be aroused and quite in contrast with the crash of exploding shells which was a common way of having our sleep interrupted at the last stop.

No, our move from the rock wall to the hillside vineyard was not more pleasant but unhealthy and we came back with less men than we had when we moved up. When this war is over there shouldn't be any shortage of men cooks for, I believe, a lot of the boys will be inclined to stay on with that sort of work when they get out of the Army.

**March 27, 1944**

The Doc in the Second Bn. used a stethoscope all over my chest and pronounced my heart and lungs O.K. but concluded that I had a cracked rib so taped me up. Vesuvius was most active again with a tremendous dark cloud of smoke boiling out of it.

**March 28, 1944**

The Col. and I made a trip up onto Vesuvius. A wind of almost gale-like proportions was the principal deterrent in keeping us from going all the way to the top. Found the surface painfully hot in spots and the climb was somewhat hazardous because of the risk of slides. We saw where one flow of lava had engulfed a community. The volcano was pouring out a huge quantity of dust.

## Further Training and Preparing to Move to Beachhead

**March 29, 1944**

Saw over a hundred forts pass over this morning and they returned some six hours later so presumably they visited southern France. Spent the morning on the range watching the three Bns. fire their co-axial machine guns. Vesuvius continues to cast a pass of dust over this area.

**March 30, 1944**

An invitation for five observers to witness and infantry, tank and artillery demonstration over on the Adriatic side sent the Colonel, myself and three Bn. C.O.s rolling over the mountains. Reached the Canadian Corps H.Q.s just before dusk and were very well taken care of in one of the officers' messes.

**March 31, 1944**

From Larino we drove on to the coast for the demonstration. Impressed by the youth of the Canadian General Officers that we met. Saw an attack on a limited objective. While urged to spend the night with our hosts, we went on to Campobasso which hasn't been touched by the war where we put up at a hotel operated by the military. A good supper with music and singing. Electric lights and running water.

**April 1, 1944**

British operated hostelries are certainly economical. Breakfast was ten lira and our rooms were one hundred lira for the five of us. We were back in camp for dinner. The Colonel just doesn't get along with the General. R.A.F. lost ninety-five bombers over Germany the other night.

The Luftwaffe is apparently very far from us though.

**April 1, 1944**

Our present mess is getting very fancy although the food isn't as good as when we were being shot at. The troops in the forward areas only averaging fresh meat once every three days but in the general's mess we are eating off of china and a tablecloth has now appeared. If I left a girl's picture in my footlocker and a bottle of liquor that was indeed an oversight. Don't remember either item. The footlocker was second hand and was well decorated and the liquor must have been some that I carried in my bedroll from the United States. You or Dad are more than welcome to use it the first time you have some real thirsty guests.

### April 3, 1944

Spent the morning on the range watching our practice firing. Played in a baseball game this evening but was in left field and didn't have much come my way. It now develops that we are slated to go to the Beachhead and fairly soon. The general feeling now is no invasion until May.

### April 4, 1944

Spent morning on the range. We are firing 75s of the tanks now. At Sunday night's party I made a date with a very attractive Canadian nurse for this week and was most disappointed this noon to receive a note from her that she couldn't keep it. Played left field in baseball game tonight.

### April 5, 1944

More range practice. Learned of heavy plane losses as a result of Vesuvius eruption.[37] Have switched over to summer underclothes completely. Reports of many deserters hiding out in Naples.

---

37    The Allied airbase at Pompeii Airfield was smothered, and up to eighty-eight aircraft were destroyed in one fell swoop. Robin Andrews, (February 16, 2017), "How Vesuvius Upstaged the Nazi Air Force During the Second World War," *Forbes*, retrieved on March 7, 2020, from https://www.forbes.com/sites/robinandrews/2017/02/16/how-vesuvius-upstaged-the-nazi-air-force-during-the-second-world-war/#4bc30800597f

Figure 30: The 1944 eruption of Mount Vesuvius (U.S. National Archives/Public Domain)

*{April 6–27, 1944, was omitted as most of the letters and diary entries involved discussions on rations and the anticipatory move to Anzio.}*

### April 28, 1944

Yesterday a very long column of Goum cavalry passed by here.[38] While they always look tough to me, this bunch looked even more wild and fierce than the others I've seen. They normally give you a cold stare but, if you smile and wave to them, they seem highly pleased and will beam all over and nearly always say "Comrade! OK."

We recently heard a story about them which was told as true, which dad would enjoy. This story came to us through one of our officers in the hospital. There was an infantry officer in the same ward

38    Moroccan Goumiers

whose nerves had gone to pieces as a result of an experience at the front. It seems he was doing outpost duty in the mountains in the sector adjoining the French. One particularly black night, while he was standing in a foxhole, straining his eyes and ears to detect any movement of an enemy patrol, he was terrified to feel a hand on his throat. He was so frightened he was unable to move. The hand followed the chain on his neck down to his dog tags. Then a voice hissed, "Americano! Ok!" and the hand was gone. This officer went to the hospital the next morning completely unnerved.

Last evening and this morning we had fresh eggs. This issue has been very generous, being ten per man. However, the cases had to be returned before we left so we ate them in two meals. No one seemed to have any difficulty in downing five at a sitting. I know of one tank crew in Africa, which hadn't eaten for several days, who finally reached an Arab settlement. The five men ate a hundred eggs before they stopped.

**April 29, 1944**

We saw a large number of heavy bombers passing over. Couldn't get a count on them because they were only visible through holes in the clouds. The balance of the second loaded out. Am switching to another diary and leaving this one behind.

*********************************

The diary which was kept from this point forward to the end of the year had two days to a page with ten lines to a day, providing more space than in the diary kept earlier in the year.

## Anzio

*{By January 1944, Allied forces were stalemated along the German Gustav Line, which was anchored around the fortifications of Monte Cassino. The mud, mountains, and rivers made an armored breakthrough*

impossible. In order to defeat this defensive line, the Allies launched Operation Shingle, the amphibious invasion of Anzio, behind the Gustav Line. Combat Command A (CCA) of the 1st Armored Division was part of the initial landings, but, as Gardiner has described thus far, CCB, including the 13th Armored Regiment, remained in the Cassino area, ready to exploit any German weakness and attack through the Liri Valley should the opportunity arise. After intense German counterattacks on the Anzio beachhead and no meaningful progress south of the Gustav Line, it was decided to reunite the 1st Armored Division in order to make a decisive armored thrust to break out of Anzio. 13th Armor was shipped north to Anzio in early May 1944 after months of waiting as described by Gardiner. There, they received extensive training on breaching and the 191st Tank Battalion was attached to the Regiment for the coming attack. After rehearsing infantry-tank cooperation, the Regiment was in its pre-attack positions near Cisterna by May 22. On May 23, the 2nd Battalion, 13th Armor jumped off at first light with D Co to the west, F Co to the east, and E Co in reserve. Attacking toward Torrecchia Nuova, the Battalion ran into an American minefield that was not properly marked. Forty total vehicles from CCB were damaged as a result. D Co had so many tanks lose their tracks to mines that E Co advanced and assumed their mission. Despite this early setback, the tanks of Companies E and F rapidly advanced. They knocked out enemy anti-tank guns, bunkers, and trenches before setting into local security positions for the night.

Meanwhile, near Carano Creek on the American left flank, the German Army had launched a counterattack in the afternoon. 3-13 Armor, under LTC Cairns in Division reserve, drove away the Germans with the help of accurate artillery support. Tank recovery operations to repair damaged tracks and return the damaged tanks of 2-13 Armor to action went on for the duration of the night. Nearly all lost tanks were operational again within 48 hours. The next day, May 24, the *attack continued. 2-13 Armor went forward, supporting 3-6 Infantry, and cleared out enemy positions in a forest and captured two artillery batteries. F Co, under CPT John C. Elliott, was sent to assist the 3rd Infantry Division to the west while the rest of 2-13 went into reserve. The light tanks of LTC Carr's 1-13 Armor passed through 2-13's lines and seized the Regimental objective, Torrecchia Nuova. The next day, May 25, Colonel Howze was ordered to seize Giulianello, and the attack jumped off at dawn.*

*Near the town of Valmontone, the 13th Armor engaged the infamous German Hermann Göring Division. 3-13 Armor blocked the road to west while 1-13 flanked the retreating Germans, capturing many. 2-13 Armor's attack went well, but a German artillery shell killed its Executive Officer, Major George Johnson, and the attack stalled. In order to capitalize on their gains, Task Force Howze (consisting of 3-13 Armor and supporting units) was formed to take Velletri and Giulianello. Working well with infantry support, the tanks of both CCB and TF Howze broke through the enemy lines while other armored units were halted by German anti-tank guns. The main highways to Rome, Routes 6 and 7, were opened for an Allied attack by June 2, 1944. During the Battle of Anzio, the 13th Armored Regiment saw its first real combat in the Italian Campaign. Although the fighting here was difficult and not ideal for armored warfare, the 13th Armor secured an Allied breakthrough and helped end the stalemate in Southern Italy. Rome, the Italian capital, was finally within reach.*[39]*}*

---

39    George Howe, *The Battle History of the First Armored Division*, (Washington, D.C.: Combat Forces Press, 1954).

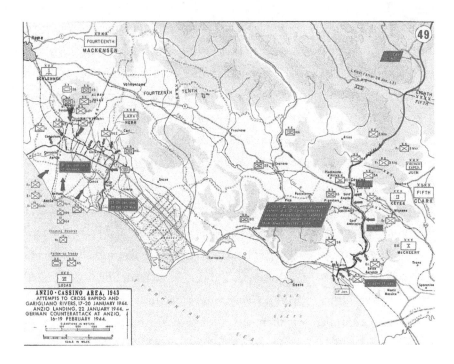

Figure 31: Anzio-Cassino, May 1943 (Wikimedia Commons/Public Domain)

## April 30, 1944

We moved down to the boat this morning and loaded out vehicles on an L.S.T. on the same dock that I landed on in Italy six months ago. The Colonel was invited uptown to have lunch with the Division Commander who was down from the beachhead for a few days. I went out on the pier, sunned myself and read until time to embark. It was an American-operated ship and the evening meal was excellent. We sailed at dark. Couldn't find a lifeboat that was operative.

## May 1, 1944

The night passed without incident and daylight found us in sight of the barrage balloons floating in the sky over Anzio. Surprised to find our convoy of three L.S.T.'s had two liberty ships, a hospital ship, and several small cargo vessels in it in addition to our escort. We moved right into port and disembarked immediately. This is being written just before sunset and as yet I haven't heard an incoming enemy shell. Our first sight as we drove inland was a shockingly large United States cemetery. The sole occupation all day was digging in. Three of us have a temporary dugout with a light steel roof.

**May 2, 1944**

About three this morning we were awakened by the scream and crash of incoming shells. This kept up until almost daylight. Several came into the regimental area, but no damage was done. We had the use of a power shovel and several bulldozers today so really made some progress in getting below ground. The walls of our home are made of empty wooden shell cases that we fill with dirt. We had a roof of light iron over us tonight, good walls and one good end but the other side was wide open.

**May 3, 1944**

The enemy planes came over at three this morning and the show lasted for better than an hour. The ack-ack was terrific making the ground tremble. The planes dived as they bombed, dropping anti-personnel and demolition bombs. This area received a lot of personnel bombs, but no one was injured although a number of vehicles were damaged. General Harmon addressed the officers of the newly arrived units of the Division. Worked most of the day on our C.P. and dug-out and have a much better setup than we had last night.

**May 4, 1944**

Devoted the morning again to our dug-out with a good working detail and made real progress finishing one of the three rooms. We have one large room off of which there are two smaller rooms that will serve as bedrooms. The Colonel and I will occupy one of these and the S-2 and the S-3 the other. The big room will serve as working space for all of us. Our roof has a base steel sheets and wire netting over which we are placing sandbags and dirt. Over to the 34th Division C.P. for a conference on a small scale attack in which we will probably be called upon to furnish a company of mediums.

## May 5, 1944

Negative reports as to an enemy activity during the night. This is being written in our completed subterranean home. We are very nicely set up. Have a skylight which we close over at night. Wet weather would create a problem. 2nd Bn. has a company tied in with one of the artillery Bn.'s doing indirect fire. The 3rd Bn. relieves a G.H.Q.'s Bn. tonight which has been supporting the 34th. Over to watch a tank infantry demonstration. General Alexander put in an appearance.

## May 6, 1944

Were awakened several times during the night by the crash of incoming shells of a heavy caliber. None landed in our area, but the Division HQ took quite a plastering with some casualties. F Co. which I visited this morning fired 1,300 rounds during the night under the direction of the Div. Field Artillery. They drew considerable counter battery, but no one was hurt. Watched a mine field clearance demonstration. We now have our dug out illuminated with electric lights and am about to go to bed in my pajamas (first time since Africa) to the tune of an exploding ammunition dump that the enemy just hit nearby with artillery.

## May 7, 1944

Our assault guns had a few come in on them during the night killing one man and wounding two. Visited 3rd Bn. They have their C.P. set up in a substantial farmhouse and from the top floor windows you have a good view of the enemy lines. Our tanks are farmed out to two infantry regiments and they are all positioned behind our buildings. Now consider our dug-out complete but spent an hour this evening shoveling dirt on top for exercise. We went over preliminary plans tonight for a coming operation of major importance.

Am sorry not to have written to you in so long but this evening is the first time I have had the opportunity and been in position where I could write. Of necessity, even now, this letter will have to be brief.

There is no way of telling whether one is going to be selected for rotation. The percentage of Lieutenant-Colonels is a very small part of the one-half of one percent that return. That is, of that group, the big proportion of officers sent back are Lieutenants and Captains.

(8 May) Didn't get very far with that previous page, a meeting having been called at that point which lasted until after lights out. As the present moment, we have the radio turned on to "Sally of the Axis." Hers is a radio program of popular pieces interspersed with sarcastic digs at the armed forces. She said the other night that Germans had regarded the Anzio beachhead as their best prison camp for the reason that it contains some hundred and thirty thousand Americans and is self-sustaining.

One reason for my not having time to write to you was that for a period of five days I spent most of the daylight hours wielding a pick and shovel and carrying filled sandbags. Until we got that job done there was no opportunity for having light after dark.

No, we are comfortably situated in a well-lighted and ventilated dugout. We have one big room in which an average of eight men in the S-2 and S-3 sections work during the daytime. We have a long narrow skylight, which we cover over with sandbags at night and then turn on the electric lights. In the daytime these bags are removed and there is sufficient light to work by. I am in here but little during the daytime. My tent mate and I are now roommates and we have a small room connecting to one end of the "office." We have our own exit, which is a twisty one, as is the main entrance. Two other officers share a similar room, which opens off of the other end of our "house." The building of this place was really a major construction job. A power shovel and a bulldozer dug a deep and fairly large hole in the ground, then we squared it off with picks and shovels. The sides were lined with wooden ammunition boxes, filled with dirt. Then a framework of heavy timbers was set up and on top of that thick planks. This was then covered with sandbags and on top of that we piled several feet of dirt.

The floor is dirt, but so far, the lace has been free from dampness, but it hasn't rained since we've been here. This actually is the best living quarter's I've been in since we landed in Africa.

### May 8, 1944

Just spent a few minutes standing in the entrance of our dugout listening to the shells whine in. The enemy is indulging in a little evening hate firing from both sides and the shells have been landing all around us. Visited the assault guns of Recon and the 1st Bn. in their firing positions. The 3rd Bn, had a platoon out with the infantry during the night on a foray and are claiming one S.F. and one tank as certain and three probables. Played volleyball this evening and added a little dirt to the roof.

### May 9, 1944

As I write the ack-ack is again making quite a fuss and has been going on and off for almost an hour. Watched it for a while and I could hear a plane droning in the distance. It seemed to be cruising back and forth just close enough to cause them to keep throwing up a barrage for fear that it would make a dive for the harbor. My activities today were devoted to studying plans for the coming operation. The 3rd Bn. lost a tank last night in an effort to recover one they lost the night before.

### May 10, 1944

The telephone seemed to be ringing most of the night. One of the calls brought the bad news that another little foray of the 3rd Bn. resulted in the loss of three tanks and one of the best officers in the outfit losing a leg. Two tanks struck mines and the officer who was wounded had his tank knocked out by an anti-tank gun. Attended a meeting at the Division at which the artillery plans for the coming operations were discussed. As it stands now the Colonel is to command the Division Reserve and the 13th staff are to assist him in that job.

**May 11, 1944**

The 2nd Bn. is in the process of moving to a forward area a company each night. As they move a British outfit is installing dummy tanks in the positions they vacate. They have a new type which they inflate with a dummy gun, etc. Toured the forward areas looking for a spot for an advance C.P. We played six games of volleyball this afternoon. Some heavy artillery shells fell in and about our area just after dark setting an ammo dump on fire.

**May 12, 1944**

Had a ride in one of the artillery observation cub planes over the forward areas with several swings back and forth over the front of our projected operations. Saw many knocked out tanks of ours. The enemy held ground looked peaceful and empty. Attended several meetings that dealt with plans for D-Day and the preliminaries there to.

**May 12, 1944**

We are sitting in our dugout listening to the radio tell of the attack that was launched on what is described as the main Italian front late last night. During the attacks that were made on that front during the first three months of this year, we were where a good share of the shells that were fired passed over our heads. We are hoping that the troops that are making the assault this time have more success than those who tried to get through before.

The principal enemy activity so far as we are concerned is usually after dark. We have resumed our volleyball games although the makeup of the teams isn't the same as it used to be. With the longer evenings, we usually average six games before the enemy guns open up and we have to go underground.

The front lines troops don't lack for fresh meat. Some soldiers in this area have acquired saddled horses that they ride about during the daytime. Several units which have found chickens in the areas that they occupy have not eaten them but instead are enjoying fresh eggs regularly. Passed one boy's dugout the other day hanging out in front there was a canary cage with a couple of canaries in it. Wondered what he was feeding them.

### May 13, 1944

Some heavy ones came in our area during the night but did no damage. Over to the hospital to see the officer from the regiment who lost a leg. He is in good spirits but not well enough so that they can evacuate him. More meetings re D-Day. The logistics of getting the various units into their proper positions for the jump-off is a most complex problem because of the congestion in the road net. Spent the afternoon looking for a position for a forward C.P. Every spot that offers cover is already occupied and most of the other country is covered with ammo.

### May 14, 1944

An air burst last evening in the Division C.P. area killed six men and seriously wounded eleven. They were gathered at a movie. Went back to a pick and shovel and spent most of the day working on a dugout for the forward C.P. Some progress is being made in the attacks on the "main" Italian front.[40] All of the artillery on the beachhead cut loose for a half hour at eight this morning. Presume it was to give the

40    Kesselring's Gustav Line

enemy the impression that we were about to attack. Played volleyball again tonight.

## May 15, 1944

This is being written with a bottle of beer before me and nice piece of cheese. Every soldier in the regiment was issued a bottle of beer today. Another series of conferences regarding various plans for the big show. The French it appears have been doing very well to the south of us. However, that has been in the mountains and it remains to be seen what can be done in the Liri valley. Our new C.P. area received some shelling as the working crews left this afternoon.

## May 16, 1944

There were some planes over last night just after we went to bed and the ack-ack kicked up quite a fuss, but we heard no bombs fall although the enemy artillery set an ammo dump on fire not far from here. Visited the H.Q. of the SSF which is a hot shot infantry outfit made up of Canadians and Americans.[41]

## May 17, 1944

The reports from the southern front continue favorable but they have some distance to go yet before we become excited. Their progress or lack of progress will form the basis of the High Command's deciding whether to order plan "Buffalo" or "Grasshopper" carried out.[42] Now that all reconnaissance that can be made has been carried out, we are falling back into just routine training. Took a sunbath this afternoon and my back is nice and warm tonight.

---

41    The 1st Special Service Force, or SSF, and also called The Devil's Brigade, The Black Devils, The Black Devils' Brigade, and Freddie's Freighters, was an elite American-Canadian commando unit in World War II, under the command of the United States Fifth Army. Ted Kemp, *A Commemorative History: First Special Service Force*, (Dallas, Texas: Taylor Publishing, 1995), p. 15.

42    There were actually four plans: 'Buffalo,' 'Crawdad,' 'Grasshopper,' and 'Turtle,' Each were a branch and sequel to the effort to breakout of the Anzio beachhead. Codenames Operation of World War II, retrieved on March 10, 2020, from https://codenames.info/

**May 17, 1944**

Yesterday we were told that we could send radiograms home, so I sent you one. Being front line troops again, we get the best they can do for us in the way of rations. Today we had fresh new potatoes which was quite a treat for they are normally dehydrated. Our present bivouac is in a vineyard and between the rows of vine in one place peas had been planted. They are now ripe, so our mess sergeant got busy and we have had fresh peas several time lately.

The worst part about sleeping in a dark hole is waking up in the morning. You don't hear the normal sounds since they don't reach you underground and if you are short on sleep someone just has to come and get you. There is hardly a night goes by but what we are awakened by the crash of incoming shells. The enemy shoots at a big ammunition dump that is not far from us and usually sets some part of it on fire during the night.

**May 18, 1944**

The radio announced tonight that Cassino had fallen at last. A heavy price has been paid for that shoulder of that one mountain. Out on a recon. on foot along a branch of the Mussolini Canal.[43] Took my tank sergeant along and he in turn took his dog, Poontang, whose home is in Northern Africa. An S.P. pumped five shells into the Division C.P. just at supper killing eight men and seriously wounding a number of others. Over to the SSF for a confab with two friends from the 106th from Chicago.

**May 19, 1944**

Within a space of fifteen minutes this morning I counted 210 heavy bombers returning from a mission either up the line in Italy or in France. The air conditions were such today that the smoke generators which are going all the time kept us more blanketed out than usual. The first rain since we've been up here fell this afternoon. Progress in the south

43    The Mussolini Canal empties into the Tyrrhenian Sea near Anzio.

continues but has slowed down. Our troops continue to rehearse for the coming operations.

**May 20, 1944**

The Division D.G. held a meeting this morning which was to address to his Commanders on what was almost the eve of what he told us he believed would be the toughest fight this Division has ever been in. Getting into the forward areas for the jump-off will require two nights and tonight was to be the first one. Just before dusk it was announced that it has been postponed. We are, of course, speculating as to the reason.

**May 21, 1944**

Well, the big show seems to be on, and the artillery and some other units are moving into position tonight. Called on a friend of mine who heads up the Ordinance units on the beachhead. He was just leaving to fly down to Naples in a cub and I went down to the air strip from which was leaving to see him off. They keep a small group of fighters operating out of that port. Watch the "Dukws" unloading the Liberty ships from out in the harbor. [44] Progress continues good to the south of us.

**May 21, 1944**

We had our first rain yesterday since we started living underground. Fortunately, it didn't last very long, so our roof wasn't put to a real test. The dust was getting bad and we were glad to have it laid. Even without dust, it is always hazy around here for during the daytime smoke generators are kept going so as to keep the enemy from seeing what is going on and to prevent his observing the effects of his artillery first.

We are playing more volleyball as the days grow longer and have gotten so we play a good game. We either play with two teams of six each or have three teams of five each and play a little round robin depending

---

44    The DUKW, pronounced "duck," is a six-wheel-drive amphibious modification of the 2 ½-ton CCKW trucks used by the U.S. military during World War II and the Korean War.

on the number of officers that turn out. Our two Chaplains are among the better players and we tease them when they miss a shot about what they said under their breath. There is always a lot of betting back and forth, the standard bet being a dollar. The Colonel and I usually choose up where there are but two teams. Last night his side won and tonight mine did, which is about the way it averages out.

Someone discovered a patch of garlic near our hole in the ground mess hall, so we usually pick a little when we have a meat course. If we stay on here, we won't lack for grapes before the summer is out.

**May 22, 1944**

This is being written in a different dugout for I moved up to our forward C.P. just before dark. That part of the H.Q.s we are bringing up closed in after midnight. We received some enemy shells in our area this afternoon, one man being killed. The interdiction fire on the main roads to the forward areas has increased which is not surprising in view of the increased daylight traffic. Tried a number of summary court cases, most "off limits" in Naples.

**May 22, 1944**

There are no natives where we are now, all of them having been moved out of here. The homes in this section are substantial nice new ones, this being an area which has only been available for cultivation since the Mussolini regime. However, the houses are gradually being knocked down by shell fire.

Just now we have a couple of young aviators staying with us. They are from bomber groups and have been on a large number of combat missions. The purpose in sending them to front line outfits is to give them some idea of how the ground combat troops live and to acquaint them with our equipment and methods of operation. We have had a number of them with us for a short time. They are nice boys but seem like such kids.

Don't be concerned if there is a considerable break between this and my next letter. We are going to be busy starting tomorrow morning.

## The Break Out

### May 23, 1944

H hour which was at 0630 preceded by a half-hour's intensive artillery preparation. The plan of attack called for the elaborate aerial bombardment and we saw the first flights come over on schedule but there was a ground mist over the target area, so they were unable to unload. It became worse and there was no aerial activity all day. Shortly after crossing the line of departure the second Bn. hit a mine field and lost thirty-one tanks. The first objective, however, was reached and work went on all night retrieving tanks.

### May 24, 1944

The Maintenance crews did a magnificent job all night withdrawing from the mine field and putting back into action twelve tanks. No mines were found about the railroad track and the tanks passed over and made good progress but encountered more A.P. fire. Our job as Commanders of the Division Reserve hasn't amounted to more so far than acting as a dispatching system. With progress all along the line we moved the C.P. across the canal just before dark and occupied a house.

### May 25, 1944

Moved at 0300 behind 3rd Bn. Spent a very uneasy two hours during the course of our march because we had to travel a good share of the distance on an R.R. right of way and were in full view of the enemy during that period. Set up the C.P. in a group of wrecked buildings just across HY-7 and a short distance above Cisterna. The area hadn't been cleared of enemy and we received sniper fire throughout the day. The tanks pushed through to all objectives. George Johnson of whom there are no finer was K.I.A.

## May 26, 1944

At daylight we joined the Colonel who was with the 2nd Bn. A new plan created Task Force Howze which consisted of the 13th A.R. (- 1st, 2nd, Bns. & Recon) and placed us under the 3rd Division. We spearheaded an attack towards Artena. The Colonel with the forward elements and I moved the C.P. up behind. Got into some mean artillery fire several times. Traffic badly snarled. Saw much knocked out enemy equipment and badly mangled dead. Our losses light. Infantry choking roads moving up behind us.

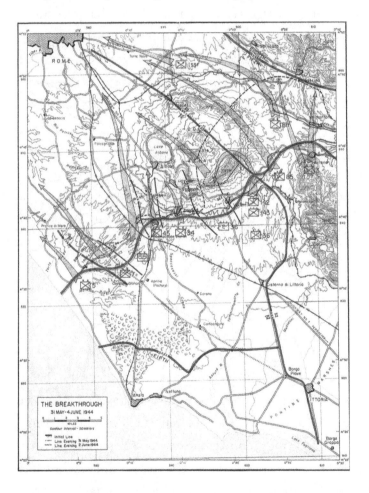

Figure 32: Shifting from Anzio, 1944 (Wikimedia Commons/Public Domain)

## May 27, 1944

Have the main H.Q.'s C.P. in a house on the outskirts of Giulianello with forward C.P. up with the 3rd Bn. three miles ahead. The Colonel is a one-man staff in himself using the rest of us as messengers. He takes off in his tank, loses communication, which all adds up to much confusion and inefficiency. I told him he was doing too much himself and was squelched. I won't raise that issue again but the first opportunity with any prospect at all in it shows up, I am moving on. Extended our advance somewhat but 3rd Infantry still not established with us.

## May 28, 1944

Enemy attacked during night and forward C.P. withdrawn about a mile. A heavy artillery barrage believed to be friendly fell on 6th infantry killing Bn. C.O. and twenty-one others with many wounded.[45] Found our C.P. sitting in an exposed position at dawn with everyone asleep. Routed them out and moved them into a defiladed position. The forward road net heavily and accurately interdicted by artillery fire and I had many close escapes. The 3rd Infantry attacked during the course of the night through our positions and we pulled back into reserve.

## May 29, 1944

Since the night of the 22nd – 23rd until last night I haven't had more than two hours of sleep in one stretch and there were but few stretches. When I was having difficulty staying awake, I took the issue Benzedrine sulphate tablets. Just at daybreak I saw six B-26 bombers going out over the enemy lines. The ack-ack was light but accurate and one plane burst into flames and plummeted to earth. Only one parachute opened up. There was increased artillery fire on the part of the enemy, and we had one right in our C.P. area, one boy being seriously wounded.

---

45    6th Battalion, Gordon Highlanders from the UK.

## May 29, 1944

We have been attacking and moving since the jump-off in the big push that started out from here to meet the forces coming up from the south. The second day after the drive commenced, we left our holes and have been staying in houses when we weren't moving at night. We don't have time to dig in during such a moving situation and these thick-walled Italian houses afford a good deal of protection. Some have been wrecked but our present abode hasn't been touched. The natives weren't here when we came in and haven't returned yet.

We have taken hundreds of German prisoners but at considerable cost. Have passed large quantities of enemy supplies and all kinds of knocked out guns, motor transports, etc. We are back in beautiful mountain country again. The dust is terrific with all this heavy traffic on dirt roads.

## May 30, 1944

Our immediate area took quite a pounding during the night from enemy artillery fire. I made a trip back to visit the other elements of the regiment who were engaged on the drive up the Anzio road towards Rome. They have met stout resistance and were taking considerable losses particularly as to tank commanders who are being killed by snipers. Their right over there is bringing a stronger reaction than that on our front.

## May 30, 1944

Conditions are somewhat stabilized for the moment and I made a trip to the rear today and picked up a few things.

Our present home seems to have been a small-scale winery. There are two large rooms with a big open doorway between them. One we found empty and that we have rigged up as our C.P. The other room is full of great big barrels and there is a wine cellar leading out of it. Investigation has shown that the cellar is flooded so no efforts have been made to see what the Germans left when they pulled out. There is an upstairs floor with four good-sized rooms. The officers sleep in two of them and the men use the other two. This is a noisy spot for there is some heavy artillery out in the gully just below us and they fire right over us. The concussion jolts the building and makes the candles flicker.

By the time you receive this, I imagine there will be a notice in the papers of the death of the stepson of a very prominent figure in the American Army.[46] This lieutenant, who was a member of the regiment, was killed in action yesterday. He joined us as a replacement last winter.

This is about as attractive a section of the country as we have been in since sailing from Africa. The mountains are lovely, and the valleys are carpeted with as fine a stand of grain as I have ever seen. Unfortunately, the dust makes things difficult when you are on the road, but we can't have everything. Everyone who makes even a short trip comes in with his face looking like it had been shoveling soft coal all day. Keep my face clean between trips but my shirt and overall collars are another matter.

### May 31, 1944

A new push is set for tomorrow and I went forward to pick a spot for our C.P. The roads are all under active artillery fire and a trip along the main one is a pretty lively affair. The spot I selected for the C.P. is about 1,500 yards from the enemy line. Walked up on the hill back of it to look around and was driven off by sniper fire. Our C.O. is certainly in everyone's hair and our staff is far from its one time happy family set-up. Enemy artillery got into our positions just after dark hitting and burning three M-7s.

### June 1, 1944

We started moving at 0200 hours and despite difficulties on the road due to congested traffic we're set up in our C.P., which is an Italian home,

---

46    General George C. Marshall's stepson, Second Lieutenant Allen Tupper Brown was killed in action on May 29, 1944, leading his platoon in an attack on Velletri. Frank A. Settle Jr., *General George C. Marshall and the Atomic Bomb,* (Santa Barbara, California: Praeger Publishers, 2016), p. 95.

before daylight. The attack which started at 0500 was preceded by a heavy artillery preparation which brought the plaster down on us. The 30th infantry drove from Artena across towards Valmonte while forces pushed towards HY-6 on their left. We were bothered by snipers and lost six tank commanders. Our tanks didn't make as good progress as the infantry. I went out to where they were in the armored car with some instructions from the Colonel. They shelled us heavily while I was there. The planes were over tonight, and we have some butterfly bombs landing in our area. Slept just on the outside of a native dugout.[47]

**June 2, 1944**

The third Bn. pushed off again at daylight and we moved the C.P. into the spot they had just vacated. Much confusion and changing of orders. We were placed under the 88th Division, then back to the 3rd, and then back to Corps, all within a matter of hours. Snipers still being cleaned out in the area through which the tanks have passed. Long columns of infantry continue to trudge ahead. Saw many German bodies. Our tanks got up and established astride of HY-6. A 155 Howitzer battery set up right in our area during the night and deprived us of what little sleep we could have gotten.

## Rome

**June 3, 1944**

I made for the third Bn. at daylight and was there when they received orders dropped from a cub plane to continue on up the Hy. We hardly came to a full halt until dark and by then we had seen the dome of St. Peter's and had entered the fringes of Rome. Several time when the tanks were moving cross country, I was in my peep on the main road with no one between me and my driver and the enemy. Saw a column of their

47    A Butterfly Bomb was a German 2-kilogram anti-personnel submunition used by the Luftwaffe during the Second World War.

horse-drawn artillery, which was trying to withdraw, cut to pieces by our guns. Became tangled up in an infantry tank attack on a strong point and spent an unpleasant half hour in a ditch while a flack wagon poured fire just over our heads.

Figure 33: From left to right: Major Gabler, Lieutenant Colonel Gardiner, Major General Keyes, Brigadier General Fredericks, and Lieutenant General Clark on the outskirts of Rome, June 1944
(Photograph from the Patricia Issel Collection)

### June 4, 1944

Moved out at daylight with the third Bn. which was carrying on its tanks member of the SSF. We went right down HY-6 to the edge of Rome proper before encountering any opposition. The lead tank was knocked out at that point by an A.T. gun, and quite a fight developed, and the infantry took some casualties. Found myself in a hot spot and had to take to the ditch. Was just starting back to the rear to report that situation when up came General Clark, the Corps. C.G., etc. I gave them the situation. Colonel

H was directed to take a tank Bn. and some infantry in a drive towards the city from the North. I accompanied it. Just at dusk all resistance stopped, and the troops continued right into the city to secure the bridges.

### June 5, 1944

The enemy strafed and bombed along the Hy during the night and we had a number of casualties. Moved the force north about four miles to just south of HY-5. We are no longer with the SSF and now await Corps orders. Took a run into town and drove around the "Eternal City". Just inside the city proper I passed some burned out enemy tanks and there were German dead still lying in the streets. There were streams of military traffic passing on through the city and I was surprised to see no rowdy nor drunken soldiers. The public was in a holiday mood, but the Army is still fighting.

**V-Mail[48]**

**June 5, 1944**

The past few days have been the same. Fighting, fighting, moving and driving on and on. Even with the big prize now ours, we are still pressing on. Everyone is worn and tired out, but of course the enemy is equally so, and they are trying to keep hot on his heels so that he can't get dug in. Our movement has been so swift that we haven't been able to keep supplied with the proper maps. My picture might show up some place along the line. Not for any reason except that I happened to be on hand when we were visited by the Army Commander as we were fighting in the outskirts of the city yesterday morning. I walked a short distance with him, and the photographers were busily engaged in taking his picture during that time. At the moment we are occupying the home of a native in the suburbs. We

---

48    V-mail, short for Victory Mail, was a hybrid mail process used during the World War II as the primary and secure method to correspond with soldiers stationed abroad. To reduce the cost of transferring an original letter through the military postal system, a V-mail letter would be censored, copied to film, and printed back to paper upon arrival at its destination. The V-mail process is based on the earlier British Airgraph process. Edward Wells, *Mailshot: A History of the Forces Postal Services,* (London: Defense Postal & Courier Services, 1987), p. 107.

just find a suitable spot, have one of our boys who speaks Italian tell the owner to clear our certain space and we move in.

### June 6, 1944[49]

We moved again just after daylight a few miles so some G-3 could straighten out the lines on his map. The eight o'clock morning news said that the German news agency a few hours before had announced that the long-expected Anglo-American invasion of the France had commenced with air borne landings at an early hour. We were left unmolested all day so listened to each news broadcast. The story was in most general terms with emphasis on the immensity of the operation and the large number of paratroopers that had been dropped. They claimed to be getting ashore in good order.

### June 7, 1944

Spent the morning in Rome and visited St. Peter's which is certainly an impressive place. Also walked around the Coliseum and other points of interest. There are troops still marching through the city and a constant stream of heavy military traffic passing westward and northward over the bridges. The street cars have resumed operations so apparently not much damage was done to the utility system before the enemy pulled out. Shortly after noon we received an order to start movement immediately and I reported to the 85th Division for orders since we have been attached to them.[50] They assigned a number of troops to us and we went into an assembly area about thirty miles N. of Rome.

## We Move On

### June 8, 1944

Only two hours of sleep during the night as we were working on plans

---

49    D-Day in Normandy, France.

50    The 85th entered the Italian capital of Rome on June 5 1944, and advanced to Viterbo before being relieved on June 10.

for the employment of Task Force Howze as it's known. Our mission was to precede the Division in its advance on the Corps' objective. We moved on two roads and encountered no resistance until mid-afternoon. Passed many vehicles and horses along the road that our Air Force had knocked out. Joined the infantry in an attack in which they assisted the tanks in overcoming a strong point. Had to hunt a hole with the boys several times. Moved the C.P. up again tonight. We encountered a number of blown bridges.

Figure 34: Destroyed German airplane at an airport near Viterbo, Italy, on June 16, 1944 (Photograph from the U.S. Army Signal Corps, Gift of Regan Forrester, from the Collection of The National World War II Museum)

### June 9, 1944

The Colonel elected to remain at the C.P. for a change this morning and sent me up to help coordinate the advance of our elements. We pushed on without making any contact and were working down on the rail and road center Viterbo when we received word not to advance any further. We just sat most of the day and were finally told that our force had been "pinched out" by elements that were also converging on Viterbo from both our flanks and that we were to be relieved. Pulled back to our C.P. site of last night. We are in beautiful mountain lake country, the best we've seen in Italy.

## Resting and Refitting

**June 10, 1944**

A movement order which came in during the night had us on our way shortly after daylight. The Division is assembling for what is promised to be a week of rest and refitting. We had the extreme good fortune to be assigned as a bivouac site an area alongside lake "Bracciano" which is a point where the Italians once had a seaplane base. We moved into the buildings which we found in good shape and no one lost any time in making for the water which proved fine. The view is lovely and once again the war seems far away.

**June 10, 1944**

We lead a life of extremes and contrasts. For days we have gone with but little sleep and not much to eat. Bathing and changing clothes has just been one of those things that wasn't being done. We have been constantly on the move and having to be careful at every turn that we didn't expose ourselves to the direct fire of the enemy.

Yesterday afternoon our force was ordered to remain in position which another one passed through us. This morning we pulled back some distance and I haven't heard a shot fired all day.

Our present bivouac is almost too good to be true. To start with this is the most attractive spot in Italy that we have seen. The mountains are similar to those that one sees in Tennessee and there are numerous lakes. Don't know just how we happened to rate it, but the regiment has really an ideal spot on the shore of a lake that is miles in extent. It is one of these crater lakes and our unit is distributed along the shore and up the sides of a slope that rises away from the water. For about a half mile from the water, the ground is clear, and, at present, the natives are just finishing cutting the hay that grows there. The ground above the hayland to the top of the ridge which is another half mile is heavily timbered with fine big trees.

*{The entries between June 10–15 were about Gardiner's time experiencing some AR&R on Lake Bracciano.}*

As to which unit was the first into Rome is a question which will never be settled.[51] The saying that all roads lead to Rome is true and there were groups pressing forward on all of the roads from the south and east and about the same time and all of them claim to have been first. We think we were first and have certain basis for saying so. The road we were on was the main road into the city and all of the press representatives congregated back of our units on that road. We had made more progress on that highway than the troops on the others and all of the high-ranking commanders dropped by to see how things were progressing. The reporters were where they thought the first break through was going to occur.

As I say, once resistance began to break up, it collapsed all along the line but, if we weren't the first in, we were tied with whoever was. I can lay no claim to being first in but was one of many others. So far as any Catholic priest being with me, that is erroneous. I know we fired at some monks who sat up in a window of a monastery that was just inside the city and watched us with field glasses. We were being shelled at the

---

51    Everyone wanted to be first into Rome, but it is wildly believed that at 1530 hours on June 4, the all-draftee 88th became the first division to enter the city. Although overshadowed by the Normandy invasion two days later, the capture of Rome was a significant victory for the Allies and a welcome event for the Romans. Jami Bryan, "The 88th Division in Italy," retrieved on March 12, 2020, from https://armyhistory.org/the-88th-infantry-division-in-italy/

time, so we chased them away from the windows with a few rounds fired in their direction.

I saw dead German soldiers in the gutters of the streets in Rome for two days after the place fell. They had been killed by our forces as they advanced into the city. While there was considerable fighting in the outskirts of the city, there was no fighting in the downtown part that amounted to anything and consequently but slight damage there.

We are continuing on at our summer resort although our lease seems to be about up. I have been going in swimming twice a day lately, once in the afternoon and again in the evening after volleyball. Have acquired a pretty good tan on my back. We have a rubber boat that we use in the afternoons. An aquaplane put in an appearance this afternoon.

### June 16, 1944

The Division has instituted quite a liberal pass policy into Rome in an effort to give all of the boys an opportunity to visit the place before we pull out. I went in this morning with two other officers. Did some shopping and thoroughly covered the city from the sightseeing standpoint and paid St. Peter's another visit. We were indignant to be denied entrance to the Grand Hotel which had been opened to the public until yesterday and has now been taken over by the P.B.S. and A.F.H.Q. Letters from home saying the "Chicago American" called Elizabeth to say that a Catholic priest and I were the first into Rome. That's stretching the hometown boy makes good.

### June 17, 1944

Movement orders came in, so we are just about to say goodbye to our summer resort. Our tank bulldozers did leave today, and they are moving by transporters. Was President and Law member of a General Court which met today. We convicted a man of going to sleep on post in the zone of the interior and sentenced him to two years' confinement. Don't view the coming operation with any pleasure. Working for the Colonel is difficult in action for he tries to do everything himself.

**June 18, 1944**

There wasn't much to do since everyone was getting ready for the move, so I was able to get some letters written and packages mailed. The news tonight was to the effect that our troops had succeeded in cutting of the Cherbourg peninsula. I wouldn't be surprised but what the whole German war machine might come toppling down once a real base is established in France and our troops begin to advance into that country.

**June 18, 1944**

Two officers and I went into Rome in the morning and stayed there into the evening. The stores are only open in the mornings and we didn't have too much time to look around. There is very little to be had except in heavier items that aren't suitable for sending home. None of the things that I sent you are special at all, but they are something from the Eternal City.

There is plenty of clothing to be had in Rome but there is a definite scarcity of food. Very few restaurants are in operation and they have but little to offer. All soldiers who go into town on pass are supplied with K rations for the trip. We ate at a restaurant at noon and at a hotel in the evening. One thing that burned us up as it always does the line troops, was to find that the nicer hotels had all been taken over by the base sections and made off-limits to us. We took the town and yet these rear echelon guys came in and took all the gravy. That was also true in Oran, Tunis and Naples.

The Tiber River is very dirty yet is filled with houseboats. These places seem to be frequented by the more well-to-do and are used primarily for sunbathing. They also serve as boat houses and there seems to be a lot of rowing on the river. We saw a few people in swimming but I can't believe that is very popular since the water is so dirty. The main streets are lined with beautiful tress, the boughs of which interlace over the middle of the street. There are many lovely well-kept parks throughout the city. For the most part, the natives that you see on the streets are a better-looking type than those one sees in Naples.

## Pursuit Renewed

**June 19, 1944**

We say goodbye to our pleasant lakeside home during the morning. The way the march was scheduled it took four hours to put the regiment on the road. Our route of march took us over some largely mountain country. Am glad we didn't have to fight through the area. We skirted the town of Civitavecchia whose port and adjacent waters were filled with shipping. Looked as though they had transplanted all of the Anzio barrage balloons there. The many dumps, airports and perambulator tents that we saw along the way made us realize how far the front had progressed beyond us. We only moved forty-five miles. Camped in open field.

**June 20, 1944**

Another march through attractive country; this time on a HY that skirted the sea. The enemy retreat through this section must have been "according to plan" for there were practically no destroyed vehicles or equipment along the way and there were frequent demolitions. We marched some fifty miles to a point S. of Grosseto. Traffic conditions are very bad with an army trying to move up this one road in which there are many places where there is only one-way traffic. To a meeting of unit C.O.s at Division. We are taking over a sector of the front tomorrow with the Pisa-Florence line as our objective.

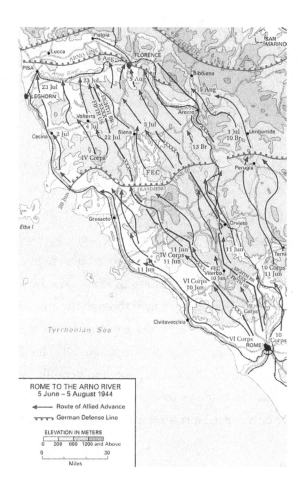

Figure 35: Rome to the Arno River, 1944
(Wikimedia Commons/Public Domain)

## June 21, 1944

Even with this the longest day in the year we were on our way by sun-up. I took a run ahead of the column to do a little reconnaissance while the Colonel went by Div. H.Q. for orders. Found the outpost line of the outfit we were supposed to pass through and continued for about a mile on foot. Concluded if I didn't want to spend the rest of the war in a German prison camp that I had better turn back. The Colonel returned with an attack order and we soon had our forces underway. They were not bothered until they reached the foot of a mountain on which stood Montemassi. There we drew artillery fire. Our own planes came over and bombed our column securing a direct hit on one of our ambulances containing three patients, a driver, and two medics.

### June 22, 1944

Was up most of the night arranging for the passage through one side of our force of a column from the group on our right. They had been stopped cold by a blown bridge, the repair of which was beyond the capabilities of our engineers. A platoon of our tanks which had worked up a mountain trail and became completely isolated had a whole column of enemy horse drawn artillery pass by them during the night but didn't open fire. Our forces collected over one hundred prisoners today. We were given another Bn. of infantry since our column, by making more progress than the other two forces, is getting to be the main axis of advance.

### June 23, 1944

I spent most of the day in a peep chasing up one column and then the other trying to keep the C.P. advised as to the Colonel's wishes, be around enough to answer some of the General's questions when he comes by and generally seeing to it that the various elements of our command are kept closed up behind us so they won't get out off from us in this heavy traffic. The dust is perfectly awful. You just aren't able to recognize one a few minutes after they have been on the road. Every community we enter blossoms out with men and boys armed with a wide assortment of weapons who claim to be "Partisans" and carrying on guerilla warfare behind the German lines.

### June 24, 1944

During the night the enemy artillery harassed the batteries attached to our force causing some casualties. Moved the C.P. before lunch to an olive grove at the base of the hill on which the town of Montemassi is perched. Our forces still confined to two roads made little progress because of demolitions and very stiff enemy resistance. Visited both of our forces and got into some hot artillery fire on one side. Heavy tanks are playing a major part in the present delaying action. A whole lot of heavy artillery has now come into firing position where they can support us.

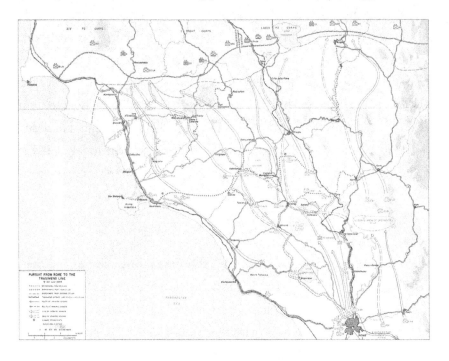

Figure 36: Rome to the Trasimeno Line
(Center of Military History/Public Domain)

**June 25, 1944**

First reports having shown that the enemy had pulled back again during the night we moved the C.P. up. The spot we originally selected was receiving artillery fire when the column started to arrive, so it pulled off the road and halted for a couple of hours until it cleared up. Went into the town of Prata with our first troops to enter that city and we were widely acclaimed despite the fact that our artillery had battered it rather severely. Our boys are doing a good job at this mountain fighting. We knocked out two Mark VI's and picked up 125 prisoners. Got caught in some nasty shelling which hit a number of infantrymen that I happened to be with.

**June 26, 1944**

The first order of the morning was to vacate our building to make way for the Division C.P which was moving up. I was burned up because there was no reason for our moving. It worked out fine, however, for we found a better set of buildings in a mining community which we occupied. More demolition troubles, rugged terrain and stiffening resistance slowed down our advance. We did succeed in taking Montieri. I commuted between our two columns. We received considerable fire, mostly artillery. There were some vehicles knocked out. Most of the casualties were in the infantry. Our boys are ravaging the potato crop in every garden they find.

**June 27, 1944**

We joined up with the columns that had been moving on our flanks this morning but succeeded in making very little progress to our front. Enemy resistance again strong and we succeeded in destroying three of their tanks. I climbed up on a mountain which gave wonderful observations and I could see enemy vehicles retiring along numerous roads. The artillery got on some of them, but we were unable to secure any assistance from the air. Casualties from that portion of the regiment operating with CCB are running higher than ours. Moved the C.P. up on a mountain top this evening.

**June 28, 1944**

Again, we moved slowly, this time the trees that had been felled across the road being so plentiful as to be quite a factor. There were two enemy S.P.'s along the road which our boys had taken care of which will never bother us again. Moved the C.P. into a little village that had been off the beaten path enough to escape being knocked out. Lovely mountain country with glorious views. Too bad it is obscured by the dust and destruction of battle. The Colonel still trying to personally fight the whole war from the head of the column. The General called to say he wanted us to get forward tonight. When I got up to the Colonel, everyone was asleep. Organized a party of engineers and infantry to check the road ahead of us for mines. Prowled around till daylight. No enemy action.

### June 29, 1944

There was no contact this morning, the enemy again having fallen back. It wasn't long before we ran into the usual blown bridges and mined bypasses. Our two columns struggled up the roads that clung to the sides of steep mountains and labored across bypasses that the engineers constructed or found for us. One column had to drop clear down into the valley floor and worm its way along the creek bed for several miles before it found a place to get out because of a bridge that had been blown by the "Partisans" who are more of a nuisance than they are a help. Enjoyed the luxury of a bath in a nice mountain stream flowed by where we camped for the night.

### June 30, 1944

We moved again. This time to a point on a high hill, vicinity [San Dalmazio]. Resumed a two-column formation again and while one force came under heavy fire late in the afternoon, the principal obstacle to our progress was demolitions and mines. In several cases after many vehicles had come down the same track, one would blow up on a mine. Engineer equipment breaking down all the time.

### July 1, 1944

Took off first thing up the route that we have been using that I haven't been over. It was extremely difficult because of the many bypasses that had been constructed in the rough ground. Found the engineers struggling with more and more demo and mines. CCB had clearer sailing than we did and got ahead of us today. Moved the C.P. up to another mountaintop near Montecastelli. We got back onto ground where we could make some progress and both columns were in contact with the enemy at dark. I was a short distance from one of our tanks when it hit a mine. Four civilians who were standing beside the road were seriously injured.

**July 2, 1944**

Moved the C.P. early to the grounds of an estate about which several peacocks strutted just outside of Pomarance. From there we had a perfect view of the arena where our force battled all day in an endeavor to continue the advance and cut HY-68. The enemy action from an artillery standpoint was the heaviest we have encountered. We had a column struggling up a creek bottom which was plastered by "Neblewerfers" all day. I spent most of the morning with one operative tank, most of the rest being out because thrown tracks. CCA took some heavy losses on our right and had to pull back.

**July 3, 1944**

We continued our attack during the night and succeeded in getting a few heavy vehicles and some infantry into the little town of "Mazzolla", which rests astride the ridge up which our boys have been trying to advance. The enemy reacted strongly and shelled that place heavily all day as well as plastering our other forward elements. I made several trips up to the tanks where the Colonel was and drove through considerable fire. Organized and got underway all of the recovery vehicles we could muster and crews which went up under cover of darkness to retrieve as many of our knocked-out vehicles that they could.

### July 4, 1944

Our maintenance crews were under fire most the night but fortunately it was not accurate and they succeeded in getting out all of the tanks which could have been moved short of major shop jobs. This was a day of conflicting orders largely brought about by a report that a major counterattack was about to be launched on our front. Our infantry made a march out of positions, were turned around and sent back in again and then recalled a second time. We withdrew all of our force except the recon elements back across Cecina River after dark. The artillery was pulled back and we set up a defensive line. Enemy activity less.

### July 5, 1944

No counterattack having developed, we were ordered to put our strong recon, establish contact with the enemy and determine whether or not Volterra was held. After they had been out for some time the C.G. called in and said he had to have that information by three o'clock. He had it all right, but it cost one dead, one seriously wounded and seven missing but believed dead. I had watched them for a while from a hilltop and at that time they were still moving in their vehicles but drawing heavy fire. A.R.C.T. of the 88th Div. came in today and plans were laid for an attack tomorrow in which we would participate. It was called off just before midnight for some reason.

### July 5, 1944

This is the first letter that I have written since June 19th. I am sorry that there has been such a break in my letters to you but there just hasn't been the time nor the opportunity.

We moved out the day after I last wrote to you and two days later were again in contact with the enemy. Since that time, we have been in action continuously. The enemy has continued to fight a delaying action and has been retiring in good order without too much loss to himself.

For two weeks he would pull out during the night, blow up all the bridges behind him, plant mines, and fell trees and demolish houses that would block roads. Some places could be bypassed but it was always slow and difficult work for the country has been just one mountain ridge after another. You would be able to proceed perhaps several miles before you encountered the enemy. He would wait until the leading elements were up close enough to [ensure] a kill before firing. It usually cost you a tank or armored car and some men to find where he had elected to delay us by other than obstructions. Then you had to take steps to drive back that force and you might be hung up the balance of the day and into the night. His normal procedure was to place a heavy tank supported by infantry just around a curve in the road and the other side of a blown bridge or slide. You would be unable to deploy and could use only a small force against him. We have apparently reached a point now where the enemy has decided to make a stand and we have been trying to break through his present position for three days now. As usual when he elects to make a stand, he is on high ground looking right down on top of us.

This has been beautiful mountain country all the way and it is too bad that we don't have time to enjoy it. Just now we are hidden under the trees that surround a very large house or I should say mansion which apparently belonged to someone of means. The natives have learned to clear out of our way because each house on the line of march is usually shelled heavily. This particular place has escaped so far. The sound of exploding shells is so much a part of our everyday life that we don't pay any attention to that, but we find the scream of the peacocks that strut around here very annoying. Our boys have threatened to shoot them, but they don't mean it although if they thought they were good to eat they would probably do so.

While we are, of course interested in the news from France and Russia, we don't have much time to think about the other fronts for we are too busy with our own problems. While this has been what has been described as a rearguard and delaying action, it has taken a heavy toll of officers and I've lost a number of my very good friends since we started out this last time. The fact that a higher proportion of officers are lost in this kind of operation comes from the reason that most of the fighting occurs at the head of a column where the proportion of officers is always high.

This war is being brought home closer to more and more families every day, but I suppose a great many people still don't appreciate what is going on and never will although they will think they do. Certainly, those who have their sons and husbands in the combat zones don't have to go to the movies to get some conception of what this war means.

Have had another ride in a cub since we took off. It was, I believe, the best plane ride I've ever had. It was a beautiful day and we flew over mountain country where the villages are all perched on the tops of mountains and it looked just like a model below us with all of the streams, forests, twisty roads and little cultivated spots. We flew quite high and I had the window open so I could look through my field glasses without any distortion.

Some place along the line our kitchen crew acquired a gosling. He has been named "Peep" because he is always making a sound like that. "Peep" is still small being in the fuzz stage but is growing fast and seems to be happy in his new association. Operating the way they are, most of the men have to prepare their own meals since the kitchen trucks can't get to them. While they have been ordered not to, there is a great deal of foraging done to supplement the 10 and 1 ration with which they are supplied.[52] As a column fights its way forward, it passes homes from which the natives have fled. The soldiers acquire a few chickens and ducks and the potato crop has suffered at the hand of the troops.

I don't know how they feel about it after we have passed through, but the natives always welcome us with flowers and press wine on the men

52    He is referencing the food parcel issued to troops intended to feed one meal for ten men.

when a non-fighting entry into an area permits them to be around. A group was standing by the side of the road, watching us go by the other day, and cheering the men on when one of the tanks hit a mine which had been buried in the road and over which twelve tanks had already passed.

### July 6, 1944

The mission of our force was to maintain contact with the enemy in our zone. After yesterday's loss to our one recon outfit, it took a lot of prodding to keep our patrols pushed out to contact. Some enemy activity was observed and plastered with artillery. News came late in the day of the death of the Exec. of the 3rd Bn. who was one of our old standbys and who had been in command of the Bn. since the C.O. was evacuated about a week ago. The Colonel was going to send me over to assume command until he found the Bn. was split up and working directly under the infantry.

### July 7, 1944

Took a run over to the 3rd Bn. to see how they were. Failed to take the correct turn off at one point which I realized about the time I was due to come under enemy small arms' fire. What made it particularly ticklish until we were able to turn around and beat it back was that it was in a barren stretch with no cover or defilade. Fortunately for some reason they didn't open fire on us. Found the 3rd Bn. in a piece of very difficult terrain with morale at a rather low ebb due largely to having their Exec. and two Company C.O.'s killed in the past several days. Their mission as was that of all the units on the 1st A.D. front was purely defensive. Another infantry division is pouring into this area.

### July 8, 1944

The 88th Division attacked through us at 0230 hours, the only support we furnished being one tank company. Watched the progress of the battle from the shadow of trees on the hilltop where we are camped. Progress was good, the main enemy resistance coming from artillery fire. Saw four heavy explosions with the enemy positions which I assumed were demolitions to cover their withdrawal. Loafed about in the sun and had a good rest.

### July 8, 1944

Yesterday the mailman brought me the fishing tackle; today one of my friends presented me with a reed pole (he had snitched it from an Italian vineyard where it had been used to support a grape vine), so all I need now is a stream or lake and a little time. The boys gathered around when I opened the envelope containing the flies as though it was a box of candy. It represented a touch of one of the pleasures at home that we had almost forgotten about.

Our group was relieved early today by another unit that has passed on through. We were more than overdue for a rest since our equipment was in need of maintenance, the men were tired, and we had lost quite a few key officers since the last push started. What the immediate future holds for us remains to be seen but we are hoping that it will involve a bivouac near the water. Since we left the lake, I have had one bath in a mountain stream and one out of my helmet. There wasn't an opportunity for anything more except shaving, which I always manage to work in some time during the day.

From the bivouac we could watch the fighting all day on the hills opposite us. I alternated between watching and dozing in the sun. For weeks a small group of us have taken turns standing by the command radio at night so that there would always be an officer on duty to answer calls. There is always an operator on duty as well. Following the taking over of our sector, we can relax on such duties so there will be no "graveyard watch" for anyone tonight.

Commencing with the Italian campaign we were required for uniformity purposes to adopt the British radio procedure. For some time, it seemed rather off but now we think nothing of it. We frequently hear the Germans jabbering away and we always know when we are near the French troops for they use the same kind of sets that we do.

**July 9, 1944**

Another day of sitting. The dope now seems to be that our movement is being held up until the 91st Division clears the road net that we will have to use. The 88th continued to make some progress but a heavy rainstorm made a mess of all the side roads and movement of equipment and supplies was brought almost to a standstill.

**July 9, 1944**

We are still sitting today, and the fighting has now progressed beyond our sight although we can hear the guns. There were planes over during the night, which is the first time we have heard any in quite a while. They didn't bother us however, and we had no shelling during the night, the enemy artillery apparently having been forced to pull back. We had a heavy shower around noon, but it cleared off this afternoon and I went for a walk. One can get plenty of exercise in a short distance for it is either up or down no matter which way you go.

## The Division Reorganizes

**July 10, 1944**

This reorganization of the Division just about cuts its tank strength in half and eliminates the armored regiments. The tanks now are formed in three battalions as against six as formerly although the new Bns. are somewhat stronger. This reorganization means that my job ceases to exist. The Colonel some time ago said that if I wanted to command one of the new Bns. he would recommend me. I said I certainly would as against going to a replacement pool. Today General Harmon told me he was going to give me command of one of the battalions. Don't know what the other choice would have been.

**July 11, 1944**

Apparently, the Col. is due to get one of the Combat commands. He didn't ask me to be his Executive for I know there is a vacancy there, so I suppose he didn't want me. The trouble with taking over this new Bn. is going to be in securing an adequate staff for we have lost so many good men. Two of the Bn. Executive officers were killed, and one transferred out. I hope we won't be too rushed on this deal and will have a reasonable opportunity to get well set before we take off again. Took a sunbath and a hike this afternoon.

**July 12, 1944**

We moved this morning to a point near Bolgheri where the Division is assembling. Our area is a pleasant one in an olive orchard on a hill which overlooks the sea some five miles distant. The Col. and I drove down to the beach this afternoon and went swimming. The water was rough and there was a strong under tow so I didn't venture out beyond where I could touch bottom. We stayed on and had a picnic supper. Am certainly going to regret the breaking up of the regiment and I must say I don't particularly relish taking over a Bn. again.

*{The entries for July 13–15 entailed the time the division reorganized and Gardiner was waiting it out in an Italian Olive Orchard.}*

**July 16, 1944**

We indeed had some news. Heard this morning that General Harmon had been relieved, and his successor was on the job.[53] That was confirmed as the day wore on and this evening a group of us were invited to meet

53    Major General Ernest N. Harmon was replaced by Major General Vernon Prichard, who led the 1st A.D. for the rest of the war.

the new General whose name is Pritchard and whom it developed I had met in Chicago through the Bradys when I was stationed there. The party was at General Harmon's villa and he openly expressed how bitterly disappointed he was to be leaving the Division. I had come to like him and have a high regard for his ability. We are all up in the air as to where this all leaves us. Had another good swim.

**July 17, 1944**

I watched both the 6th Infantry and the 1st A.R. pass in review for General Harmon today. The 6th looked particularly well and the General in his brief remarks to them said that while he had the Division, they had never failed to take an objective, nor had they given up any ground that they had secured. We held a memorial service this evening for the thirteen officers and eighty enlisted men from the regiment who had been killed during the Italian campaign. A platoon of tanks fired the salute. It was held just at sundown and proved very impressive. Swam again.

**July 18, 1944**

The regiment passed in review for General Harmon is what may well have been the last parade of the 13th A.R. I was the C.O. of troops and we went through one "dry run" before we went for record. The regiment looked splendid. There was a meeting which the new C.G. called this afternoon. He startled us all somewhat by announcing the 5th Army has dispatched a cable today to the War Department requesting that reorganization of the A.D. be held up. Nevertheless, we were told to make plans for the change, and I was named C.O. of the 13th Tk. Bn.[54]

---

54    The 13th Armored Regiment was reduced in size and was redesignated as the 13th Tank Battalion. 1-13 Armor was disbanded, and its tanks and crews went on to replace others lost in combat. Companies D, E, and F of 2-13 Armor became Companies A, B, and C of the 13th Tank Battalion (M4 Shermans). B Co of 1st Armored Regiment became D Co, 13th Tank Battalion (M5 Stuarts). Companies G, H, and I of 3-13 Armor left and formed the 4th Tank Battalion. The 13th Tank Battalion now had an effective strength of 804 tanks, and it soon began preparing to meet the next formidable German defensive position: the Gothic Line. George Howe, *The Battle History of the First Armored Division,* (Washington, D.C.: Combat Forces Press, 1954).

Figure 37: B Co 13th Tank Battalion in Italy (Photograph from the Patricia Issel Collection)

### July 19, 1944

A fairly busy day working on the problems that are arising in conjunction with the transfers that are necessary in order to form these new tank Bns. An allotment of five officers and sixty men to be rotated is going to enable us to take care of some of the older men for whom there is no position. Went swimming this afternoon and again grubbed about in the sand for the small clams that one finds and ate those I was able to capture. The radio was full of good reports. Capture of Leghorn and Ancona, etc.

### July 19, 1944

Was invited out to dinner last night and had a meal like the kind one expects to get on returning home. The Colonel and I were invited to dine with a friend of mine from Cornell who I met while I was in Ithaca through George Floyd. This boy's name is Jack Detweiler and I may have mentioned him before for I have seen him in Africa over here last winter and on the beachhead.[55] He was rather badly wounded during the break through from the beachhead but is fine again now.

He commands all of the ordnance groups in this general area which is a big important job. Since his headquarters are not in the combat area and he has so much engineering facilities at his disposal he doesn't lack for modern conveniences. His quarters are in the nature of a trailer home in that a shop two-and-a-half-ton truck has been converted into his office and quarters. It is air conditioned, has running water, beautifully lighted and appointed and has most of the comforts and appearance of a deluxe drawing room on one of our crack trains.

The mess he operates is complete with linen, silver, china, and menu. Last night we had tomato juice cocktails, soup, salad, main course consisting of steak, mashed potatoes, fresh peas, then ice cream and finally watermelon. There were several table wines and finally cigars for those who were interested. Some of his officers in all seriousness were telling us how they had found the Louisiana maneuvers more strenuous than campaigning it Italy. Considering the way they live, I am not surprised.

Went swimming this afternoon. The other day we watched a native gathering clams a short distance off shore. He has a sort of rake which he pulled through the sand in order to collect them. They were all small, none of them being longer than the first joint on my middle finger. He broke one open and offered it to me, indicating that it was good to eat. There wasn't much to it, but the taste was good. Now, when the colonel and I go in swimming, we always dig up a few clams and eat them raw. The pickings are pretty slim and those that you do get are so small that there is no danger of spoiling one's appetite.

---

55    Major and then Lieutenant Colonel John "Jack" G. Detweiler, commander of the 45th Ordinance Battalion, commanded all Ordnance troops at the Anzio beachhead, including the 62nd Ammunition battalion. Lida Mayo, *The Ordinance Department: On Beachhead and Battlefront*, (Washington, D.C.: Center of Military History, 1991), p. 196.

**July 20, 1944**

This reorganization is certainly a headache and there are times when I think it would be better to be slated for replacement center than a Bn. Commander. We are faced with an acute shortage of competent officers, particularly among the tank platoon leaders. My entire day was spent in conferring with various individuals over problems brought about by the reorganization. As of today, the 13th A.R. ceased to exist and the 13th Tank Battalion came into being. Our regiment is also making up the 4th Tank Bn. while the 1st A.R. only make the 1st Tank Bn.

**July 21, 1944**

While at breakfast this morning we heard the crackle and rip of airplane guns' firing. We rushed outside of the tent to find two spitfires attacking a JU-88 just over our heads. We saw them make two passes at it before it burst into flames, slowly began to circle and then plunged to earth. Spent the day stewing over reorganization and rosters. I sure hope we get a couple of months before they put us back in action again.

**July 22, 1944**

We worked all day preparing long reports required by the A.G. in connection with the transfer and assignment of personnel on the reorganization only to find this evening that most of our work had been thrown out the window. I was summoned to a meeting where we were told that a ruling had been made by Army that no one could be rotated unless they were excess as a result of this reorganization provided excess men in those grades. Was given three captains whom I consider wholly unsuited to fill vacancies competent lieutenants were holding.

**July 23, 1944**

Our clerks and company commanders worked for most of the night revising lists and then more army red tape and contradictory rulings developed today and again everything had to be done about completely over. Perhaps we will have an organization when this thing is finished that will satisfy the paper requirements of a reorganized tank battalion, but it's combat efficiency will be much less than if some common sense were allowed in the elimination of unfit personnel. Considering the mess we are in, I wish I could review my decision not to be rotated.

**July 24, 1944**

Thought I would be able to get to the beach today but it was more of the same damn thing. On top of the present shifting, the property transfers have started and to climax it all we learned that the 6th Infantry is going back into the line this weekend and we are apt to be close behind them. About the only solution to our problems is for the discontent which Germany is continuing to be reported as being of serious proportions to overflow to the point where this war can be wound up without our help.

**July 25, 1944**

While the 13th has been dissolved on paper for several days now the real physical dissolution started this morning. Col. Howze moved over to CCA with a number of officers and men from the 13th that he had drawn back to work with him there while I moved down to the 2nd Bn. area which is where I am going to set up the 13th Tank Bn. We have started to transfer equipment and the present situation is still a long way from being a clear one so things are a mess. I took off for the beach anyhow this afternoon and had a good swim.

**July 27, 1944**

In view of the reorganization the Division had been given a special rotation allotment which when broken down gave the regiment sixty men and five officers. They left this morning and it was saying goodbye to a lot of friends and as fine a bunch of soldiers as one will ever find for we sent the most deserving and the best.

*{Partial entries from July 27 to August 2 included discussion about replacements and reconstitution and the availability of the Division for IV Corps in the future.}*

### August 2, 1944

I've mentioned to you before about calling on my friend Detweiler, who is with the ordnance. Had dinner again with him last night and it was the usual super eight course affair. He had some interesting guests in the persons of several R.A.F. pilots who fly night missions from a nearby airport. Detweiler had been in Rome for a few days and while there purchased two fine brand-new German cameras. One of them is now mine to the tune of two hundred and fifty dollars. These cameras aren't on the market but come out of hiding when you know where to look. If I can secure film, I will soon be sending you pictures. They will be small but will enlarge well for this is an extra special lens.

Lily Pons and her hubby performed for the division the other night, but I couldn't go.[56] Most everyone got there, and they all enjoyed the program immensely. Kostelanetz conducted the division bands. We have had fresh eggs three time in a week. Those who got into this war late will never fully appreciate what we had in the way of rations the first six months we were in Africa.

### August 3, 1944

Today we started to clean up twelve of the new 76 mm tanks with the Ford motor that we are getting in the Bn.[57] They are a much-improved

---

56  An opera singer, Lily Pons canceled her fall and winter season in New York in 1944 and instead toured with the USO, entertaining troops with her singing. Her husband, Andre Kostelanetz, directed a band composed of American soldiers as accompaniment to her voice. "Lily Pons Here," *The Last Roundup*, April 11, 1946, retrieved on March 14, 2020, from https://archive.is/20120630212338/http://home.comcast.net/~cbi-theater-5/roundup/roundup041146.html#selection-27.43-27.58

57  There were a wide variety of M4 Sherman Tanks. Based on the Ford Motor, this was most likely the M4A3.

tank over our present one and it is a fine-looking gun, but no one know anything about it. We had the rest of the gun crews firing on targets out on the water, but it wasn't very satisfactory for they were continually destroying them. Supper with Jack Detweiler and then up to look over some A-20's at a nearby field.[58] The British use them for night work and run a series of flights every night on road bombing in the Po valley.

### August 4, 1944

We had a snafu parade this morning with the color company, among other things, failing to arrive on the parade ground with the colors. Told that we were to move up the middle of next week. The way the Germans are reeling back on all fronts if they postpone our employment much longer, we may not have any live targets when we do go up. Jack Detweiler told me today that Army was already tooling up an occupation force in Munich. Had a good swim. General Pritchard addressed us this evening.

### August 5, 1944

Had an inspection of the vehicles and area this morning. The vehicles in fine shape. It always amazed me how clean the boys can make a tank when they really apply themselves. We drew twelve of the new tanks today. While there are many improvements in it one of the minor faults in our tank design has not only not been corrected but has been made worse. The new tank is six inches higher than the old one.[59] Had a good swim this afternoon. My swimming has improved a lot since we have been here.

### August 6, 1944

The Division artillery moved up during the night to take over positions in the sector we are going to occupy S. of the Arno river. Our troops continue to flood into the Brittany peninsula with breath-taking

58    Douglas A-20 Havoc
59    Meaning it presented a bigger target

rapidity. They are also making some progress to the east. Now if the 7th Army would just clear up on the speculation and land in southern France. Another good swim this afternoon. We were issued four cans of American beer so the shipping situation must be getting fairly easy. Things are shaping up for our move.

**August 7, 1944**

Division H.Q.'s moved up to the front today. The dope so far is that we are going to be in a strictly defensive role up there but while that may be their intention now, I don't think they will let us sit around idly for very long without using us. With everything pointing towards an end of the war in Europe within a matter of months, I find myself wondering how I will adjust myself to my old ways. One wonders if all the headaches of a businessman that are bound to exist are going to be worth the dividends, if any.

**August 8, 1944**

We had an extra special meal today noon with steak, new French-fried potatoes and fresh tomatoes. The kitchen, of course, can't take credit for the ingredients they serve but we do have a very good mess here in headquarters company. During the shuffle of personnel as a result of reorganization we were able to weed out some of the less desirable cooks for with many units being disbanded there was a surplus in cooks.

## The 13th Tank Battalion Starts to Function

**August 9, 1944**

I went on ahead of the column which wasn't to start until after dark. The trip was just under forty miles and over very mountainous roads. I got a couple of hours of sleep before the first elements commenced to arrive and stayed up from then on. We are quite congested but defiladed from the enemy. While we are within artillery range, none have been coming in here. The General at a meeting this afternoon said it had been determined that we weren't to take over a sector here, that those elements in the line were coming out and we were moving back for training.

**August 10, 1944**

Our area is filled with fruit trees, heavily burdened with fruit and you can reach up from most any spot and pick a plum, pear or peach. We devoted the day to work around camp and maintenance of vehicles. Took a run over to IV Corps to see a couple of friends from the 106th that I understand were there but found only one. On returning to camp found General Pritchard there. He had just dropped in for a visit and spent some time giving us his views with regard to our employment. Col. Howze asked me to come over to dinner at his mess. They are set up in a lovely villa with magnificent view to the North.

**August 11, 1944**

We broke camp right after breakfast and commenced infiltrating to a new area that we had been ordered to move into which meant about an eleven mile move over the mountains. The reason for this shift was to put us near a training area. We are better off there being able to spread out somewhat but there is little shade. The news reports spectacular advances in France. For some time, we have been expecting to hear the 7th Army had started to land in southern France. Something seems to be holding it up. Venereal rate starting up.

**August 12, 1944**

A training area which we moved over here to be nearby is just outside of our bivouac. Had the whole Bn. out there this morning maneuvering over the hills. I drove one of the new 76 mm tanks for a while. We had an unfortunate and freak accident. While there were known to be mines still along the main highways, we didn't expect to find any. A tank hit an S mine which exploded in the air killing the tank commander and seriously wounding another.[60] The General at a meeting this afternoon informed us that the Division was taking over a section of the line tomorrow.

**August 13, 1944**

I had learned yesterday that the other two tank Bn. C.O.'s were taking a four-day leave as well as several members of the Division staff so I concluded to put in my bid for a similar vacation. While some tanks are going into defensive positions and an intensive training program is set up, I thought it would be a good idea to get a complete change of scenery. I arranged to go down with the C.O. of the 1st Bn. We started out in a sedan but knocked the bottom out of the oil pan in a bypass so had to call up our peeps. Put up at the Excelsior Hotel in Rome which is the 5th Army officers' rest camp. Some of our crew lost no time in picking up local gals. I had a pleasant evening drinking, dining and singing.

**August 14, 1944**

The General couldn't have been concerned much about anything happening while we were away for all three tank Bn. C.O.'s, one infantry Bn. C.O., and the G-2, 3 and 4, are all down here. I don't believe any of the officers who are sent to the hotel go in much for the cultural opportunities in Rome but spend their time in the bar, in the dining room, or in bed. The girls aren't permitted to come into the hotel alone, but you can pick one up in front any time and take her in. It seems to be the accepted practice to pick one up, feed her and sleep with her during your stay. No one objects.

**August 15, 1944**

A fine big bathroom that I am sharing with the infantry Bn. C.O. is our greatest luxury with its big tub and ample supply of hot water. One

60    The German anti-personnel S-mine was also known as the "Bouncing Betty" on the Western Front.

sleeps late, finds after a short walk that it's too hot to do much sightseeing and returns to the coolness of the hotel bar. The meals are excellent. Managed to get a date with a nurse in one of the local hospitals. Took her out to cocktails at a lovely home of some local English-speaking people and then back to the hotel for supper and the usual evening dance and floor show. The "Stars and Stripes" put out an extra telling of the landing in southern France.[61]

*{At this point in the diary, Gardiner shifts to the third person stating that "the writer did not fail to fill each page in this diary from the time it was started through the end of the year. However, at some time after the entries were made, it is not recalled now when, the leaf covering August 16th, 17th, 18th, and 19th was torn out and destroyed. This is now regretted. The part that was voluntarily censored covered an amorous interlude in Rome".}*

**August 19, 1944**

We are once again up within the sound of the guns and we can see the flashes of them at night. Our present bivouac is in a grape vineyard and the grapes are just now becoming ripe. It has rained hard several times during the last days and we aren't troubled with the dust now, but our old friend Gen. Mud is back with us. This is our second camp since we were back near the seashore. There has been no swimming since we left that area and there won't be any so long as we are here. To start with, we are too busy but, if we weren't, the coastline is too far away.

**August 20, 1944**

We fired all of A company this AM that have the new 76's. One difficulty we are experiencing is being able to observe the burst of the

---

61    Operation Dragoon (initially Operation Anvil) was the code name for the landing operation of the Allied invasion of Provence (Southern France) on August 15, 1944. The goal of the invasion was to secure the vital ports on the French Mediterranean coast and increase pressure on the German forces by opening another front. Jeffrey J. Clarke & Robert Ross Smith, *Riviera To the Rhine. United States Army in World War II: European Theater of Operations*, (Washington, D.C.: Center of Military History, United States Army, 1993).

shell because there is so much smoke and dust produced by the gun that it is some time before you can see. Otherwise we like the gun and its performance very much. Dropped in to see Col. Howze who is laid up in bed with a bad knee. He wrenched it playing volleyball and it had to be drained.

### August 21, 1944

A unit C.O.'s meeting at the Division brought word of a change in plans which will require the 13th to do some moving. A movie tonight included a short "The Liberation of Rome" taken by the U.S. Signal Corps. Surprised to see a brief shot of myself walking along the road with General Clark. Few people would recognize me.

### August 22, 1944

Spent the day out in the training area. We were going over company problems involving an assumed enemy. The enemy with the new tanks put considerably more into the problems than they do the boys with the old M-4's. Everyone wants to go to France. Not that they are anxious to get back into the fighting but rather because we are tired of Italy and want a change of scenery. We had a very pleasant Bn. officers' dinner party prepared by some natives in the patio of what had been a pretentious mansion in Italy's better days.

### August 23, 1944

We again made use of the training area all day for company problems. The enemy with some of his super binocular instruments could have observed us as we went through our maneuvers. Our assault guns left this evening to work with one of the artillery Bn.'s and I had the Bn. H.Q.'s and H.Q.'s company move to the new area, but I remained behind to check on the move of the Bn. proper. Am reading the "Autobiography of [Ephraim] Tutt."[62] Col. Howze recommended it to me and aroused my interest by saying that the character Mr. Tutt reminded him of me.

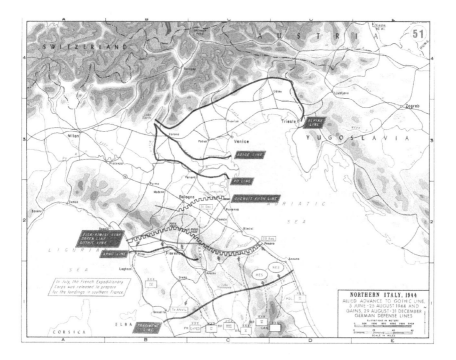

Figure 38: Advance in Northern Italy to the Gothic Line (Wikimedia Commons/Public Domain)

### August 23, 1944

It is after seven in the morning and the sun is almost ready to drop behind a mountain which borders our valley to the west yet I'm dripping with perspiration. This has been a sweltering hot day as have been the past several. I never have become accustomed to the lack of good water and what I miss more than anything on these hot days is being able to get a good drink of cold water. Fortunately, it cools off at night and one needs one blanket to sleep warm, but we sure melt away during the day. The natives all take a siesta during the heat of the day.

---

62    The 1943 book is actually titled *Yankee Lawyer: The Autobiography of Ephraim Tutt.*

No, my old tent mate is no longer closely associated. He is still in the division but in a higher command echelon. His old job was eliminated by the reorganization, but he was well taken care of and, if the war lasts much longer, may collect a star. He went to the right school. My present tent mate is one of my old associates from the 2nd Bn. His name is George Williams and he is a major. George comes from North Carolina, is married and has two children. He was badly wounded just before we got into Rome and has a silver plate in his head.

## August 24, 1944

The Bn. commencing at day light moved to a new bivouac area about twenty-five miles to the east. We are again in an area of vineyards, alfalfa and corn. Without moving from my present position in my office tent I can pick grapes from the vines which form the background of my tent. Two of our companies are now under CCB and I visited them this afternoon in their forward assembly area. Took a run down towards the Arno River which is as far as we go.

## August 25, 1944

With the war against German apparently drawing to a close I have been given to thinking about my plans for civil life. Was sort of jolted back to the reality of things today when the enemy threw a barrage in on an infantry outfit killing sixteen and wounding thirty. We still have a strong enemy to defeat before we can count on seeing home again. Shipped one of our captains off to France this afternoon. Division called saying we had to furnish one of three who were going there to a tank Bn.

## August 25, 1944

We have moved again since I wrote to you last. Our new area is much like the last. This section of the country is made up of a series of sharply rising hills and narrow valleys. The low ground is divided up into tiny fields in which there is corn and alfalfa. All of these fields are bordered with fruit trees which are trained grape vines. There is no difficulty about laundry for the place is overrun by women soliciting such work. I never stop thinking about what a shock it must be to the natives to hear the roar of motors and the creak clank of the tanks during the night and to find at daylight that they have a new community set up and keeping house all around them.

**August 26, 1944**

Went by CCB to discuss a plan of theirs for an attack across the Arno which they had submitted to the units involved for comments. Saw some of the 370th infantry which is a colored outfit that is now going into the line on our left.[63] They are under the 1st Armored. The night they moved in resulted in a charge of rape against three of their soldiers which is to be tried by a Division General Court. Went to an O.P. from which I was able to secure a good view of the country through which we are supposed to attack. It's covered with houses.

**August 27, 1944**

Visited our two forward companies and assault guns this morning but was careful to be back at H.Q.'s in time for lunch since we are having fried chicken. One platoon of tanks fired 750 rounds last night. It was indirect fire under supervision of the artillery. That is 150 rounds per tank which is a lot of shooting and most of the loaders become sick because of the gases.

**August 27, 1944**

There is an infantry outfit in the Fifth Army made up entirely of American born Jap boys. We have seen quite a bit of them and there was a group of their officers at the Excelsior Hotel when I was there. Most of

---

63    The regiment was assigned to the 92nd Infantry Division fondly known as the "Buffalo Division," thus the moniker "Buffalo Soldiers."

them I understand, came from Hawaii. They have a reputation of being fine soldiers.[64]

The blurs on this paper are the result of my trying to eat some grapes at the same time. One of the boys just came in and presented me with a particularly nice bunch of grapes that his washer woman had given him. We have a constant stream of women and girls soliciting laundry. They are prompted largely, I think, by the fact that the boys are pretty generous at handing out candy, etc.

**August 28, 1944**

Am concerned about George Williams' physical condition. He gets about with difficulty which I believe is traceable to his recent wounds. He is an excellent executive officer but if he doesn't show some marked improvement shortly, I am going to ship him off to the hospital. Went out to one of our platoons of light tanks that is backing up an advanced infantry position and they stopped by the platoon of mediums that is firing indirect. They are in a different spot from yesterday. Didn't encounter any enemy fire.

*{Entries for August 28–31, 1944, omitted.}*

## Back to the Wars

**September 1, 1944**

The plan of attack which we were all familiar with was jettisoned yesterday and a new one produced and the troops jumped off in accordance with that at 1000 hrs. During the night we moved two medium companies into position with the infantry and they crossed the Arno with them. No opposition was encountered but their progress was slow because of the mines and demolitions. The Arno is being crossed on a ford. The 13th

64    The 442nd Infantry Regiment

(- two companies) is in CCB reserve. We moved twice and spent the night just short of the river.

## September 2, 1944

We moved across the river at daylight, the reserve going into an assembly area just short of a canal which was still holding up the tanks. One group soon made it and I tagged along with them. They made good progress only encountering small arms' fire. The objectives of CCB having been achieved, consisted of [Orentano] and several small villages. We were ordered to hold up because of the outfits on either side had not been able to keep pace with us. We were showered with flowers and fruit by the natives. Moved the reserve well forward just before dark and camped in a pine forest.

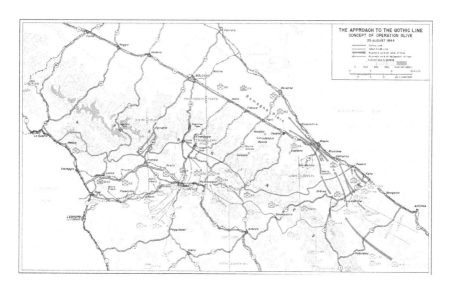

Figure 39: The approach to the Gothic Line (Wikimedia Commons/Public Domain)

## September 3, 1944

The moon was shining brightly when we turned in last night and no one bothered to pitch a tent. About two this morning I was suddenly awakened with a feeling that someone had thrown a bucket of water in my face. A regular torrential downpour had suddenly come up. By the time I clawed my way out from under the mosquito bar I was soaked. Constructed a makeshift shelter out of my tarp but it was not long before the other leaks developed, and I was finally forced to get up. No move developed and the sun came out, so we are in good shape again. The High Command was satisfied to have us just sit.

*{Entries from September 3–11 are omitted.}*

### September 12, 1944

Today we ran two companies through a joint tank infantry exercise, and I commanded the column in the afternoon problem. The General who has been supervising this instruction and who is the Assistant Division Commander didn't agree at all with my plan of attack which I had formulated at one point in the exercise.[65]

*{The intensity of the combat of September and October 1944 had a detrimental effect on the morale, readiness, and capability of the Allied forces in Italy. The already critical manpower shortages in Fifth and Eighth Armies were becoming so severe that their commanders predicted that if they continued to lose men at the same rate, both armies would have to cease operations for lack of replacements. Between September 10 and October26, II Corps' four divisions had suffered over 15,000 casualties, with the U.S. 88th Division alone losing over 5,000 men. During roughly the same period, Eighth Army casualties approached 14,000 men.*

*Losses were so severe that on October 10, Prime Minister Churchill asked the United States to send at least two additional divisions to the Italian front. His request was turned down by U.S. Army Chief of Staff General*

---

65    Gardiner is referencing Brigadier General John E. Wood, the Deputy Commander of the 92nd who during this period commanded Task Force 92 which included CCB. Ulysses Lee, *United States Army in World War II Special Studies: The Employment of Negro Troops*, (Washington, D.C.: Center of Military History, 1965), p. 542, retrieved on March 15, 2020, https://history.army.mil/books/wwii/11-4/chapter19.htm

*George C. Marshall, who preferred to send new U.S. units to France where significant progress was being made rather than to Italy for an increasingly bloody and stalemated campaign in a secondary theater. The black U.S. 92d Infantry Division, Brazilian Expeditionary Force (FEB), as well as the South Africans were sent into the fray.*

*To focus the reader on the actions Gardiner experienced in combat, the majority of the following sections have been omitted "We Tackle the Apennines and Its Defenders" starting on September 27, 1944; "The Enemy Elects to Make a Stand" starting on October 3, 1944; and "Working with the Brazilians" starting on November 10, 1944, to December 22, 1944, where we pick back up with the "Winter Stalemate."}*

## We Tackle the [Apennines] and Its Defenders

### September 27, 1944

There was a series of changes in the set up today and by evening all units had moved to new locations. Assembled the medium tanks in vicinity of Montecatini but took H.Q.'s and "D" companies up into the clouds on a mountain road that was a series of switch back for ten miles. Am in command of a force consisting of a company of light tanks, a reconnaissance troop and two batteries of field artillery. We relieved some S. African and British units on our right flank and have the mission of continuing on to contact.[66]

### September 28, 1944

We are 750 meters above where we were camped before we moved, and everyone is having difficulty keeping warm because it has been raining and blowing. Fortunately, we have a good building and all of the men are under cover. We furnished two hundred men from the medium tanks to pack supplies into the infantry. I turned our recon. and mortar

66    6th Armoured Division (South Africa)

platoons into engineers and they lifted mines and filled in blown spots in the roads. I walked all morning checking the road over which we will try to advance. Church bells in the villages let the natives know it was safe to return. We picked up three prisoners. On patrol drew small arms' fire.

## Winter Stalemate

### December 22, 1944

No specific news of the German offensive. General Eisenhower called up his troops in an order of the day to take advantage of this 'gamble' of the enemy to strike him down. This success of the enemy has the powers that be here nervous and undoubtedly that is true on all fronts. I moved up to what we have been terming our rear C.P. which is the place we left early in the morning of October 29th. Called up to Brazilian H.Q.'s tonight for consultation on how our tanks are to support the infantry in the sectors where they are located.

### December 23, 1944

This morning in company with representative of the B.E.F.'s G-3 office and an interpreter I visited the regimental C.P., the Bn. C.P., the Company C.P., and then the platoon C.P. of the outfit that we are working with in the Bombiano sector.[67] I believe we have things on a workable basis with them now as to the liaison set-up so that they can get support from us when it is needed. The Corps C.P. pulled out on short notice and headed for the west coast. They seem to be expecting something to pop over there.

### December 24, 1944

Went out with the same party this morning and visited the Gaggio-Montano sector this time. Am doing the best I can to educate these Brazilians as to the advisability of traveling with their windshields down,

67    Bombiano-Marano Sector

not driving up to forward positions in the day-time, do more patrolling for security, put their outposts out at night away from the buildings, etc., but they just nod their heads in agreement and then don't do a damn thing. The Germans are still making progress in the west but at a slower pace. It started to snow just before dark.

**December 24, 1944**

It is the "Night before Christmas" and it will be a white one. I have moved since my last letter and am now back where I was before we moved up the Bailey Bridge the latter part of October. We had continued to maintain a headquarters here all of the time and because of a reshuffle of the troops I decided to come back here so as to be more in the center of things. This is the place where I took the picture of the youngsters waiting to get left-overs from our kitchen.

This place is not as close to the enemy positions as the other spot and they can't reach us with mortar fire. However, it is within medium and heavy artillery range and the road and the communities in front and behind us are shelled a good deal. They were dropping all around us last night at this time but so far this evening it has been quiet.

It turned cold enough several days ago to freeze the ground to a point where the mud ceased to be a problem. Just after dark last night it commenced to snow and by morning there was close to six inches. So far it hasn't drifted any so the roads are open although we had to put chains on both the front and rear wheels to negotiate the roads that I was travelling this morning.

The mail has been piling in on us, both letters and packages. Yesterday I received sixteen letters and today almost as many packages. I opened the packages and expect to pass on a lot of the items I received to Italian children tomorrow. Most of our boys are living in homes that are jammed with natives. There are the regular occupants as a rule plus as many refugees as can move in. The boys are planning Christmas parties for the youngsters and I have seen a number of Christmas trees. The trimmings are all improvised but some of them are very good. The Italian custom is to put a doll on the top of the tree.

There are ten youngsters in the buildings that we occupy here, and the boys are playing Santa Claus for them tonight. I gave them some extra candy that I had plus cigarettes for their fathers and a little soap for their mothers.

In the room that we use as an office in this building there is a gasoline stove which works very well, and we have electric lights powered from a half track. There are smoke generators all around us, but they aren't as close as in the other spot, so we aren't suffocated by it here as we were there.

There are about as many officers here as there were at our other C.P. but not as many men. We have a radio and this evening has been devoted to opening packages, writing letters and a lot of interruptions. Just now we are trying to help an outfit that doesn't have the facilities to get some vehicles out of a spot where they are installed. This is the first snow that most of the men who are in this area have ever seen. They don't like it, or perhaps I should say they don't like the cold weather.

### December 25, 1944

These was almost six inches of snow this morning. I spent the morning visiting the companies and had dinner in Riola. During the afternoon I visited the outlying platoons. In addition to a lot of candy which I passed out to children as I saw them along the way, I gave two boxes of assorted things to two particularly needy Italian families. All of the boys said that this was the best Christmas they had spent overseas despite the fact that they were being shot at. Most of them were in houses occupied by civilians and they all played Santa Claus to the kids.

### December 26, 1944

Visited the platoon in Gabba which was one I wasn't able to get to yesterday. While that little community is practically on the front line, it strangely enough still enjoys electricity. The news is of continued progress by the Germans in Belgium although the improved weather has permitted the Allied Air Force to get at Runsted's supply columns. The big news today was the flight of Churchill and Eden to Athens to try and effect a settlement with the Greeks. Considerable flare up in enemy artillery and we had one man wounded.

**December 27, 1944**

I sure hope the Army and Corps G-2's are right for if they aren't we may have a rough time of it one of these days. They pulled another Bn. of artillery out of this sector this morning and headed it over to the west coast. The troops are not plentiful over there to start with and then they are wholly unreliable being American colored. Took the Corps G-3 representative at Brazilian H.Q.'s with me on a run around the Riola sector this afternoon. Considerable increase in the artillery on Silla and some heavy stuff was falling in Porretta.

**December 27, 1944**

The past two days I have been out both morning and afternoon visiting the units. We have been issued really more winter clothing than we need and there is no trouble keeping warm. I usually drive up to a point beyond which I think it is inadvisable to take a vehicle and then walk the rest of the way, so I leave an overcoat or two with my driver. Have been taking quite a few pictures the past several days and am certainly sorry that I can't get them developed and printed.

On Christmas I tried to see as many men in the battalion as I could. Started out by a run back to Service Company, which is located five miles to our rear. On the way I dropped off a package I had fixed up at the home of the brunette partisan girl who was in a picture alongside of a tank with me and a blonde. Found her mother, father, brother and two sisters all at home. Their house consists of one room on the ground floor and apparently an attic. Couldn't get away until they had given my driver and me some coffee.

The Service Company boys had the prize Christmas setup. They had a large tree which was beautifully decorated even to electric lights. They had made the lights from signal wire and peep light bulbs and were drawing on one of the vehicles for electricity. That afternoon they had a Christmas party for some thirty-five youngsters in the immediate neighborhood and gave them all presents.

### December 28, 1944

Visited Service Company area this morning and held a unit C.O.'s and staff meeting this afternoon. The news is now carrying reports of an attack on the west coast. It was against the colored troops and they have fallen back. There is no reliable report yet as to the strength of the attack, but the top side is apparently worried for the 1st Armored has also been moved over there. That sounds like there will not be any push soon on the II Corps front.

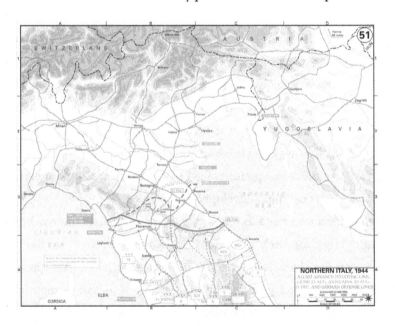

Figure 40: Northern Italy through December 31, 1944
(Courtesy of the U.S. Military Academy at West Point/Public Domain)

**December 28, 1944**

The sector now has its own artificial moonlight and on what would be dark nights a series of searchlights stay on all night thereby making driving very easy.

After I left Service Company on Christmas morning I stopped by "C" and "D" Companies and visited their kitchens in accordance with a time-honored custom in the 13th. From there, I had another officer with me, we visited a platoon that is out in a forward position. The men there were going to walk down the hill in two relays to a point where a peep would bring them their dinner without being exposed to the enemy.

We made it down to where I was just before this last move for dinner. It was a particularly good turkey dinner. Lt. Selby came over to have Christmas dinner with us. He is quite a character and we have all become very attached to him. Selby says that he has become a great admirer of American foreign policy in view of certain associations he has had lately in his contacts with us and he is a firm believer in the Monroe Doctrine.

One group at Christmas dinner included a Chaplain who had kindly agreed to fit us into his busy schedule. His services were to be a one o'clock, but I could not stay and make the other stops that I wanted to. In walking up to another platoon, I delivered a box of things I had prepared to an Italian family which are in sort of an out of the way place. Their house had been destroyed and everyone was living in the barn with the livestock. We could not get away without having a drink of wine.

Everyone was in the open the previous two winters which meant in the mud and the rain. This year everyone has some sort of a building to sleep in, they had a good meal, they have plenty of warm clothing and sleeping bags and there was a homelike atmosphere to the occasion with a Christmas tree most of the places and the children to play Santa Claus to. Another thing is that they are all satisfied that they will be home for their next Christmas.

**December 29, 1944**

They are now reporting that the Germans seem to have shot their wad on the western front. The Third Army is reported to be making some progress. The one fact that we don't like about that is it will mean more plaudits for Patton. Up to visit the boys in Combiano this morning. They are crowded into a badly torn up building with some Italians. Yesterday I had a letter from my U.S.O. singer friend saying she was back in Florence and hoped to see me. I wrote her a note saying I would be down tomorrow night. This morning there was an order out cancelling all passes and leaves until further notice so I relayed a message that I could not make it after all.

**December 29, 1944**

Please don't send me any more nuts for a while. We are now getting them in our PX ration and Christmas packages brought others. I just had some smoked herring that you sent me and a bottle of beer. You asked me to make a request in every letter. There really isn't anything I want just now, and it keeps me busy holding down my extra possessions to where I can haul them around. Additional winter clothing makes one's possessions much more bulky. In one package I received a pair of shorts size 38. Someone must have confused Dad's measures with mine.

My peep has received several battle scars. I believe in each case I was in the ditch not far away. Captain Clay got a new peep the same time I did but has had much worse luck with it and had it badly shot up several times oftener than I have mine. I had not started to wear any heavy underclothes yet. The shorts and undershirt I wear are of the summer variety. I wear woolen trousers and a wool shirt, a sweater and coveralls. Over that I wear a jacket when I go out and as many coats as the temperature makes it advisable. I wear a wool cap under my steel helmet.

Some heavy shells just came in. We don't get any mortar fire here but medium artillery and the "Anzio Express" comes roaring in a few times each day.[68] Of late that type of shelling starts around four in the afternoon and stops about eleven. This cold weather and snow on the ground makes the report of the explosion much louder than it is under normal conditions, which is plenty noisy.

### December 30, 1944

Yesterday marked the heaviest artillery and mortar fire that has fallen on the B.E.F. sector since they have taken over but today passed without any follow up on the part of the enemy. A few heavy shells continue to fall in Porretta, and the Brazilians have moved some of their installations out of here. I visited the boys in Gaggio-Montano this morning. No news of any further enemy action in the Lucca sector. My guess is that our High Command has suffered a case of nerves and been stampeded into abandoning its plans for an attack and shifted large forces over to meet nothing but feint, if that.

*{Entries from December 30, 1944, and January 1, 1945, omitted.}*

### January 1, 1945

Just at midnight last night every gun in position on the front fired two rounds on enemy targets. They made quite a racket but not as much as the German New Year's getting which came crashing in just a few minutes later. They kept it up for a while and some of them were very close. We arranged to have all of the American officers at Brazilian H.Q.'s eat at one of our messes. I took two of them to Service Company where we had a particularly good meal. Over to the 68th this evening for a farewell party for their CO who is leaving in the morning for the U.S.A.[69]

---

68    Anzio Express was the nickname for one of the Krupp K5; heavy railway guns used by the Nazis against Allied soldiers stuck on the beach. The other gun was named "Anzio Annie." The moniker "Anzio Express" was due to the express train-like sound the shells made. Krupp K5, retrieved on March 16, 2020, from https://www.militaryfactory.com/armor/detail.asp?armor_id=526

69    68th Armored Field Artillery Battalion

Dear Elizabeth,

We have a lot of troops here with us from Brazil who are seeing their first snow. One of our boys saw an officer of theirs out the other day doing a little experimenting with a pair of [skis] which he had borrowed from some Italian. He would slide down to the bottom of a hill where a soldier would pick up the skis and carry them back up to the top of the hill for him. It has been too cold and so far the soldiers don't seem to mind it particularly. I have seen several snowmen that they have built and one snow woman who favored the Mae West lines.

January 1, 1945

Happy New Year! Bueno Anno! So far it is still only 0800 hours, but things have been just like any other day recently. There was some little attempt at New Year's Eve celebrations last evening.

Our headquarters is pretty well scattered and there were only five of us here last evening. We sat around and visited about previous New Year Eves, drank a little and ate crackers and the Roquefort cheese that you had sent to me in one of the Christmas packages. The men had a little party in a garage across the road, with music provided by some Italians playing stringed instruments. The girls in the immediate vicinity attended.

I never cease to marvel at the way the Italian women wash clothes in the open streams during the wintertime. The pictures of this community wash tub shows a better setup than is normally encountered. Most of the time they are on their hands and knees using a rock on a stream back as a wash board.

Am afraid I ate too much. Had dinner at Service Company and they have one of the better messes in the battalion. The meal got off to a flying start with oyster soup. Then there was a roast turkey, dressing, gravy, sweet potatoes, beans, cranberry sauce, and hot rolls. The grand finale was hot mince pie and then oranges. I don't intend to eat any supper.

Figure 41: Major General Crittenberger and Lieutenant Colonel Gardiner inspect a captured enemy 170mm gun near the Po River, April 1945 (Photograph from the Patricia Issel Collection)

### January 2, 1945

Our present house has some defilade but has escaped injury so far principally because it hasn't been a suitable target or in the gun target line of something the enemy was interested in. While I was shaving this morning a 170 landed nearby blowing in all of the windows on that side of the house.[70] I was hit by some glass but not injured. Considerable fire down Riola way and we had two men wounded while the Brazilians had three killed and several wounded. Visited the boys in Gabba. We seem to have the initiative on the western front again and are making progress.

*{Entries from January 2–18, 1945, covering post-New Year activities and Battlefield circulation are omitted.}*

70    170 mm artillery

**January 19, 1945**

Each news broadcast brings word of another breathtaking advance of the Russian Army. Everyone is beginning to get in the frame of mind that this may be the blow that will bring an end to all of this organized killing in Europe. As to what can be expected to follow is not causing the average soldier to worry. The situation in Greece, however, is most disturbing for it might be a fore taste of what will follow in other countries. Rained and things are awash.[71]

**January 20, 1945**

The news continues to report more orders of the day by Stalin and there appears to be no checking the on rush of the Red Army. Even with all of the reversals the Germans have had the strength to mount a drive against the Seventh Army which is making considerable progress. Col. Howze and Jim Simmerman came up to pay us a call. I had a phone call this evening from the G-1 saying that I was slated to fly home right away for a thirty-day furlough.

## Home Leave

**January 21, 1945**

Did a little rearranging of the staff this morning, paid a farewell visit to Brazilian HQ where I had a drink with the Commanding General and collected a list of people to call when I can get where one can reach them on the phone. Drove down to the 1st Armored Division HQ which are just outside of Lucca and put up for the night to await further orders.

**January 22, 1945**

It now appears that we aren't due to leave until the 25th and that our stay will be for only twenty-one days as against the originally scheduled

71    He is referencing the Greek Civil War pitting the U.S. and UK-backed Greek Government Army against the communist Democratic Army of Greece.

thirty. The Division was asked to submit the names of four officers to go on a special plane to the States and return and I happen to be one of the four who were recommended and approved. The others are the Chief of staff, the G-4 and the Infantry Bn. Commander that I shared a room with in Rome. Dinner at CCA, and a supper at CCB. The Russians are now reported only 160 miles from Berlin.

### January 23, 1945

One night in the hot stuffy room where all of the Division Staff Lt. Colonels sleep was enough for me and I moved my cot out into the hall last night. The Division surgeon sleeps next to the gas heater which runs all night and he has a dirty pup sleeping on his bed. Now know why it is so difficult for us to get a Special Service radio for any of the companies. They are all in Division HQ. Every office and sleeping quarters seems to have one. Lunched at 4th Tk. Bn. The Russians roar on. Can this be this beginning of the end?

### January 24, 1945

The Div. C.G. is in Rome on leave and the Acting Div. C.G. is General Daniels who is referred to by everyone as the "Moose." This is not a term of endearment but a descriptive of his features and his rather ponderous face. Went into Florence in time for lunch putting up at the Army transient hotel. Did a little shopping acquiring some small leather items as well as a few handkerchiefs. Met a few more officers that are to be in our party which it now appears totals fifteen. Sent radiograms home which if delivered prior to my arrival will tip them off to the fact that I am en route being in a code of our own.

### January 25, 1945

This morning was spent in securing our orders at Fifth Army rear, having money changed to proper type, etc. Our orders read only 21 days

T.D., so this will indeed be a whirlwind trip. Our party which is headed by a B.G. and mostly full colonels, took off from the Florence airport at 1430 hrs. Had a good flight to Naples and saw some of our old stamping grounds including a good look at Anzio beachhead which appeared pretty thoroughly sodden. We took off for Africa just before dark in the same plane which is a regular commercial airliner type of the two-motor type generally at home.

**January 26, 1945**

We landed at Oran shortly after midnight. Gave one a feeling of accomplishment to use an airport that we had helped capture, it being one of the initial objectives of our force when we made the invasion of Africa. We stayed only long enough for a meal and then flew on to Casablanca. There we got a few hours' sleep at a hotel before returning to the airport for briefing in ditching that consists of instructions in how to abandon ship if forced down at sea, living on a rubber raft, etc. Midafternoon found us headed out over the Atlantic in a four-motored cargo type plane.

**January 27, 1945**

We put down at the Azores for a couple of hours during the night before taking off for Newfoundland where we had breakfast. Our big ship set us down gently on LaGuardia airport at 2:30 in the afternoon, our elapsed flying time from Florence being thirty-five hours. They cleared us rapidly and we were up town by late afternoon.

************

{Gardiner refers to himself at this point, describing "during this time that the writer was on leave he visited his mother, father and sister Alice in Montana, his sister Elizabeth in Evanston, Illinois and his Aunt Annie in St. Catherines, Ontario".

Shortly before going overseas in May 1942, [I] accompanied General Daley to dinner at the home of friends and the latter in New York, where [I] *met Rita Singstad. Out of this acquaintanceship, an intensive and extended correspondence developed. The latter part and the major portion of [my] leave was spent in New York City. The day [I] left there to return overseas, an announcement was carried in the newspapers of the engagement of Rita Singstad to Lt. Col. H. E. Gardiner.}*

## Return to Duty

### March 8, 1945

Awakened at 0300 and informed that we were to leave for the airport within half an hour. There was not much of a delay and we took off at 0530 in a C-54 "plush" job we came in on. On arriving in Bermuda, we were informed that there would be a twelve hour delay. We took advantage of that to tour the island, visit Hamilton, eat a lobster dinner and get some sleep. We soared into the night just after 2300 hrs.

### March 9, 1945

Since we were travelling light most everyone had a double seat to themselves. The center arm rests were removable, and I did a pretty good job of napping on the ten hours' jump to the Azores. We had an uneasy few minutes coming in there for it was raining hard with the clouds so low that we had to skim along just above the water to get down where the pilot could see at all. The navigation was perfect, however, and they hit the runway right on the nose. There just long enough to eat and refuel. We were glad to find on arriving at Casablanca that we would be spending the night there in a hotel.

### March 10, 1945

Had a good night's sleep. Found that we were not due out until evening, so Jim and I took a stroll about the city this morning. Someday I'd like to return to Africa and backtrack over the areas I've travelled and fought over. This afternoon Jim and I took another walk, this time going out to the end of the main jetty that forms the breakwater between the ocean and harbor. Saw a number of mute examples of the decadence of the French Fleet being rusting battle ships going to pieces at anchor. We got a 2300 east-bound plane out.

**March 11, 1945**

Made a stop at Oran where I had four fried eggs which held me over until I got one during a brief breakfast halt at the Tunis airport. We had enough daylight this morning to have a good look at Beja, the "mouse trap" and Mateur. Sure hope to be able to leisurely look that area over again one of these days. We had a good flight across to Naples where we were billeted at a transient hotel for the night. Spent the evening and afternoon writing letters. The main development on the fighting fronts since we left has been the crossing of the Rhine on a bridge that was seized intact by elements of the First Army.

**March 12, 1945**

We got a plane out of Naples that landed us in Florence in time for lunch. Called the G-1 and he kindly suggested that we put up at the hotel and get a good night's rest before reporting for duty. Jim and I secured a room overlooking the river and just loafed around during the afternoon. Learned that Col. Howze was located but a short distance out of town and he came in and spent the evening with us. Reported on my "date" with his wife and he brought us up to date on the Division. Learned of many changes. The Division is in the line but the 13th is out having been relieved the week I left.

**March 13, 1945**

Jim and I had a long dusty ride out to the Division C.P. where we reported in and were relieved to find that we were not in the doghouse for having taken the thirty days that were offered to us as against the twenty one that our orders called for. Returned to find the Bn. comfortably quartered in undamaged houses.

**March 14, 1945**

Oh, how I hated to get up this morning! My holiday was really over this morning when I had to get up at 6:30 and fall in for calisthenics fifteen minutes later. Spent the morning going over "Poop sheets" and periodic reports so that I know what has gone on in my absence. Out this afternoon to observe some tank firing on the range and a platoon problem. Paid Col. Howze a visit at his establishment which is a school teaching means of crossing ditches, etc. My accumulated first class mail yesterday totaled 65 letters.

**March 14, 1945**

Returned to the battalion yesterday afternoon and found the whole outfit all lined up with a S. African band on hand to pass in review for me. It was complete surprise and, of course, made me feel good. Will write you in detail about it in my next letter.

The battalion was relieved the same week I left and we are at present set up as comfortably as we have been and so far back of the lines that we can't hear the guns fire and you would hardly know there was a war on except from reading the "Stars and Stripes." The weather has been perfect here and we are strictly rear echelon troops at the present. How long that pleasant situation will continue I don't know. Our boys were in the lone from the 2nd of September until the 31st of January, which is something of a record. There is a small group of my boys still up there, but they are being rotated so it isn't bad. Everyone is in a house and while the one I'm in is not one of these large villas that we have sometimes taken over, it is very comfortable. The area we are in now didn't suffer a scratch from the fighting or bombing so we have all of our windows. We are busy training and I have been out all day watching various activities, range practice, etc.

*{The next few sections are omitted, starting with "Training in the Non-Combat Zone" starting on March 15, 1945, until April 9, 1945, including the resting, refitting, and training of the battalion and, notably, the issuance of M-24 light tanks to replace the M5s at the beginning of April 1945—only to be turned in and the old tanks reissued some weeks later.}*

## The Battalion Moves into Position for the Attack

### April 9, 1945

The stupidity of the Army seems to continue to grow rather than lessen as its battle streamers increase. A call this noon ordering us to detach seventeen tank drivers to drive the new tanks we had to turn back. Spent the morning cleaning up some inactive matters and drove over the mountain to our new location which is on a hillside just beyond Silla. All of the real estate that we occupied last winter is now populated by fair weather tenants. Am sitting up in my Italian pup tent. The Division is assembling in this general area and two more companies of the Bn. came up tonight. The searchlights are on all night.

*{Omitted sections from April 10–12, 1945, which entailed letters and diary inserts on administrative actions}*

### April 13, 1945

Everyone was shocked to hear on the radio this morning that President Roosevelt had died suddenly. One reason why I was so opposed to his election was because of the man who was on the same ticket and who is now the President of the United States. Our new President, Harry Truman, is the product of one of the most corrupted political machines that has ever flourished in America. He will be built up as much as possible by the press but the material they have to work with is mighty poor. Out on recon. this morning. We received word at 1930 hours that the attack for tomorrow was on.

# The Spring Offensive Commences

## April 14, 1945

Was out on an O.P. at dawn with the Bn. S-2, my driver and tank gunner to watch the fireworks. Had excellent radio communication with all of our participating units. The opening of the attack was a series of bombings by the fighter bombers on the objectives. It was most spectacular for they were using an oil bomb which gave a big splash of liquid flame all over the area that was hit followed by a dense cloud of black smoke which later changed to white. We had two companies of tanks giving direct fire support and one platoon in the assault. Aside from our tank fire the Division was committed until late afternoon when the 10th Mountain had taken its first objective.[72]

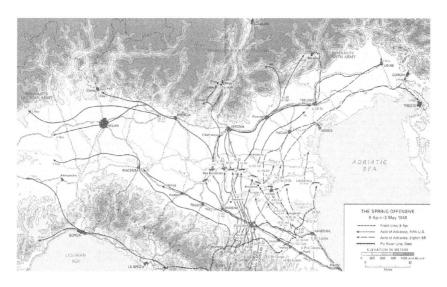

Figure 42: The Spring Offensive, 1945 (Wikimedia Commons/Public Domain)

72    In early March, the division fought its way north of Canolle and moving to within 15 miles (24 km) of Bologna. On March 5, while Brazilian units captured Castelnuovo, the 85th and the 87th Infantry took Mound Della Spe and Castel D'Aiano, respectively, cutting the Axis routes of resupply and communication into the Po Valley, setting the stage for the next Fifth Army offensive. The division maintained defensive positions in this area for three weeks, anticipating a counteroffensive by the German forces. The division resumed its attack on April 14, attacking Torre Iussi and Rocca Roffeno to the north of Mount Della Spe. On April 17, it broke through the German defenses, which allowed it to advance into the Po Valley area; the 10th crossed the Po River on April 23, reaching Verona April 25. A.B. Feuer, *Packs On!: Memoirs of the 10th Mountain Division in World War II*, (Mechanicsburg, Pennsylvania: Stackpole Books, 2006).

### April 15, 1945

Moved the C.P. just before daylight to a more advanced position and brought a medium tank company along which was attach to the infantry. Trails that our tanks negotiate during peace time maneuvers would have been considered as doubtful mule trails as compared to what we are now going over. Our C.P. area received some artillery fire but I think it was intended for some of our tanks which are firing from the ridge in front of us. The Division gained some ground during the day and the tanks were able to advance as far as the infantry did – in fact, preceded them. Just as I was about to turn in for the night, I received a call to report to Col. Dewey at the C.P. of the infantry Bn. that was in the attack. It was after dark by the time I reached there, and they had gone. From that point, which was a steep ascent I proceeded on foot, in fact, I walked, climbed and slipped all night.

### April 16, 1945

Finally, located the colonel. He had been sent up to put some push into the attack on Mt. Pero which, it was felt, was dragging and he wanted me along to advise him as to the use of tanks. That was easy. After all of the climbing around we did it was obvious tanks couldn't help, at least in an assault. It was a noisy night with German rockets adding to the usual mortar and artillery fire.

### April 17, 1945

Had a good eight hours' sleep last night. Sort of like old times in Africa for it was on the ground without the benefit of any tent. He had breakfast at CCB. Their plans were in a turmoil except that I was told I could start assembling the Bn. but not to bring the tanks we had up on top of the mountains down. I started up to see that group but was impeded by roads choked with mule trains, guns, infantry, tanks, supplies and ambulances. Got caught in some nasty artillery fire in the town of

Tole during which a number of casualties were sustained by the troops that were passing through. Saw several hundreds of German prisoners marching to the rear.

## April 18, 1945

During the morning the last unit of the Bn. that had been away from us rejoined. We sat alongside of HY-65. We watched over 400 heavy bombers pass over. The Bn. was ordered to move this afternoon to an assembly area the other side of the mountains and I went ahead to the Division C.P. for orders. Traffic was at a standstill for miles. We are to be in Division reserve.

## April 18, 1945

We took part in the opening attack on this front and have been involved ever since. Don't know how much the papers are devoting to this front, but we have been making good progress and now have the worst of the mountains behind us. Getting the troops and supplies over the bad mountain roads that we have had to use is the biggest problem at the moment. The first-class roads at the moment are still impassable because of demolitions.

Since we have been living outside and on the ground again, the weather has been fine. It gets pretty chilly at night but hot during the middle of the day. The dust is terrific. One night since we jumped off, I didn't get any sleep but the rest of the time I've been able to secure a few hours up to a normal amount. Yesterday I passed mule trains which extended for miles and one troop of American horse cavalry. I'll wait for my return to that branch of the service until after the war.

Ran into Bill Mauldin, the cartoonist, the other day and had a nice visit with him. He was spending the night with an infantry outfit in our area. Was flattered to have him recognize me from our previous meeting. Guess it was the haircut which is back to the bone again.

**April 19, 1945**

Last night's march was about the worst we have ever experienced. It took us fourteen hours to move the Bn. eleven miles. It was just a case of moving ahead a few yards at a time and then waiting until the vehicle which had slid off the tortuous road or become bogged in a soft spot had been extricated. Some heavy British guns were the worst offenders. Our bivouac was near Tole which was shelled throughout the day. Late in the afternoon I was ordered to report at once to the Division C.P. and we were alerted to move immediately. By the time I got through the traffic, the picture changed. At first, we were being farmed out to the 10th Mountain Division but they got a Recon. Bn. instead.

**April 20, 1945**

A task force Gardiner consisting of the 13th and one infantry and one other artillery Bn. which was to be attached to the 10th Mountain Division existed for about forty-five minutes this morning before it was cancelled. The next order which came in shortly after noon attached us to CCA and I was ordered to report to Col. Howze for orders. We were given a mission of attacking what seemed to be the last enemy defensive positions hinged on a community called Oliveto. An infantry Bn. was attached and after a brief artillery barrage we jumped off with about an hour of daylight left. We attacked on a three-company front. The center company which was "C" lost three tanks to a S.P. They burned and two men were killed. I followed the attack in my peep. We secured Oliveto.

## Out of The Mountains

**April 21, 1945**

Midnight found us out of the mountains at last. While we had secured our initial objective, we were told to continue on through the night in the direction of HY-9. Much confusion as to presence of friendly elements on right flank and we moved slowly with infantry on foot leading the tanks. I moved with the infantry. Came upon the still warm body of an American lieutenant lying in the middle of the road. Just getting well organized after the confusion of early in the evening when still another change of mission occurred, this one requiring a split of our force. The group I was with reached HY-9 at 0730 and I received an order to proceed at 15 m.p.h. to the Po river. Ridiculous. An S.P. had traffic that was trying to move up 9 stopped. Had a very close one when a shell hit just in front of my peep. Also drove into a town to find it occupied by about fifty Germans. Got out and in a hurry. The Bn. was pretty well assembled and took and passed through Castel-Franco just at dusk and we were ordered to continue to push on. General Pritchard and Col. Howze were both riding near the head of the column at this point getting in Johnny Elliot's way.

**April 22, 1945**

I took over the running of the column at 0300. "C" leading ran into a fire fight. Daylight found us stopped by a blown bridge. Recon. opened a way around and we pressed on crossing the Secchia river. Col. H. was relieved of command of CCA by General Daniels (alleged failure to get his troops forward fast enough). We pushed on well into the night taking over 200 P. W.'s, knocking out some enemy artillery fire vicinity Carpi. We seemed to be in the midst of fleeing enemy columns. Our Doc wounded.

**April 23, 1945**

While the orders were not to stop, we found that we didn't have enough gas to refuel our tanks. I accordingly ordered a halt of two hours for everyone was just about out on their feet with fatigue. At 0230 we started out but the light company platoon that was leading became lost twice and we didn't make much progress until it became light. No opposition encountered. We moved along rapidly being stopped just short of the Po by a blown bridge. While halted there two Germans on a bicycle appeared on the dike ahead of us trying to escape. Directed my gunner on them with M.G. fire killing one and the other came in with his hands up. Situation much confused. Reports of enemy tanks moving south and the 91st Artillery asks for help. Made a detour to south over the bridge that was intact and took our positions in and around Guastella, on banks of Po. Midafternoon we were detached and told to report to the 10th Mountain Division at San Benedetto P.O. I went ahead of column and Col. Darby, whom I knew, formerly of the Rangers, and General Hayes gave me our orders.

## Across the Po

### April 24, 1945

The Bn. closed in during the night receiving some strafing on the way in. I took two of the company C.O.'s with me and we went across the river to look for an assembly area in the bridgehead which the 10th had established. We went across in the second dukw to make the crossing. The enemy was shelling the part of the river where crossings were being made with 88's that were part of their ack-ack defensive along the river. Breakfasted with some natives on fried eggs, wine and bread to the sound of air bursts and mortar shells of the enemy. Walked out to advanced positions which reported no enemy contact. Work commencing on platoon bridges and ferries (captured) put into operation late in afternoon with priority going to our tanks. Ferries kept breaking down and movement of our tanks extremely slow.

### April 25, 1945

By daylight we had three mediums and seven light tanks across. These tanks were attached to one of the Infantry Bns. and pushed on. The ferry operation improved somewhat and by mid-morning a light pontoon bridge was in and by late morning wheel traffic began to stream across. A terrific traffic jam developed largely as a result of the simplified march table of the Mountain Division which amounted to a case of the highest ranking individual who happened to be in one of the three columns that were converging on the entrance to the bridge went across first. The Corps Army and Army Group commanders also snarled up traffic when it became necessary to have them photographed out on the bridge. We had close to a company of mediums across by early afternoon. Formed the armored spearhead of a column organized under the command of Col. Darby and we set off for Verona. We closed in back of our light tanks and the force they were with at Villafranco without incident except that we were strafed along the highway.

**April 26, 1945**

An attack was planned on Verona and at three in the morning we took off in two columns, the tanks leading the way. Col. Darby and I followed the column on the main road. No opposition encountered but just at daylight a demolition to the north of us threw a column of dust into the air that looked like Vesuvius on the rampage. We entered the outskirts of Verona just at sunup to find that our 88th Division with some T.D.'s had preceded us during the night. One crossroad was littered with knocked out German vehicles and bodies. Later learned that a number of the enemy were still alive. Verona was the most damaged of the large cities that I've seen. We had some difficulty in getting the tanks into the city proper. It was quite a stirring spectacle moving through the town with the populace rushing out to greet us. All bridges blown. Dispatched two groups of tanks out to accompany infantry columns pushing on. We were relieved late in the afternoon and reverted to Division control, but the 10th Mountain refused to let those tanks that were committed loose until they had reached their objective.

**April 27, 1945**

We remained in an assembly area in the vicinity of Verona during the night and I got fourteen hours of uninterrupted sleep and most everyone else did as well. All units being released to us we started out to rejoin the Division. Caught up to them and were able to feed one meal out of the kitchens when we were ordered to pull out just at dusk in a force under command of Col. Howze. Marched all night and had considerable difficulty with parts of the column getting lost. One F.A. battery which got behind and failed to make a turn ran into a force of Germans including four tanks which were holding a platoon of our infantry as prisoners. The Germans surrendered and the infantry took over the job of covering them. We skirted Brescia and Bergamo, reaching a community called [Breno] shortly after daylight.

## We Reach Lake Como

**April 28, 1945**

CCA which had preceded us by a few hours went on direct to Como, so the Division was pretty well deployed across all escape routes of the enemy. Prisoners were pouring in from every direction. We established roadblocks in our sector and kept a steady stream of P. W's heading into the Division cage which was overwhelmed with business. The influx was so great that all they could do was just crowd them into one building where generals, officers, and enlisted men were placed without any attempt to segregate. Everyone is grabbing hold of a German passenger vehicle but that is a luxury which will be short lived, I am sure. Late in the afternoon we were ordered to send a company of tanks to intercept a German column which had shown up at Bergamo. The column had cleared that point by the time our boys got there, and they were stopped and brought back after a short pursuit.

**April 29, 1945**

Drove over to Lake Como this morning and called on CCA who are set up in a lovely hotel. That is beautiful country over there and shows evidence of having been damaged by the war. In fact, with the exception of Verona, what we have seen of the country since entering the Po valley has been almost unaffected visibly by the war. One of our outposts captured a passenger train last night headed in the direction of Germany. The dope is that El Duce and some of his group has been captured by the partisans and killed. The war in Italy certainly is over with and it appears that Germany is just about through everywhere. We are supplying our light trucks for escorting P. W.'s back to the Army cages. Rumors of some units to our west who have declared that they have no intention of surrendering, so we may be headed their way.

**April 29, 1945**

We participated in the initial big push in the mountains and have had no rest since. Our tanks were the first into the Po Valley and the first astride of Highway 9, which is the main artery running the length of the valley. Both of those operations were at night and cost us some good men. It was then a case of two more days, continuous fighting and moving until we reached the Po River.

Our battalion was then detached from the division and assigned to a division which had secured a bridgehead across the river in order to give them some armor to exploit their success. No time was lost after we got over the river. We pushed on all the rest of the day and through the night and the next morning were in the foothills of the Alps and astride the highway which leads up into the Brenner Pass. The city we took that morning is identified with Romeo and Juliet. From there we made more all night forced marches and yesterday were admiring the snow-clad Alps at close quarters. This is being written but a few miles from the Swiss border.

Our work today and yesterday has been one of round up prisoners. We have been getting them by the thousands and they are still coming in. In our swift move to the north we cut off tens of thousands of Germans and we are still capturing convoys of hundreds of vehicles trying to escape through the passes. At the moment we have a fleet of small German convertible cars but there is already an order out requiring us to turn them in.

The natives and the Germans tell us the war is over. However, there is still a certain amount of fighting. Musso and some of his crew were executed a few miles from here this morning. I went for one seventy-two-hour period without lying down and the following twenty-four-hour period I had two hours sleep. Last night I had seven hours sleep and the night before none. Tonight, I am hoping for some. Am fine except tired.

### April 30, 1945

This morning we were ordered to send a company of tanks into Milan to assist in taking over the city and a force to Monza where a garrison of S.S. troops were scheduled to surrender with the balance of the Bn. moving down closer to the auto strada. I went along to see the S.S. crowd and picked up a few pistols and some other loot. We moved the garrison out of there in their vehicles under considerable tension for feeling was running high among the natives and partisans and they crowded the road where the column pulled out on the highway, shouting and threatening their former overseers. Drove on into Milan and had considerable difficulty getting through the streets because of the crowds of people who were still anxious to personally slap the back, kiss, embrace, shake the hands of, and cheer all Americans. Visited the German garrison where our tanks are lined up ready to move them out of the city after dark.

# The War Ends in Italy

**May 2, 1945**

There was not much more than time to assemble the Bn. and re-gas when we moved out on a march that lasted through the night. There was a driving cold rain and it was a mean move for the road was poor. We halted for the day a few miles south of [Vercelli] and then moved to a little community for the night, named Villanova. On the way there the radio operator picked up word that the Germans in Italy and western Austria had surrendered unconditionally. It hardly caused a ripple. Invited and accepted the invitation of one of the local citizenry to supper and for a bed both of which proved to be excellent.

**May 3, 1945**

You would probably have been surprised at the lack of reaction to the announcement yesterday that the Germans in Italy had surrendered unconditionally. We first received the news over BBC at six o'clock in the evening and were moving at that time. I listened to the eight o'clock news as did many of the men for we were halted for the night then. There was no outburst, no cheering and no attempt at any sort of celebration by our troops.

To start with everyone was very tired. We had marched all the night before over a difficult road and that was on top of prior nights of little sleep and hard days. Our march last night before last was further complicated by a driving cold rain. I was pretty well soaked early in the game. We were just feeling our way and there were frequent halts which was fortunate for that enabled us to get warmed up somewhat. I was riding in my peep just back of a tank. When we would stop, I would get out and stand alongside of the tank so that the exhaust gases from the engine hit me in the back. They are nice and hot and that is a favorite way for the men to warm up at halts.

An additional reason why the formal declaration that the war in Italy was over didn't create a ripple because that has been apparent for several days. We haven't fired a shot now in four days, but we have been taking thousands of prisoners.

Day before yesterday I accepted the surrender of a German Corps Commander, another general and twenty-five hundred of his troops. As per arrangements I took some tanks and infantry to a designated crossroad at eight o'clock in the morning. There I was met by a German officer. He led the way in his car, and I followed in my peep with an interpreter for several miles back into German lines.

On the way in we passed German roadblocks, heavily manned and armed. We went directly to the Corps Commander's headquarters which was in a group of farm buildings. He was a very large man, standing, I should judge, six foot three and weighing about two hundred and twenty-five pounds or perhaps more. I would guess his age around fifty. His hair was iron grey and he was a very fine-looking man and although he didn't smile he appeared capable of doing so which is more than I can say for many of the German officers we have seen lately. The day before I supplied the tanks that escorted a German S.S. General and his staff and troops to the P.W. cage. They were a tough looking lot. Tough in the sense of hardness for they wore handsome uniforms and were all shined up.

This general the other morning had a blue uniform with a lot of red on it and shiny black boots. There was a lot of heel clicking by his staff and men and they all gave the salute with their arm extended.

This outfit had enough of their own motor transport to move the twenty-five hundred men. When the arrangements were completed, they all mounted up and I had them pull out on to the Autostrada and halt. As they passed the road junction where the tanks were located, we cut tanks and infantry into the column. They served a dual purpose. One was a guard on the prisoners and the other was to protect them from violence by the partisans who were all along the way, armed to the teeth.

Once we had the column on the road formed and halted, we took five trucks and drove them from the rear to the front, picking up all of the rifles, machine guns, bayonets, pistols and grenades. We kept the artillery in the column and the anti-tank and anti-aircraft guns until we reached our ordnance company that was located on the main highway where we pulled these off and left them. There were quite a few German WAACS in the group and a number of their nurses.

The only trouble we had were with a couple of groups which had been drinking. They announced they weren't going to give up their arms. The delay they caused us was slight.

Another reason why there has been not much change in our routine since this announcement of capitulation is because they are still fighting in parts of Germany and Austria and no one knows yet what part this division or elements of it may have to play in the war in the Pacific.

Last evening, we halted in a small farming community and the headquarters arranged to billet in the local schoolhouse. I was just about to spread my bedroll out on the floor of one of the rooms when Major Elliott came in and told me we had been invited by some local residents to stay with them and from what he could gather we should do so.

A short distance from our headquarters we passed through a gateway in a dingy wall and found ourselves in a lovely garden. The house we entered from the garden had a beautiful interior and was richly furnished. We had to pinch ourselves when we were escorted to adjoining bedrooms as handsomely furnished as one will find any place, each with its own tiled bathroom and big tub, all fixtures being of the most modern type. The hot water was boiling, and the bath towel was as big as a blanket.

We had eaten at five but when we learned that we were expected for dinner at nine we gladly accepted. Our host was a retired doctor, who had taken this place some years ago and fixed it up. He spoke some English, but his wife didn't. Their daughter, who is about my age, is living with them at the present time, with her two daughters, the oldest being fourteen. The daughter is most charming and speaks English very well. She is a "refugee" from Turin, having left her home there because of the bombing. Her husband who is a doctor is still in that city.

Our hostess and her daughter both dressed for dinner, saying that was a custom they followed both in the city and in the country. They weren't the least concerned by the fact that Johnny and I were both in coveralls. Fortunately, they were clean, and I had a good jacket to wear over the top of mine.

We had an excellent many course dinner. Two maids in uniform did the serving. One novel feature which they said went back two generations for its origin simplified the work of waiting on table. A great grandfather, who did not want the servants eavesdropping on the table conversation developed a turn table for the center of the table. All of the food, wine bottles, salt, etc. are placed on this part of the table and when you want a particular item you just spin the table around until what you need comes opposite you.

Our headquarters is less than half a block from this establishment. During this last operation when we could use our kitchens, we have been eating breakfast at five-thirty. However, with the war about over, I dropped it back to seven this morning and asked our hostess if she could have us called at seven. We were awakened then, and I found myself eating breakfast in bed.

The maid brought us tea, bread, butter and what they call marmalade, which is made out of chestnuts. It has the consistency of a thick paste and is sweet. They are much better off for food in this area than any section of Italy that we have been in so far but there is still practically no fresh meat.

In this community and the surrounding ones, the natives wear wooden shoes. Much of the area is underwater and is used for the purpose of growing rice. Was told that with the ground so wet, wooden shoes were more practical. They stuff straw in them to act as socks and a sort of cushion. Hope to be able to fill up the blanks soon.

## May 4, 1945

Breakfast again in bed this morning. Perhaps I could become accustomed to such a luxury, but I just don't like the idea. While Johnny Elliott and I couldn't ask for better accommodations, the Bn. is not at all well set up and I sent out a recon. party to look for a new area. The boys have a lot of bicycles that they took from German P. W.'s and I used one to visit the companies. We sent "B" Company to Turin to join a force that is being set up to maintain peace in that community. Dined with our host and hostess this evening. Another fine meal and much wine. The ladies dressed.

## May 4, 1945

The end of the war does not mean any immediate return for the troops. There is the problem of rounding up all of the Germans, policing the Italian communities until it is felt they can take care of themselves and then depending on the higher strata decision it will be a question of waiting your turn for a boat home.

Last evening, I was invited to have dinner at eight with the Dr. Ferrarise's who are the family that Major Elliott and I have been staying with. At seven-thirty I received a call ordering me to report to division headquarters at eight-fifteen for a meeting. Sent Major Crittenden over to eat in my place. I got back in time for a night cap before going to bed. This morning I again had a breakfast tray delivered to me at seven o'clock. The menu was the same. We had Dr. Ferrarise and his daughter for dinner with us this noon. They didn't experience much of a treat for we had spam, carrots and Italian beans.

## May 5, 1945

We made a short move this morning to a larger community by the name of Trino where everyone has a good roof overhead and there is good standing for the tanks. Our C.P. is set up in the local jail. The community is filled with heavily armed partisans. We have been called upon for a number of details which will be used in P.W. escort work. The radio reports further German collapses and predicts it will all be over at any time. Still no celebrating among the troops.

**May 5, 1945**

We have moved again, and our present headquarters is a strong position being set up in the local jail. This is a larger and more attractive community than the one we were in last but that still leaves room for much improvement. There is quite a modern school building adjoining the jail which is in operation. We secured one room there which we are using as an officers' mess.

Major Elliott and I have a room in a civilian home, but it is quite a come down from our last residence. There are no toilet facilities or running water.

The family that we stayed with were all out to wave goodbye when we left this morning and the daughter took pictures with her movie camera. Last night we had an excellent meal with them, and it was a case of breakfast in bed again this morning, which is a luxury we may not enjoy again during the remainder of our stay in Italy.

The first course last evening was steamed rice, with some sort of meat sauce on it. Then there was fried chicken and fried potatoes, followed by a lettuce and egg salad, then cheese, then a cake with a sort of whipped cream on it and finally topped off with what amounted to a small baked apple, with wine and champagne throughout the meal. We aren't too far from there and if we stay around here will probably get back over there again for they seem to really want us to return and appeared quite disappointed when they learned we were leaving. I supplied them with magazines and gave them my cigarette ration.

Learned last evening from our host who is quite a distinguished looking elderly gentleman with a very bushy white moustache that just before the war he represented Italy in an international chess tournament which was held in New York.

**May 7, 1945**

It is now stated that the war with Germany is officially over but that it will not be so proclaimed until tomorrow. Still no news of Hitler although it is mentioned that he is dead. The Germans tried to make a deal whereby they wouldn't have to surrender their troops to the Russians but that was turned down. We still don't get excited over the fact that the fighting is at an end. It just seems as though we are in a rest period and may be started out on another operation any day. I don't believe that Japan will hold out more than a year.

## It's All Over

**May 8, 1945**

This was the official V.E. Day and we listened to Prime Minister Churchill make a brief statement this afternoon confirming that fact. It is still hard to realize it's all over. Guess one reason is that we have been in and out of so many rounds that we haven't come around to understanding that there isn't another one ahead of us. Paid Division HQ a visit and had lunch there with the C.G. and staff. They don't have any idea of what lies ahead for the Division. Was paid sixty-five dollars of the money I have bet as to the war being over by June 1st.

**May 9, 1945**

Drove into Turin this morning to see our one company of tanks which is part of the force that is kept there to serve as a warning to the local partisans to restrain from any violence. The city, aside from the railroad installations and industrial plants, has not been battered about a great deal by the bombing. Johnny E. and I had supper with our friends the

Ferrarises and had as usual an excellent meal the main event being turkey.

*{The entries and letters for portions of May 10–11, 1945 are omitted as the information is already conveyed in previous entries.}*

### May 11, 1945

From now on your letters will be filled with questions and speculations as to when I will be returning home. So far there isn't anything I can pass on to you in that connection. All sorts of lists are being prepared by our G-1, showing those men that have been overseas the maximum amount of time, have certain decorations, children, etc.

In a matter of a couple weeks the situation ought to be pretty well clarified but until then I doubt if I can give you any definite information. We may know just what our position will be before long, but the big wait will be for a boat home. There is to be no more rotation or temporary duty and the boys who were home on T.D. when the war ended will not be returned over here.

We have found a little ice cream plant here in town and they are now making ice cream for the companies as we furnish the ingredients. This noon we had our first batch which made it quite a good meal for we had fried chicken. We have been faring pretty well of late on butter.

## Marking Time

### May 13, 1945

The main news of the day so far as many of the men were concerned was the statement of General Eisenhower's carried in the "Stars and Stripes" to the effect that no soldier who had fought in Africa and Europe would be required to go to the Pacific.

*{Letter on May 13, 1945, that described a sightseeing tour of Aosta and*

*Mount Bianco as well as a brief discussion that the Germans are allowed to retain sidearms to protect themselves against Partisans until they can be brought to the P.W. cages.}*

## May 14, 1945

We were supposed to move to a new area this morning but that was cancelled at the last minute. The story now is that when we get through evacuating P.W.'s we will take over the 34th Division sector in the mountains while they go to Montecatini to be processed before going home and we will follow them there. Took a walk this afternoon and watched a native catching frogs. There were so small I don't see how one could get enough of them to make any sort of meal.

### May 14, 1945

Our move for today was cancelled late last night after everyone had finished packing everything but their bedrolls. We were going to get up at five this morning instead of six thirty as normal and many of the men were asleep when the change came in. No one complained for the area where we were headed was not near as pleasant as this one. That particular move is off and now gossip has it that we may go up into the mountains after the evacuation of the German P.W.'s that is now in progress is completed.

## May 15, 1945

If it continues to heat up as the days grow longer like it has for the past several ones, we will soon be flattened out with the heat. Ice drinks and strawberries for lunch and ice cream for supper. We had been scheduled for an inspection by Division on Monday. Now they have jumped it up to Thursday which is going to make us hustle to get ready. I imagine we will get to send some E.M. home within the next month but I don't think I can expect to make it before July.

## Heading Home

**May 21, 1945**

Up before six and took off in a cub for an airstrip on the shores of Lake Garda. 'Twas a grand flight. Over the rice paddies and well cultivated fields and toy-like villages of the Po Valley. Fifth Army was living like royalty having moved in on all of the best that Lake Garda had to offer. Reported to the Fifteenth Army Group G-1 who is a B.G. It seems that the Army Group Commander is going to Chicago, Illinois, with a group of men eligible for discharge from the Fifth Army and I am being considered for inclusion in that group. I had none of my personal effects with me which made things rather awkward when I was ordered to proceed on to Florence which I did by air. There we were told to stock up on shining and polishing equipment and were issued new clothes.

**May 22, 1945**

Another increment arrived during the day and by evening there were some sixteen officers here. Everything was pretty well shrouded in mystery during the day but by evening things were taking shape so far as I was concerned. A group of us were interviewed this evening by General Gruenther, the C/S of the Fifteenth Army Group.[73] I was first of the lot and he told me I was one of the ones that was definitely going and asked that I remain in his office while the others were selected. No decision was reached because of more pressing tactical, where I suppose in the H.Q.'s of this strata it would be more proper to say strategical matters. My peep arrived from the Bn. with all of my personal effects. Understand the field officers selected to make this trip will return to the theatre.

[73]    General Alfred Gruenther

## May 23, 1945

The Army G-1 turned things over to me so far as this detail is concerned, and I now have the complete story. Six groups of Army personnel headed by prominent General officers are returning to the United States to go to that many large cities to take part in certain demonstrations or ceremonies dealing with the completion of the European phase of World War II. Group II which is to be headed by General Clark is to proceed to Chicago by air via Paris. The Ground Forces portion of this group, in addition to the General officers, is to be made up of two field officers and sixteen men. In the directive it is provided that in the group there is to be at least one colored officer and two-colored soldiers. The basis of the selection is supposedly those with the most combat awards. That wasn't true throughout the group selected, however, much weight being given to appearance, hometown Chicago, etc.

Figure 43: General Clark addressing a group selected to accompany him to Chicago. Gardiner is to the back left of the general. Florence, Italy, May 25, 1945 (Photography from the Patricia Issel Collection)

**May 24, 1945**

Had a showdown inspection of the men to check on completeness of uniform and status of pressing. This afternoon we turned out for General Clark who talked to us. His remarks sounded more like that at times of a politician than a General, i.e. the backslapping and praises that were distributed. Noticed that the photographers who gave us the once over seemed to be primarily interested in photographing the colored men in our party. Out to the Hospital to see General Pritchard, our Division C.G., who is laid up with a stomach ulcer, and seems to be headed back for the States. Was asked if I preferred to remain in the United States and be discharged or return to my unit. I chose to stay at home.

**May 25, 1945**

When we reached the Florence airport this morning, we were lined up by the two planes that we were going on while we were serenaded by the band. A Guard of Honor was provided by the M.P.'s and the ceremony finished off with the National Anthem. General Clark and his party left in another plane and were due to stop in Cannes for lunch. We flew out to sea between Leghorn and Pisa and then headed towards Paris where we landed shortly after noon. We weren't received in the style in which we had been dispatched because there were too many General officers descending on the overtaxed visitor's bureau of Shaef. The officers in our party were put up in the Ritz and I rated a beautiful room. The lounge was filled with stylishly dressed women. Another officer and I went to see the Casino de Paris and saw a performance featuring bare breasts of various contours. Very few civilian vehicles to be seen. The shop windows look very attractive.

**May 26, 1945**

Did a little shopping this morning. With the franc pegged at a value of two cents and actually being much less in value, everything is sky high.

I bought some ladies' handkerchiefs and paid thirty-five dollars for a bottle of perfume. Had a brief session with General Clark and he divided up the General officers for our trip between the three planes which are to carry our party and told me to complete the rosters out of the remaining personnel. Lunched with an old 1st Armored friend who is now tied in with the Public Relations Office of Shaef. This evening he went along with another officer and me to the Follies Bergere and arranged to take us backstage where we spent the entire second act. I had my camera along and in photographing several tableaus, found myself very calmly using as the point on which I was focusing the nipple of the strutting breast of one of the show girls.

### May 27, 1945

From the newspaper accounts it appears that the Air Force isn't waiting for any deployment to get on with the war against the Japs for the raids in their cities grow in intensity every day. This hotel is jammed with visiting senators and General officers. Ran into several people I knew, including the Senior Senator from Montana, B. K. Wheeler. Took an American Red Cross tour of the city this morning and then a run out to Longchamp and Versailles in the afternoon. Deferred a night club trek to visit with Major Tom Carter, an old Black Horse associate who is now the A.T.C. head at their Paris airport.

### May 28, 1945

I still have my watch set on Paris time and it's a little after eleven in the evening. However, it is still perfectly light, and the sun hasn't quite set. Our party boarded three C-54's in the mid-afternoon. I am in the one with General Clark and General Twinning of the Fifteenth Air Force.[74] There is also on board another Major General, one B.G., and Ambassador Murphy.[75] This morning in Paris was mostly getting ready to leave.

74   General Nathan Farragut Twining
75   Robert Murphy was the eventual Ambassador to Belgium. In 1945, he was a U.S. Political Advisor.

**May 29, 1945**

During the night we came down to the Island of Santa Maria in the Azores where we had ham and eggs and the planes were refueled. This is a different island from the one I landed on in that group on my other trip. There are two beds on this plane. General Clark slept in one and the other General officers took turns on the other. I found the floor more comfortable than trying to sleep in my seat. We landed in Newfoundland for refueling and another breakfast and then on to Presque Isle, Maine. We were permitted to make calls from there and I called Elizabeth. Talked to Mrs. Singstad who told me Rita was en route to Chicago. The tailoring establishment did a good job of pressing for us and I had some information General Clark ordered on our personnel typed up. Everyone was tired and we turned in early.

**May 30, 1945**

We took off at 7:30. Spent some time in Control compartment and it being a perfect day had a grand look at things. When we passed over Michigan City, we picked up a fighter escort of twenty four planes. We flew directly over the Loop and then out to the Municipal airport. I spotted Rita before I got off the plane. Elizabeth and the kids were also on hand to meet me. I got to see them a few minutes before we climbed into open cars and paraded up town and through the Loop. There was some speechmaking at the Congress Plaza. We were put up at the Palmer House. There was a banquet and entertainment and more speeches. Talked to mother. Saw quite a few old friends.

Figure 44: Lieutenant Colonel Henry E. Gardiner at the end of the war in May 1945 in Northern Italy, days before he returned to the U.S. (Photograph from the Patricia Issel Collection)

## A Civilian Again

**May 31, 1945**

Said goodbye to Rita after breakfast, she being on her way back to New York. The date for the wedding has been set for the 19th. Out to Fort Sheridan with the boys who made the trip over here and they started us through channels for separation. They are beginning to get quite a flow of personnel headed in that direction. Had a complete physical, records checked, was paid and told that I was out of the Army. I am so far as the records go drawing my terminal leave which extends to October 1st. Lunched with the Post Commander and his wife. They are using 1,500 German P.W.'s on the Post. Would have liked to have completed my service in the Army as a full colonel.

*{Gardiner ends his 1,271 day odyssey by writing in the third person, once again, that "the writer was commissioned a full colonel in the Organized Reserve shortly after being discharged from the Army. He then joined the 77th Infantry Division (Reserve) of New York in which he was promoted to Colonel and served as a regimental commander until moving to Chile in 1948. At that time, he was transferred to the Inactive Reserve.}*

# Bibliography

## Service Records

Compiled service record, Henry E. Gardiner, Colonel, National Personal Records Center, St. Louis, Missouri.

## Interviews and Correspondence

Patricia Issel. Henry E. Gardiner's Niece.

## Archive and Library Collections

General George Patton Museum Archives, Ft. Knox, Kentucky
George S. Patton, Jr. Collection
James R. Pritchard Collection
Robert E. Van Zant Collection

## Articles, Books, Magazines, and Unpublished Documents

Abbott, Henry P, Major (Chaplain), *The Nazi "88" Made Believers*, Dayton Ohio, Otterbein Press, 1945, found at http://depothill.net/abbott.pdf

Aboul-Enein, Youssef, *Infantry Magazine*, September-October 2010, found at http://findarticles.com/p/articles/mi_m0IAV/is_3_99/ai_n56541299

Anderson, Charles R. *Tunisia*, Center for Military History Publication, CMH Pub 72-12.

Andrews, Robin. "How Vesuvius Upstaged the Nazi Air Force During the Second World War," *Forbes*, February 16, 2017, found at https://www.forbes.com/sites/robinandrews/2017/02/16/how-vesuvius-upstaged-the-nazi-air-force-during-the-second-world-war/#4bc30800597f

*Armor. The Cavalry Journal* 48: 93, 1939.

Atkinson, Rick. *The Army at Dawn: The War in North Africa, 1942–1943, Volume One of the Liberation Trilogy*. New York, New York: McMillian, 2007.

Atkinson, Rick. *The Day of Battle: The War in Sicily and Italy, 1943–1944*. New York, New York: Henry Holt and Company, 2007.

Barry, Steven Thomas. "Battle-Scared and Dirty: US Army Tactical Leadership in the Mediterranean Theater, 1942–1943," found at https://etd.ohiolink.edu/!etd.send_file?accession=osu1313541748&disposition=inline

Blumenson, Martin. *Kasserine Pass: The Epic Battle Where Patton met Rommel in the African Desert*, New York, New York: Tower Publications, Inc. 1966.

Bowlby, Alex. *Countdown to Cassino: The Battle of Mignano Gap, 1943*, United Kingdom: Leo Cooper, 1995.

Brown, John Sloan. *Draftee Division: A Study of the 88th Infantry Division, First all Selective Service Division into Combat in World War II*. Lexington, Kentucky: University Press of Kentucky, 2014.

Bryan, Jami. "The 88th Division in Italy," found at https://armyhistory.org/the-88th-infantry-division-in-italy/

Budnik, Ruslan. "The Smoking Snakes: The Brazilian Expeditionary Force in WWII," *War History Online*, May 7, 2019, found at https://www.warhistoryonline.com/instant-articles/the-brazilian-expeditionary-force.html

Calhoun, Mark T., *Defeat at Kasserine: American Army Doctrine Training, and Battle Command in Northwest Africa, World War II*, CreateSpace Independent Publishing Platform, 2014.

Caraccilo, Dominic J. *Forging a Special Operations Force: The US Army Rangers*, Warwick, UK: Helion & Company, 2015.

Caraccilo, Dominic J "The Battle of Buna," *Infantry Magazine*, 83, no. 3. (May–June 1993).

Clarke, Jeffrey J. & Smith, Robert Ross (1993). *Riviera To the Rhine. United States Army in World War II: European Theater of Operations*, Washington, D.C.: Center of Military History, United States Army, 1993.

Conn, Stetson and Fairchild, Byron. Office of the Chief of Military History, Department of the Army. *The Framework of Hemisphere Defense*, 1960.

*Cornell Magazine*, October 1994 Notes: Obituary in Cornell '31 JD - Henry E. Gardiner of Bozeman, MT, April 5, 1994; retired vice president of Anaconda Company; active in community, professional, and alumni affairs. Sigma Alpha Epsilon. '31, p. 91.

Crabb, Brian James. *The Forgotten Tragedy: The Story of the Sinking of HMT Lancastria*. Lincolnshire, UK: Paul Watkins Publishing, 2002.

Crowther, Rosley. "The Screen; 'Sahara,' an Exciting Picture of Desert War, With Humphrey Bogart as a Heroic Sergeant, Is New Feature at the Capitol," *New York Times*, November 12, 1943.

Davis Jr., Henry Blaine. *Generals in Khaki*. Raleigh, North Carolina: Pentland Press, Inc., 1998.

Edwards, John. "Commodore James Bisset," *Ocean Liners Magazine*, found at http://oceanlinersmagazine.com/2015/07/15/commodore-james-bisset/

Elting, John R. *Military Uniforms in America: The Modern Era from 1868*. New York, New York: Presidio Press. 1988.

Failmezger, Victor. *American Knights: The Untold Story of the Men of*

the *Legendary 601st Tank Destroyer Battalion*. Oxford, UK: Osprey
Publishing Co., 2015

Falkenberg II, J. C. "History of Task Force 45," January 30, 2008, found
at http://ww2f.com/threads/history-of-task-force-45.12270/

Favager, D. J. *The Illustrated History of the Gardiners of
Whitchurch, Liverpool, and Wallsey Volume 1: Herefordshire.*
Calameo Publishing, 2019, found at https://en.calameo.com/
read/00476044921a85e3064e9

Favager, D. J. *The Illustrated History of the Gardiners of Whitchurch:
Volume 2 Liverpool, Canada, Wallsey, and Montana.* Kindle Direct
Publishing and Calameo Publishing, 2019, found at https://
en.calameo.com/read/004760449628a26c946d7

Favager, D. J. *The Illustrated History of the Gardiners of Whitchurch,
Liverpool, and Wallsey Volume 3: Canada and Montana.*
Calameo Publishing, 2019, found at https://en.calameo.com/
read/00476044938611724fd32

Favager, David. *War Heroes: Gardiners at War: Extracted from The
Illustrated History of the Gardiners of Whitchurch: Volume 2
Liverpool, Canada, Wallsey, and Montana.* ISSUU Publishing, found
at https://issuu.com/davidgalina/docs/gardiners_at_war_

Favager, David James. *The History of the Gardiners of Whitchurch:
Volumes 1 and 2.* Independently published, November 22, 2019.

Feuer, A.B. *Packs On! Memoirs of the 10th Mountain Division in World
War II.* Mechanicsburg, Pennsylvania: Stackpole Books, 2006.

Forty, George. *M4 Sherman.* New York, New York: Blandford Press,
1987.

Franks, Norman L. R. *Royal Air Force Losses of the Second World
War. Volume 2. Operational Losses: Aircraft and crews 1942–1943.*
London: Midland Publishing Limited, 1998.

Freeman, David. "Winston Churchill & Eamon De Valera: A Thirty Year
Relationship," The Winston Churchill International Society, 2008,

found at https://winstonchurchill.org/publications/finest-hour-extras/churchill-and-eamon-de-valera-thirty-year-relationship/2008

Gardiner, Henry E. Interview with the Montana Historical Society with Michael Malone, Montana State University, and Bill Lang, Montana Historical Society. Bozeman, Montana. November 10, 1987.

Gardiner, Henry E. "We Fought at Kasserine," *Armored Cavalry Journal* (March–April 1948): 8–13.

"Grand Hyatt New York Shares Update on Timing Around Proposed Redevelopment Project," August 20, 2019, found at https://www.hyatt.com/en-US/hotel/new-york/grand-hyatt-new-york/nycgh/news-events

Heise, Keith. "Tribune Writer John Thompson," December 15, 1995, found at http://articles.chicagotribune.com/1995-12-15/news/9512150109_1_cuban-missile-crisis-mr-thompson-troops

Hogg, Ian. *Twentieth-Century Artillery*. New York: Barnes & Nobles, 2000.

Holmes, Colin. *Searching for Lord Haw-Haw: The Political Lives of William Joyce*. New York, New York: Routledge, 2016.

Holt, Thaddeus. *The Deceivers: Allied Military Deception in the Second World War*. London: Phoenix, 2005.

Holzimmer, Kevin C. *General Walter Krueger: Unsung Hero of the Pacific War*. Lawrence, Kansas: University Press of Kansas, 2007.

Howe, George. *The Battle History of the First Armored Division*. Washington, D.C.: Combat Forces Press, 1954.

Howe, George F. *United States Army in World War II Mediterranean Theater of Operations Northwest Africa: Seizing the Initiative in the West*, Washington, D.C.: Office of the Chief of Military History, 1957, found at https://www.ibiblio.org/hyperwar/USA/USA-MTO-NWA/index.html

Jervois, W.J. *The History of the Northhamptonshire Regiment: 1934-1948*. The Northhamptonshire Regiment Committee, Northampton, 1953

Keegan, John, *The Face of Battle.* London: Viking Press. 1977

Kemp, Ted. *A Commemorative History: First Special Service Force.* Dallas, Texas: Taylor Publishing, 1995

Knighton, Andrew. "Life at Thélepte, a US Air Base in WWII North Africa in World War Two," War History Online, December 12, 2017, found at https://www.warhistoryonline.com/world-war-ii/life-thelepte-us-air-base.html

Knighton, Andrew. "The First Battle for Tunisia in World War Two," War History Online, September 29, 2017, found at https://www.warhistoryonline.com/world-war-ii/first-battle-tunisia-world-war-two.html

Kurowski, Franz. *Endkampf in Afrika: Der Opfergang der Heeresgruppe Rommel in Tunesien 1942/43.* Druffel-Verlag, 1982, p.54.

Laurie, Clayton D. *Rome-Arno 1944. CMH Online bookshelves: WWII Campaigns*, Washington, D.C.: U.S. Army Center of Military History CMH Pub 72-20, October 3, 2003, p. 24, found at http://www.army.mil/cmh/brochures/romar/map4.JPG

Lee, Ulysses. *United States Army in World War II Special Studies: The Employment of Negro Troops.* Washington D.C.: Center of Military History, 1965, found at https://history.army.mil/books/wwii/11-4/chapter19.htm

Mauldin, Bill, *Up Front,* New York, New York: W.W. Norton & Company, 2000.

Mayo, Lida. *The Ordinance Department: On Beachhead and Battlefront.* Washington, D.C.: Center of Military History, 1991.

Millett, John, D. *United States Army in World War II: The Army Service Forces.* Washington, D.C.: Center of Military History, 1987.

Painton, Frederick C. "Comeback at Kasserine Pass," *The Saturday Evening Post*, May 29, 1943.

Parker, Ray. *Down in Flames*, Minneapolis: Mill City Press, 2009.

Pratt, Sara E. "Benchmarks: March 17, 1944: The most recent eruption of Mount Vesuvius." *Earth*, March 17, 2016, found at https://www.earthmagazine.org/article/benchmarks-march-17-1944-most-recent-eruption-mount-vesuvius

Rame, David. *Road to Tunis*. New York, New York: The Macmillan Company, 1944.

Risch, Erna, *The Quartermaster Corps: Organization, Supply, and Services. Vols. 1-2. United States Army in World War II. The Technical Services*, Washington, D.C.: Center for Military History, 1952.

Robinett, Brigadier General Paul McDonald. *Armor Command*, Washington, D.C.: McGregor & Wheeler, 1958.

Sandler, Stanley. *World War II in the Pacific: An Encyclopedia*. New York: Garland Publishing. 2001.

Selective Service System. "Selective Service in Peacetime First Report of the Director of Selective Service, 1940-1941," Washington: Government Printing Offices, 1942.

Settle Jr., Frank A. *General George C. Marshall and the Atomic Bomb*. Santa Barbara, California: Praeger Publishers, 2016.

Steele, Richard W. "American Popular Opinion and the War Against Germany: The Issue of Negotiated Peace, 1942," *Journal of American History*, 65 no. 3 (December 1978), found at https://doi.org/10.2307/1901419

Stentiford, B. "Forgotten Militia: The Louisiana State Guard of World War II," *Louisiana History: The Journal of the Louisiana Historical Association*, 45 no 3 (2004), found at www.jstor.org/stable/4234033

*The Armored Division as an Assault Landing Force: Military Monograph 320*. Bennington, Vermont: Merriam Press, 1990.

Tomlin, Barbara Brooks. *G. I. Nightingales: The Army Nurse Corps in World War II*. Lexington, Kentucky: The University Press of Kentucky, 2001.

University of Minnesota Human Rights Library, "The Atlantic Charter, Joint Declaration by the President and The Prime Minister,

Declaration of Principles, Known as the Atlantic Charter, Aug. 14, 1941, U.S.- U.K., 55 Stat. app. 1603" found at http://hrlibrary.umn.edu/education/FDRjointdec.html

Vanzo, John P. "U-boat Attacks during World War II," *New Georgia Encyclopedia*, January 31, 2011. Found at https://www.georgiaencyclopedia.org/articles/history-archaeology/u-boat-attacks-during-world-war-ii

Von Luck, Hans. *Panzer Commander: The Memoirs of Colonel Hans von Luck*. New York: Dell (Random House), 1989.

Wells, Edward. *Mailshot: A History of the Forces Postal Services*, London: Defense Postal & Courier Services, 1987.

Wheal, Elizabeth-Anne, Pope, Stephan, and Taylor, James. *A Dictionary of the Second World War*, New York, New York: Peter Bedrick Books, 1989.

Whitlock, Flint. *The Rock of Anzio: From Sicily To Dachau, A History of The U.S. 45th Infantry Division*, New York City, New York: Basic Books, 2005.

Zaloga, Steven J. *M3 Lee/Grant Medium Tank 1941–45*. Oxford, United Kingdom: Osprey Publishing, 2013.

Zaloga, Steven J. *The Sherman Tank in US and Allied Service*, London: Osprey Publishing Ltd, 1982.

Zeiger, Sue. *In Uncle Sam's Service: Women Workers with the American Expeditionary Force*, 1917-191. Philadelphia, Pennsylvania: University of Pennsylvania Press, 2004.

## Web Resources

"1st Armored Division History," found at https://army.togetherweserved.com/army/servlet/tws.webapp.WebApp?cmd=PublicUnitProfile&type=Unit&ID=252

"13th Armored Regiment in Tunisia Part II," found at https://www.flamesofwar.com/Default.aspx?tabid=112&art_id=581

"1942: Declaration of the United Nations," found at https://www.un.org/
en/sections/history-united-nations-charter/1942-declaration-
united-nations/index.html

"443rd Antiaircraft Artillery Battalion in World War II Italian
Campaign Battle for Mt. Maggiore," found at http://www.
texasmilitaryforcesmuseum.org/36division/archives/443/44363.htm

"Ballykinler Camp: The First Seven Decades, 1900–1969," found at
http://www.downcountymuseum.com/getattachment/Collections/
Down_Survey/Ballykinler_Camp_compressed.pdf.aspx

Belfast Hills Partnership found at http://belfasthills.org/visiting/divis/

"Camp Livingston," *Densho Encyclopedia*, found at http://encyclopedia.
densho.org/Camp_Livingston_(detention_facility)/

"Christian missionaries in Tunisia," found at http://www.tunisia.com/
community/threads/christian-missionaries-in-tunisia.7117/

*Codenames: Operation of World War II*, found at https://codenames.
info/

"Durban Castle," found at http://www.bandcstaffregister.com/page186.
html

"French Language Guide," found at https://www.eisenhowerlibrary.gov/
sites/default/files/file/French_Language_Guide.pdf

"Fort Devens, Massachusetts," *U.S. Army Bases*, found at http://
armybases.org/fort-devens-ma-massachusetts/

Hight Point Ireland Website, found at https://www.highpointireland.
com/province-high-points.html

"Historical Resources About the Second World War," found at https://
historicalresources.wordpress.com/category/ww-ii-second-world-
war/ww-ii-maps/war-maps-war-in-north-africa-and-italy/

"History of Fort Dix New Jersey – 50 Years of Service to the Nation
1917-1967," prepared by the Information Office, United States
Army Training Center, Fort Dix, New Jersey 08640, found at
http://whitedeercafe.blogspot.com/2017/05/history-of-fort-dix-

part-i-1917-1967.html

"History of the 32nd Infantry Division," found at http://www.lonesentry.com/usdivisions/history/infantry/division/pacific/32nd_infantry_division.html

"History of the 37th Infantry Division," found at https://history.army.mil/html/forcestruc/cbtchron/cc/037id.htm

"HMS Aquitania," *Scottish Built Ships: The History of Shipbuilding in Scotland*, Caledonian Maritime Research Trust, found at http://clydeships.co.uk/view.php?official_number=&imo=&builder=&builder_eng=&year_built=&launch_after=&launch_before=&role=&propulsion=&category=&owner=&port=&flag=&disposal=&lost=&ref=3293&vessel=AQUITANIA

Hollis, John D. "Honor our WWII veterans while they are still among us," *The Washington Post*, May 26, 2019, found at https://www.washingtonpost.com/opinions/2019/05/26/honor-our-wwii-veterans-while-they-are-still-among-us/

Indian Army in Italy, see https://montecassinotours.com/index.php/page/id/19/the-indian-army-in-italy.html

"Krupp K5 (Anzio Annie)," found at https://www.militaryfactory.com/armor/detail.asp?armor_id=526

Landing Ship Tank (LST), found at https://www.globalsecurity.org/military/systems/ship/lst.htm

Letter from General George C. Marshall 3-198 To Major General Edmund L. Daley, May 18, 1942. The George C. Marshall Foundation, found at https://www.marshallfoundation.org/library/digital-archive/to-major-general-edmund-l-daley-3/

Light Tank M2. found at https://tanks-encyclopedia.com/ww2/US/M2_Light_Tank.php

"Lily Pons Here," *The Last Roundup*, April 11, 1946, found at https://archive.is/20120630212338/http://home.comcast.net/~cbi-theater-5/

roundup/roundup041146.html#selection-27.43-27.58

Mining in Beja, found at https://thediggings.com/tun/beja-tun4084

Minnesota National Guard 34th Infantry Division Artillery, found at https://minnesotanationalguard.ng.mil/documents/2018/10/34th-infantry-division-artillery-history.pdf/

Monte Cassino Abbey, found at https://www.atlasobscura.com/places/montecassino-abbey

Moroccan Goumiers, found at https://www.warhistoryonline.com/world-war-ii/mountain-warriors-wwii-goumiers.html

National Park Services NPGallery Digital Asset Management System, found at https://npgallery.nps.gov/AssetDetail/NRIS/79001084

Operation Dickens, found at https://codenames.info/operation/dickens-i/

Ponic, Jason. "Whatever Happened to the RMS Queen Elizabeth, RMS Queen Mary's Sister Ship?" OwlVacation, December 29, 2019, found at https://owlcation.com/humanities/RMSQueenElizabeth

"Sibley Stove Stover," found at http://www.afn.org/~micanopy/html/sibley_tent_stove.html

*The Camp Claiborne News*, July 6, 1944, found at www. http://www.campclaiborne.com/

"The Fifth Army's Where My Heart Is," found at http://www.fiftharmymobileradio.com/

The Wartime Memories Project – 1st Battalion, Argyll and Sutherland Highlanders during Second World War, found at https://wartimememoriesproject.com/ww2/allied/battalion.php?pid=790

"Troops and Cargo Transported During World War II under U.S. Army Control," found at http://www.usmm.org/armycargo.html

U.S. Air Force Biographies, found at https://www.af.mil/About-Us/Biographies/Display/Article/107211/brigadier-general-christian-f-dreyer/

"U.S. Army Officers 1939-1945," found at https://www.unithistories.

com/officers/US_Army_officers_K01.html#Knuebel_JH

"United States Army in World War II: United States Army Forces in Northern Ireland," found at https://history.army.mil/reference/ireland/IRECHR.htm

University of Illinois Veteran's Memorial Project, found at http://chiuiaaweb1.admin.uillinois.edu/illinois/veterans/display_veteran.asp?id=348

"Wall of Valor" extract, *Military Times Magazine*, found at http://valor.militarytimes.com/recipient.php?recipientid=31043 and https://valor.militarytimes.com/hero/23123

*West Point Association of Graduates Memorials*, found at https://www.westpointaog.org

"William Stoneman, 83; Foreign Correspondent," *The New York Times*, found at https://www.nytimes.com/1987/04/14/obituaries/william-stoneman-83-foreign-correspondent.html

WW2 American M1 Steel Helmet, found at https://www.dday-overlord.com/en/material/uniforms/m1-steel-helmet

# Biographies

Henry Edward (H.E.) Gardiner was called to active duty on November 25, 1940, when Troop "C" of the 106th Cavalry was inducted into Federal Service. He served as a battalion commander and regimental executive officer until his discharge at the rank of colonel in October 1945. In February 1943, then-Lieutenant Colonel Gardiner was awarded the nation's second highest combat award, the Distinguished Service Cross (DSC), for actions as a Lieutenant Colonel in command of a squadron in North Africa. Gardiner was a colonel at his time of discharge in October 1945.

Colonel (Ret.) Dominic J. Caraccilo culminated a 27-year career as the Deputy Commander of the 101st Airborne Division. His 65 months of combat during multiple deployments included Desert Shield, Desert Storm, Kosovo, and a series of deployments to Afghanistan and Iraq. Caraccilo's other works include *Achieving Victory in Iraq: Countering an Insurgency* (Stackpole Books, 2008), *Beyond Guns and Steel: A War Termination Strategy* (PSI, 2011), and *Forging a Special Operations Force: The US Army Rangers* (Helion & Company, 2015).

H. R. McMaster served as National Security Adviser from 2017–2018, culminating a distinguished military career as a combat leader and soldier/statesman. Lieutenant General McMaster was awarded the Silver Star, Bronze Star with V, and the Purple Heart in a career that saw service in the Gulf War, Afghanistan, and Iraq, where he commanded the 3rd

Armored Cavalry Regiment. A West Point graduate, he holds a doctorate in history from the University of North Carolina and is the author of the award-winning *Dereliction of Duty*.

CPSIA information can be obtained
at www.ICGtesting.com
Printed in the USA
BVHW061025130621
609463BV00011B/693